FORMING NEW FAMILIES

WILEY SERIES

in

CHILD CARE AND PROTECTION

Series Editors

Kevin D. Browne
School of Psychology
The University of Birmingham, UK

Margaret A. Lynch
Newcomen Centre
Guy's Hospital, London, UK

The Child Care and Protection Series aims to further the understanding of health, psychosocial and cultural factors that influence the development of the child, early interactions and the formation of relationships in and outside the family. This international series will cover the psychological as well as the physical welfare of the child and will consider protection from all forms of maltreatment.

The series is intended to become essential reading for all professionals concerned with the welfare and protection of children and their families. All books in the series will have a practice orientation with referenced information from theory and research.

Published

Michelle Aldridge & Joanne Wood	Interviewing Children: A Guide for Child Care and Forensic Practitioners
Ann Buchanan	Cycles of Child Maltreatment: Facts, Fallacies and Interventions
Dorota Iwaniec	The Emotionally Abused and Neglected Child: Identification, Assessment and Intervention
David Quinton *et al.*	Joining New Families: A Study of Adoption and Fostering in Middle Childhood
Jacqui Saradjian	Women who Sexually Abuse Children: From Research to Clinical Practice

Forthcoming

Lenard Dalgleish	Risk and Decisions in Child Protection
David Middleton & Jayne Allam	Child Sexual Abuse: Working with Offenders
Janet Stanley & Christopher Goddard	In the Firing Line: Relationships, Power and Violence in Child Protection Work

Potential authors are invited to submit ideas and proposals for publications for the series to either of the series editors above.

JOINING NEW FAMILIES

A Study of Adoption and Fostering in Middle Childhood

David Quinton, Alan Rushton,
Cherilyn Dance and Deborah Mayes

JOHN WILEY & SONS
Chichester · New York · Weinheim · Brisbane · Singapore · Toronto

Copyright © 1998 by John Wiley & Sons Ltd,
Baffins Lane, Chichester,
West Sussex PO19 1UD, England

National   01243 779777
International (+44) 1243 779777
e-mail (for orders and customer service enquiries):
cs-books@wiley.co.uk
Visit our Home Page on http://www.wiley.co.uk
or http://www.wiley.com

Other Wiley Editorial Offices

John Wiley & Sons, Inc., 605 Third Avenue,
New York, NY 10158-0012, USA

WILEY-VCH Verlag GmbH, Pappelallee 3,
D-69469 Weinheim, Germany

Jacaranda Wiley Ltd, 33 Park Road, Milton,
Queensland 4064, Australia

John Wiley & Sons (Asia) Pte Ltd, 2 Clementi Loop #02-01,
Jin Xing Distripark, Singapore 129809

John Wiley & Sons (Canada) Ltd, 22 Worcester Road,
Rexdale, Ontario M9W 1L1, Canada

Library of Congress Cataloging-in-Publication Data

Joining new families : adoption and fostering in middle childhood /
   David Quinton . . . [et al.].
      p. cm. — (Wiley series in child care and protection)
   Includes bibliographical references and index.
   ISBN 0-471-97837-X
   1. Older child adoption—Great Britain. 2. Special needs
adoption—Great Britain. 3. Foster home care—Great Britain.
I. Quinton, David. II. Series.
HV875.58.G7J65 1998
362.73'4'0941—dc21   98–28949
                                                               CIP

British Library Cataloguing in Publication Data

A catalogue record for this book is available from the British Library

ISBN 0-471-97837-X

Typeset in 10/12pt Palatino by Mayhew Typesetting, Rhayader, Powys
Printed and bound in Great Britain by Biddles Ltd, Guildford and King's Lynn
This book is printed on acid-free paper responsibly manufactured from sustainable
forestation, for which at least two trees are planted for each one used for paper production.

CONTENTS

ABOUT THE AUTHORS

David Quinton – Professor of Psychosocial Development in the School for Policy Studies at the University of Bristol

David Quinton has a background in anthropology and developmental psychopathology and has worked for many years on long-term outcome studies of children whose early experiences put them at risk for psychosocial problems. He is author, together with Michael Rutter, of 'Parenting breakdown: the making and breaking of Intergenerational links.' Aldershot: Gower.

Alan Rushton – Senior Lecturer in Social Work, Institute of Psychiatry

Alan Rushton has a degree in psychology and was for many years a mental health social worker with children and adults in the UK and in Canada and currently directs the MSc programme in Mental Health Social Work based in the Maudsley Hospital, London. He has conducted research into a range of social work topics including adoption and fostering, child protection and post-qualifying training. His special interest in this study is the evaluation of the social work intervention. He is author, together with Judy Treseder and David Quinton, of 'New Parents for Older Children.' London: BAAF.

Cherilyn Dance – Research Co-ordinator Maudsley Family Research Studies, Institute of Psychiatry, London

Cherilyn Dance originally trained as a nurse and Health Visitor and has a degree in developmental psychology. She has been involved in a variety of placement related research studies since she joined the team in 1989 and has recently worked with BAAF in producing their report of adoption patterns in England ('Focus on Adoption', London: BAAF, 1997). Her particular research interests concern the experiences of birth children in new families when older children are placed with them and placed children's experiences in the school system.

Deborah Mayes – Research Worker, Maudsley Family Research Studies, Institute of Psychiatry, London

Prior to joining the research team in 1993, *Deborah Mayes* worked as a child and family social worker in a London Borough and as a researcher for the Economist Intelligence Unit. She has a particular interest in understanding how the process of attachment may be assessed in placements of older children.

SERIES PREFACE

The **Wiley Series in Child Care and Protection** is a series of books primarily written for all professionals in policy making, research and practice concerned with the care, welfare and protection of children and their families.

The aim of the series is to publish books on child care and protection covering both the psychological and physical welfare of the child, including legal and social policy aspects. The series was prompted by the need to view child protection within the wider concepts of child care and social welfare. After three decades of remarkable growth in child protection work, which has led to widespread public awareness and professional understanding of child maltreatment, it has become increasingly recognised that child protection is enhanced by the improvements in the welfare of families and the promotion of positive parenting and child care. Indeed, child care, family welfare and effective child protection are inter-linked and cannot be separated.

Books in the series are from a wide range of disciplines and each book is encouraged to link research and practice to inform, in an easily accessible way, professionals, policy makers and the public in general. Consequently, it is hoped to further the knowledge and understanding of health, psychosocial and cultural factors that influence the development of the child, early interactions and the formation of relationships in and outside the family.

'*Joining New Families*' is the fourth book in the series. The authors, David Quinton, Alan Rushton, Cherilyn Dance and Deborah Mayes report on a study of establishing permanent placements in middle childhood. Such late permanent family placements by adoption or long term fostering are often the most problematic in terms of the social and emotional development of the child and the difficulties experienced by the new families. The book investigates the first year of placement for these children and families. The first year is the most vulnerable to placement breakdown and this is exemplified by the fact that young people currently resident in secure accommodation often experience eight to ten care placements by the time they are sixteen years of age.

This book is the first in the series to concern itself with issues surrounding the public care of children and we would welcome further books in this area.

Kevin Browne
Margaret Lynch

PREFACE

The focus of this study is on one of the most problematic groups of children in care – older children with disrupted pasts where return home is undesirable or has already failed and where placement with relatives is not possible or appropriate. These children's interests may be best served by permanent family placement with approved, alternative parents, through adoption or long-term fostering arrangements.

This book tells the story of 61 children who were each placed with a new family with the intention of permanence. The placements were all arranged by local authority adoption and fostering teams or by specialist independent adoption agencies working on behalf of the authorities. The research study which forms the basis of the book aimed to document the first year of placement for these children and families and compare progress throughout the year according to a number of characteristics of the children and the families. The information was obtained by talking at length to both the families and the social workers at three points during the first year. These interviews covered a variety of aspects of daily life for the families as well as detailed information about the children's earlier experiences. We have tried to identify the most salient points made by the families and the social workers we spoke to as well as describing what the first year was like for those involved.

Because of the variety of information to be presented we decided that it made easier reading to deal with different aspects of placement and family life in separate chapters, and each chapter is designed to stand alone, with a brief introduction, presentation of relevant data, a section on practice implications where appropriate and a summary.

ACKNOWLEDGEMENTS

We should like to thank the children and the new families for seeing us at a time when they were heavily engaged in the task of getting to know each other; the authorities for agreeing to take part and the social workers for helping us to make contact with the new parents and for giving their time to talk about the placements. We wish to thank the Department of Health for funding the study and Dr Carolyn Davies and the Department's research committee for their support. We are grateful to the Buttle Trust for funding the development of a new measure. Nicola Dooley deserves special thanks for assisting with the interviewing and data collection. We are indebted to Professor Ian Sinclair and a number of other colleagues for their very valuable comments on earlier drafts of the material.

BACKGROUND AND RESEARCH ISSUES

INTRODUCTION

Permanent placement in alternative families has been found to be a viable option for many children who cannot grow up in their own homes. While the outcomes for the majority of such placements have been shown to be successful, that is, the children have remained with their new families, earlier research by other workers has shown that such children have often had very adverse experiences in their early lives and their behaviour can be extremely challenging. Not surprisingly the level of behaviour problems has been found to be closely related to placement disruption. The other very consistent finding of early studies has been that the older a child at the time of placement, the greater the risk of breakdown.

While these studies were informative about the stability of placement for different groups of children, little was known, when we began this study, about the experience of placement for the children and the new families. In the interests of providing relevant preparatory information to prospective parents and appropriate support systems, it seemed to us that it was particularly important to learn more about day-to-day life for the families, the challenges that arose and the help that was needed. We were interested to discover the extent of problems among placed children; whether some groups of children had more difficulties than others; whether these difficulties persisted or improved over time; which factors helped children to settle in their new homes and what helped the new parents to cope with the children's needs and challenges.

The bulk of this book tells the story of the first year of placement for 61 children who joined new, unrelated families during their middle childhood (five to nine years). We describe the backgrounds of the children and the preparation for placement they and their new families received and explore the relationship of both of these factors to the placement experience and the one year outcome. We examine the types of behavioural problem the children show and their level of problems in school, exploring whether either of these features are related to earlier experiences for the children. Finally, we examine the way in which relationships developed in the new family both between parents and children and between siblings, again looking at whether this is affected by earlier experiences.

However, before we move on to looking at our study placements in detail, the remainder of this chapter will provide an overview of developments and research in adoption and fostering. To begin with we will address the policy and practice context of this research and then go on to explore the way in which our work relates to selected areas of theory and evidence concerned with permanent placement. We have chosen to restrict this review to four major topics: the evaluation of placement outcomes for older children; emotional and behavioural problems of children with adverse early experiences; the development of relationships in new families; and finally, theories of parenting and their application to permanent placement. More specific fields of enquiry are discussed, where appropriate, in the introductions to relevant chapters.

PERMANENT PLACEMENT

The move towards permanent placement for older children began at a time when the number of infants available for adoption was decreasing but also at a time when a clearer picture was emerging of what may happen to children looked after by local authorities, including the recognition that the care system could itself present hazards. Children were shown to remain 'in limbo', drifting with no clear plan for permanence (Rowe & Lambert, 1973); to experience adverse care environments, such as poor quality residential provision; and to suffer multiple changes of placement and of caregivers, with the long-term psychosocial difficulties that this can produce (Wolkind & Rushton, 1994).

Such findings, along with concern about the increasing costs of keeping a large number of children in care, led to greater efforts to avoid drift and either to work towards rehabilitation or to decide on permanent substitute care. It was rightly seen to be of paramount importance to reduce the level of unplanned change, and, when rehabilitation was not possible, to provide an alternative that engendered a sense of permanence that was conducive to children's normal development (Maluccio et al., 1986). This view, which encouraged a rapid move to permanence when this was thought necessary, was probably most influential in the late 1980s. The aim of permanency planning for such special needs children was to secure stable and nurturing homes. Although the principle still holds good, it has since been tempered somewhat by the emphasis in the Children Act on children remaining with their own families if possible, together with a recognition that an alternative family may not be the solution for every child.

THE AGENCY CONTEXT OF PERMANENT FAMILY PLACEMENT

Although the field of adoption and permanent family placement has been undergoing considerable scrutiny in the UK in recent years, the routine collection of national data is very under-developed and it has been impossible to obtain a sufficiently detailed picture of adoption and fostering practice from the annual Department of Health (DoH) statistical reports ('Children Looked After by Local Authorities'). In practice, it is difficult to obtain accurate information even on relatively straightforward characteristics, let alone the equally important but more complex information that is needed to monitor placement practice. A recent survey conducted by British Agencies for Adoption and Fostering (BAAF, 1997) has provided a more detailed picture of local authority and voluntary agency adoption practice. This study was able to show that in many agencies practice has developed to embrace DoH recommendations, although there is considerable variability across types of agency and much needed data remains unavailable. A further source of information has been the periodic investigations by the Social Services Inspectorate (SSI) into adoption services (DoH/SSI, 1991, 1993, 1996a, 1996b, 1997). Authorities have been advised to avoid harmful delays in moving children to permanent placements, of the need to develop post-adoption support and to establish separate and accurate costing of adoption services.

These SSI investigations are only representative, of course, of a minority of the local authorities in England and Wales and do not necessarily include the authorities involved in our study. Our data collection took place at a particularly significant moment: just before the provisions of the Children Act 1989 were beginning to take effect and during the time that the review of adoption law was taking place (DoH, 1992). These changes generated considerable debate and, therefore, we conducted our own brief survey so that we might be aware of developments in policy formulation in older child placement and to help us to understand the context of placement practice in our referring authorities. The full details of this survey are available elsewhere (Rushton, 1994).

A Survey of Adoption and Fostering Policy and Practice

In May to July 1993, we surveyed those authorities that had referred substantial numbers of cases into the main study. This was not, therefore, a comprehensive survey of representative adoption and fostering units. The agencies in question had agreed to collaborate with the main study by making referrals of new placements, which indicated that they were dealing with a considerable volume of permanent placement work, and were therefore more likely to be engaged in the current issues. The survey focused solely on the permanent placement of older children in non-related families by the referring agencies at the time of the study, and aimed to record the agencies' views on the key policy questions.

Eighteen authorities participated in the main research. The policy survey was based on the seven authorities that had referred 69% of the cases into the study (42/61). Nineteen cases entered the study via one authority and three to six cases each from the remaining six. There were two London Boroughs (one inner, one outer) and five counties in the Midlands and the South of England. Each Principal Officer for adoption and fostering agreed to complete a 33 item questionnaire followed by an interview (conducted by AR) used to clarify and extend the answers. The interviews were conducted in the agencies, often in the company of a colleague or an administrative assistant who had helped to collate the information. The authority's manuals on its permanent placement philosophy and procedures were also consulted.

Policy Statements

One indication of policy development is the document social services agencies are required to produce at least every three years reviewing their policy and procedure. The respondents described their frequent involvement in setting up working parties with the intention of producing more specific guidance. However, several Principal Officers said that guidance and procedure on arranging substitute family care was much less specific than that for child protection. The documents tended to state the general child care policy of the agency with separate sections on adoption and fostering. These sections varied in their level of generality but staff members who wanted to know, for example, their responsibilities towards new parents and their children in a placement would often find little more guidance than that they should 'provide appropriate counselling and support'.

In spite of the growth of research into outcomes of older child placements (Thoburn, 1992), reference to specific research in the documents in support of a policy choice was rare. One authority, indicating its preference for adoption over permanent fostering, quoted research evidence that the latter offers less security and has more ambiguities than adoption. The practice implication drawn in the document was that adoption needs to be considered first and ruled out before opting for permanent fostering.

The Need for Placement for Older Children

The decision to make plans for a child to live permanently in a substitute family is clearly influenced by the social worker's initiative and workload, the quality of case reviews and the efficiency of case management systems to prevent planning 'drift'. The questionnaire was designed to reveal how many five- to nine-year-old children (boys and girls) looked after by each authority had been identified as in need of permanent, substitute families, and to establish the average waiting time for a placement and how many were actually placed (between 1990 and 1992).

Figures on the numbers placed for adoption are fairly easily obtained by reference to adoption panel minutes. These authorities placed an average of 15 older children each year but there was a broad range of between 4 and 30 and numbers fluctuated widely from year to year within each authority. During any one year, between 5 and 36 older children were waiting for a suitable family in these authorities. However, the way numbers waiting were reported varied, depending on whether they included those children for whom social workers had indicated the possibility of substitute placements at reviews, or whether they were in the queue for consideration by the panel, or whether panel approval had been given but they were waiting for a matched family. This lack of agreed definition makes for difficulties establishing precisely, and consistently across authorities, how many were waiting for placement.

The waiting time between the panel's decision that adoption was in the child's interests and the date of placement varied from 3 months to 4 years, with an average of 15–18 months. The accumulation of difficulties in the child or sibling group, when added to specific requirements, clearly increases the delay, and some matches may have been preceded by several months of circulating information about waiting children. Once the families were found, most authorities said they spent no more than 3 to 4 months on preparation before complete transfer to the new placement.

Recruitment of Applicants

Agencies generally used their own home-finding services before making a referral to another agency. The cost of inter-agency placements played a part in these considerations. Recruiting adequate numbers did not guarantee the ability to make planned choices, as agencies might still not be satisfied even with a plentiful supply of applicants if this did not produce a good match of child and family. Most agencies reported difficulties in recruiting adopters for older children and the commonest obstacles were:

1.   Insufficient numbers of applicants prepared to cope with older, disturbed and/or disabled children.
2.   Difficulty achieving appropriate matching, especially where the child has a dual cultural heritage.
3.   Large sibling groups, especially with a broad age spread.
4.   The difficulty of persuading new parents to take sexually abused children.
5.   Complicated contact arrangements.
6.   Insufficient staff, resulting in waiting lists for potential adopters to be assessed.

Achieving Permanence via Adoption or Permanent Foster Care

The major distinction to be made between permanent fostering and adoption is that foster parents only *carry* parental responsibilities whereas adopters are applying for full parental responsibility to be *transferred* to them. Authorities use both fostering and adoption regulations depending on the placement plan. Although many agencies prefer to place for adoption, they find that some substitute families will only accept permanent fostering. Rather than lose the placement, the authority may comply with this wish. More than one authority reported that the proportion of children in permanent foster care placements had recently reversed the usual preponderance of adoptions. This apparently increasing route to permanence leaves many questions unanswered about the decision-making process, which may differ in quality from that undertaken by an adoption panel. Written policies did not indicate when permanent fostering was appropriate and these important placement considerations did not routinely come before a permanence panel and the consequences of the decisions were not regularly monitored.

Adoption and Fostering Panels

The Adoption Agencies Regulations specify that each agency must establish adoption panels to act on its behalf. Their major task is to consider whether adoption is in the best interests of a child and whether prospective adopters would make suitable parents in a particular case. In arriving at recommendations, the panels must take into account and balance the needs and interests of all the parties: the child, the birth parents and potential adopters. They then make recommendations, which have to be confirmed by the Director of Social Services or the Social Services Committee.

A considerable amount of time was spent on panel meetings in the authorities surveyed. One authority, for example, had five panels (four UK, one overseas) meeting monthly. The composition of the panels was a balance of professional, independent and political appointments and disputes could surface between lay and professional members. A concern from the professional perspective was that lay members might take a less enlightened view of the acceptability of potential adopters, although most respondents said their panels worked efficiently and harmoniously with a strong desire to avoid delays which might prejudice the child's welfare.

Panels can be of central importance in promoting consistent practice, especially when scrutinising social work plans. They would be likely to have the greatest influence on overall quality of service in the agency when they were involved in all new permanent placement decisions, including where the plan was permanent fostering. Some panels wished to have referred back to them any proposals to change a placement plan. This was seen as an important safeguard against inappropriate or unsupervised decisions by inexperienced social workers.

A common difficulty panels faced with older children was in ensuring that rehabilitation to the birth family had been given the fullest consideration prior to making plans for adoption. A child might be returned home in one last effort at family preservation. If this were then to fail, it could cause distress merely in order to provide stronger evidence for adoption. This type of decision caused much heart searching for panel members.

Continuing Contact with Birth Families

'Openness' was a live issue for all the authorities and many were preparing a new policy statement. There has been increasing acknowledgement that severance from the past, 'a clean break' – as was common in infant adoptions – is frequently not appropriate, or possible, for older children and may have adverse effects. Many children will have had continued contact with their original families while in care and so the question for them is less one of how to open doors to birth families than how to keep them open. One authority's policy statement read:

> The older the child, the greater the likelihood that s/he has developed important relationships with significant people in her/his life and will want contact to be arranged to sustain these relationships.

The issue of contact was forcing some hard thinking about the most beneficial pattern of relationships for all concerned, especially in the light of the power of the courts to attach 'contact orders'. Concern was voiced by one respondent about the possible consequences of local court decisions:

> The courts are routinely making fairly high face-to-face contact arrangements even for small children. This would appear to be made more on the basis of meeting the parents' needs than the child's. Such high levels of contact are making family finding difficult and adopters feel pressurised into accepting more contact than they are comfortable with because they want to adopt the child.

On the other hand, if potential adopters express their discomfort with the idea of contact, the extent of contact may be restricted to prevent the agency from losing a family which has been regarded as a scarce resource.

In general, the respondents favoured 'openness' and wished to persuade prospective adopters of the reason for the policy. However, they also had reservations about the danger of a premature march into uncharted territory. They were cautious about contact leading, in some cases, to

divided loyalty in the children and the risk of destabilising the placement. Concern was felt at the lack of research evidence to show when
contact was likely to be beneficial.

Race and Culture Matching

The authorities varied considerably in the number of black and mixed
parentage children waiting for permanent placements. Matching placements by race was much more debated where numbers were larger and
here policy tended to be formulated in more detail. All the authorities
appeared to accept the general principle that 'in the great majority of
cases, placement with a family of similar ethnic origin and religion is
most likely to meet a child's needs as fully as possible' (DoH, 1990).
However, policy documents were often silent on the more taxing issues,
for example, on the selection of a placement plan in circumstances
where, after a long wait for the children, the ideal match had still not
been found.

One Principal Officer said black children in need of permanent placement are almost never placed with a family of a different race by the
authority. Other authorities made trans-racial placements only in very
exceptional circumstances, such as short-term care when demand
exceeds the supply of foster homes. In one set of policy guidelines a
non-matched placement was permitted, but only when a matched
placement had not been found within an agreed period of time. In such
a case, the reasons had to be clearly recorded and 'preparation, training
and support' had to be given to the families involved.

Some authorities saw the race dimension as paramount and sought first
to match by race before considering other characteristics. Others wished
to consider race alongside many other features and to decide on placement according to individual circumstances. Some respondents were
concerned that Same Race Placement policy can become inflexible and
may sometimes work against the needs of individual children.

Post-placement and Post-adoption Support

The actual volume of service provision for post-placement support was
largely unknown to the authorities. Lack of such knowledge prompted
us to collect data on the specific activities of both the child and family

social workers and to make this a major aim of the main study. The authorities' views on providing a social work service after legal adoption raise an important issue. The first SSI study (1991) found that little specific action was being taken to implement section 12 of the 1976 Adoption Act (which came into force in January 1988 and required authorities to provide a post-adoption service). The authorities in this survey were keen in principle to offer continuing services, especially to families who had adopted children with special needs and where there were complex contact arrangements. On the other hand, authorities were uncertain of their capacity to take on more responsibilities and accompanying costs. Agencies pointed out that as no extra resources had been allocated to provide these services they had to argue their case alongside the competing claims of child protection.

This brief survey of local authority adoption and fostering work has provided the opportunity to explore the professional considerations, value conflicts and resource issues that form the backdrop to the decision to place for permanence. It was evident from the responses that there was a need for a secure knowledge base to inform the development of policy and practice.

EVALUATIVE RESEARCH ON THE PLACEMENT OF OLDER CHILDREN

That late placement *can* have successful outcomes is illustrated by retrospective studies of adolescents or young adults, which have generally reported high levels of satisfaction from the new parents and from the children placed with them (Kadushin, 1970; Triseliotis & Russell, 1984). These studies have been a spur to confidence in placing older children, but the design does not allow for the identification of factors associated with differential outcome.

In trying to evaluate variations in placement outcome, three types of measure have commonly been employed: the disruption rate, parental satisfaction with continuing placements and, more rarely, assessment of the child's functioning or 'adjustment'. With all types of outcome, comparisons across studies can be misleading when these are based on dissimilar samples, different follow-up periods and different outcome measures. However, the most robust findings concerning risks related to the *child's characteristics* are that poorer outcomes are associated with older age at placement and a high level of behavioural difficulty.

With regard to *placement patterns*, poorer outcomes have been associated with children placed in families who have a birth child of similar age. The main factors discussed in the research literature are outlined below, but the limitations in the outcome measures are very noticeable.

Factors Associated with Disruption

Different research strategies have been selected to unravel which factors discriminate between disrupted and continuing placements. Some studies have focused on disruption: that is they have used the strategy of identifying samples of previously placed children and track down the placements and assess their status. This establishes the frequency of disruption and permits a search for predictors of it. Both Barth and Berry (1988) and Festinger (1986) used disruption as the key outcome variable rather than a parent satisfaction rating on the outcome of continuing placements.

Borland, O'Hara and Triseliotis (1991) conducted a prospective study of a representative series of local authority placements. The sample contained all the 'hard to place' children (n = 95) who moved to permanent family placements during one year (1983). Data collection was by semi-structured interview combined with questionnaires to parents, older children in the sample and social workers. Interviews took place at three years after placement but not at the time of placement itself. The sample was collected in the 1980s, a decade earlier than ours, and included children with disabilities and a full age range (except for the infant placements which were considered at low risk of disruption). Placements were monitored prospectively for three years, at which point 34% (33/95) had disrupted. The best predictors of disruption were found to be severe behavioural difficulties in the child and being over age 12 at placement.

Fratter, Rowe, Sapsford and Thoburn (1991) have conducted the largest UK survey of special needs adoptive and permanent foster placements. The sample comprised all special needs children (1165) placed from local authority care by 24 UK voluntary agencies into permanent families (1980–84). Data were gathered retrospectively by questionnaire, completed on the basis of agency records. Outcome was defined in terms of placement survival, with 21% of placements having disrupted by the time of the survey. However, the period at risk for breakdown was not standard, follow-up occurring between one and a half and six years after placement. A logit analysis was performed with disruption as the dependent variable and this identified nine risk factors. These included: age at placement and behavioural and emotional difficulties (factors making their usual appearance); being of mixed parentage; and having a history of institutionalisation, abuse or deprivation.

An important late placement study was conducted in the USA by Barth and Berry (1988) of 898 out of 1000 placements, set up by public adoption agencies in California between 1980 and 1984. The sample was of similar age to ours with a mean age at placement of 8.2 years. Seventy-two per cent of the sample were white, 23% were in sibling groups, and 13% were trans-racial placements. However, a quarter had mental or physical disability or a medical condition: a group we excluded. Barth and Berry found a relatively low disruption rate of 10% over 18 months. Five variables were found to discriminate between the stable and disrupted outcome groups. Disruption rates were higher the older the child at placement; the greater the number of child problems; where children had a previous adoptive placement; and where adoptive mothers were college, rather than high school, graduates. Children adopted by long-standing foster carers had lower disruption rates and it may be the presence of this group that lowered the overall rate.

Outcome as Measured by Parent Satisfaction

Outcomes beyond 'disruption' involve recording subjective judgements about levels of satisfaction with the continuing placements. Nelson's adoption study (1985) pays the greatest attention to measuring new parent satisfaction systematically. This was an interview-based study of 177 families who adopted 257 special needs children. The children had emotional, physical and intellectual impairments and their average age at placement was seven and a half years. This was a relatively short-term follow-up with few disruptions, which limits the analysis in some ways but shifts the interest to more detailed assessments of continuing placements. A seven item satisfaction scale was devised and produced an index of satisfaction. Most of the sample families (73%) were shown to have a high (good to excellent) satisfaction score. A regression analysis showed the most important predictor of poor satisfaction to be if the new parents found the child 'isolated'. This meant having few friends, being mistrustful and holding people at arm's length. This was interesting in that it suggested that a particular type of relationship difficulty influenced the capacity of the new parents to feel positively about the placement.

A follow-up of adoptions has recently been conducted with special attention to the adolescent years. Howe (1996, 1997) has reported on a retrospective, interview-based study of a volunteer sample of adoptive parents ($n = 120$) followed up when their adopted children were in early adulthood (at least 23 years old, mean age 26). This method, of course, favours the continuing placements and adoptive families in which disruption had taken place would be less likely to participate. In fact only two of the 211 placements studied had broken down.

Of the 211 children, 89 were late placed and the majority (69) were classified as having had a 'poor start', that is, they had experienced inconsistent, neglectful, rejecting or abusive parenting from their birth families. The interest was on the level of behavioural problems and quality of parent–child relationships during adolescence. Rates of problem behaviour were highest on every item for the poor start/late adoptions and mean scores were three times as high as for the other two groups (early adoptions or good start/late adoptions). This group also had much poorer parent–child relationships at age 16. However, it was found that relationships had improved when young adulthood was reached. Sixty-seven per cent of parents felt they had a positive relationship with their adult adoptive children compared with only 38% during adolescence. Increased confidence and security appeared to develop later and adoptive parents and children were often reconciled after the stormy period.

In summary, in most studies of placement outcome in older children, age at placement and level of child difficulty stand out as the most frequently identified predictors. Research has not consistently found differences by gender, ethnicity, race matching, single parent adoptions or age of new parents. These variations in associations may arise because the confluence of negative factors in particular cases may be more important than the individual factors *per se*. In addition, there may be protective factors that work against poor outcome. For example, siblings may offer each other support, or adverse experiences may have been counteracted by positive ones such as good relationships with other adults. Protective factors have been less studied than risks.

In our study the intention was to go beyond an inquiry into influences on disruption to a prospective examination of the developmental progress of the children and the stability of their placements at the end of the first year of placement. Because of this focus it will be possible to examine, through further follow-up studies, the predictors not only of disruptions but also of differences in outcome within placements that remain intact.

Studies with Systematic Assessments of Children's Psychosocial Functioning

There are few studies that use systematic evaluations of children's behaviour at placement and document changes prospectively. Tizard and her colleagues (Tizard, 1977; Hodges and Tizard, 1989a, 1989b) followed up a group of children who were in institutions from infancy and were then placed with new families or restored to their own parents after the age of two. Adopted ex-institutional children followed up in adolescence developed selective attachments to their parents and showed a reduction in the restless, distractible pattern exhibited at eight years. However, they still showed problems at school and had more difficulty in close relationships with peers. This difference on peer relationships was not shown by children restored to their birth parents, but, otherwise, the latter group had poorer outcomes than the adopted group.

The first study in our research programme followed 18 boys from disrupted backgrounds prospectively over eight years in their placement with unrelated foster and adoptive families (Rushton *et al.*, 1988, 1993, 1995). Data were collected by parental interview and questionnaire at 1, 6 and 12 months after placement and again at 5 and 8 years. Poorer outcomes at one year were found for the older boys and for those who had experienced multiple changes of pre-placement environment. A modest reduction in problems in the first six months was followed by more rapid improvement by the end of the first year, accompanied, for the majority, by the steady development of affectionate relationships with the new parents. Restlessness and lack of creative play were persisting problems.

At the five year follow-up, two-thirds of the boys continued to show modest improvement but the remainder exhibited a high level of problems, which had either been present throughout or were associated with an upswing of difficulties in early adolescence. At the eight year follow-up there was a 19% breakdown rate but 54% of the surviving placements had a good outcome. Having spent more than a year pre-placement in residential care predicted disruption or poor outcome in placement. Very high quality and consistency in parenting predicted better outcomes. The commonest and most persistent problem experienced by the boys in continuing placements was restlessness.

This brief review of permanent placement research emphasises the very strong association of age at placement and behavioural problems with

disruption. Studies that have explored difficulties in continuing placements have found isolated, restless behaviour to be a particular feature
for placed children. There is also some indication that schooling and
peer relationships can remain problematic.

EMOTIONAL AND BEHAVIOURAL PROBLEMS IN CHILDREN WITH ADVERSE PARENTING EXPERIENCES

The data reviewed above suggest that the developmental recovery of
many of the children for whom new permanent family placements are
sought is not a matter of a 'quick fix' via the provision of a stable loving
environment. Rather, these children often arrive in their new families
with a multiplicity of difficulties that may take many years to diminish
and indeed may, in some cases, persist through adolescence and into
adult life. Although the great majority of these children have manifestly
been deprived of consistent, loving relationships, it does not follow that
the provision of these in new permanent families will lead to rapid
psychosocial recovery. Since the great majority of these children have
been maltreated in a variety of ways, what is known about the emotional, behavioural and cognitive development of such children will now
be briefly reviewed.

Most children for whom permanent substitute family placements are
now sought have experienced very poor parenting, often for a number
of years. They will have suffered emotional, physical or sexual abuse or
neglect, and many will have experienced several of these forms of maltreatment from more than one parental figure. Psychosocial development rests on the accomplishment of a range of tasks and failure to
progress through these satisfactorily increases the probability of mal-
adaptive outcomes (Cicchetti & Garmezy, 1993).

By the time children in the age range of our studies are placed they may
have experienced five years or more of markedly inadequate developmental environments and thus be lacking in a whole range of com-
petencies necessary for more stable and successful functioning. Cicchetti
and Toth (1995) have summarised the problems that may arise for
abused and neglected children with respect to: *the regulation of emotions*
(control of anger and frustration, and emotional responses to anger
between others); *the development of attachment* (particularly in the development of stable internal models of attachment figures); *the development
of the self-system* (identity and self-esteem); *the quality of peer relationships*;
and *adaptation to school*.

Emotional regulation

Adequate control over the expression of feelings is very important for the development and maintenance of stable social relationships, with both peers and adults. Physically abused infants have been observed to express high levels of negative emotions and a lack of positive ones, whilst neglected infants tend to be low in the expression of both kinds of emotion. A tendency to a lack of self-control and higher levels of expressed negative feelings have also been observed in maltreated pre-schoolers (Allesandri, 1991), together with increased fearfulness and a lack of empathy and concern (Main & George, 1985). Not surprisingly, these behavioural features continue to be shown in school (Shields *et al.*, 1994), and appear related to a heightened arousal and vigilance. This results in over-reactions to real or imagined threats to the children themselves or disagreements between carers (Hennesey *et al.*, 1994).

The development of attachment

Current developments in attachment theory stress not only the secure or insecure behaviours shown by children towards their carers, but also the mental representations – or internal working models – they carry of these relationships. Thus, models formed on the basis of past experiences are thought to influence the children's approach to new relationships with adults. Maltreated children tend to show a lack of any kind of organised response or strategy in dealing with separations – the most usual test for attachment problems. Children who have not been maltreated, but whose attachments are problematic, tend to be either consistently anxious or resistant in their reunion behaviour, whereas maltreated children appear disorganised and disoriented, and even appear frozen, dazed or appre-hensive (Main & Solomon, 1990). This pattern has appeared in as many as 80% of maltreated infants in some studies (Carlson *et al.*, 1989), and appears to be persistent.

The development of the self-system

It now seems clear that children's representational models of themselves and others are markedly influenced by the stability of the early care-giving environment, especially during the second half of the second year of life (Sroufe, 1990). Maltreated toddlers tend to use fewer words referring to internal states (Beeghly & Ciccheti, 1994), and engage in less symbolic play (Allesandri, 1991). In later years maltreated children have lower self-esteem (Egeland *et al.*, 1983), lower perceived self-competence (Vondra *et al.*, 1989), and tend to be more depressed (Kaufman, 1991).

Peer relationships

It is not surprising that the problems in emotional regulation, development of attachments and poorer self-image are associated with markedly
poorer peer relationships. Physically abused children tend to show
much more physical and verbal aggression in their interactions with
peers (Mueller & Silverman, 1989), which may even occur in response to
friendly approaches or to signs of distress (Main & George, 1985).
Neglected children also have disturbed peer relationships but these are
more likely to involve withdrawal and social isolation (Hoffman-Plotkin
& Twentyman, 1984). In new situations, maltreated children are less
positive, initiate fewer interactions and engage in less complex play.
Moreover, this lack of social competence appears to be persistent and, as
a result, maltreated children are often disliked (Salzinger *et al.*, 1993).

Adaptation to school

School provides one of those potentially rewarding environments that
might improve maltreated children's self-image and social competence.
Unfortunately, the adaptation of these children to school tends to be poor.
Physically abused children tend to be aggressive and non-compliant and
to show poor cognitive performance (Erikson *et al.*, 1989). Neglected
children tend to be anxious, inattentive and unable to understand their
work, and to be uncooperative and lacking in empathy. These ill effects
affect boys and girls equally and have been shown across the entire range
of grade levels (Eckenrode *et al.*, 1993).

Of course, these problems do not apply equally to all maltreated children since individual differences in resilience, presence of compensatory
experiences, the timing, frequency and severity of the abuse and the
degree of emotional or psychological maltreatment accompanying
abusive episodes will make for considerable variation in the children's
experiences and very probably in their subsequent responses.

Summary

In summary, it is clear that maltreated children show a very wide range
of emotional, behavioural, cognitive, social and attachment problems.
These problems are related not just to the facts of maltreatment itself,
but also to the consequences of the broader parenting difficulties the

children may have experienced. By the time our group of children entered their new families between the ages of five and nine, many of them had experienced these environmental adversities for most or all of their lives. This involved not just an absence of love or caring, but also the lack of stable relationships needed for the development of attachments, the stimulation and input needed for cognitive development, the positive regard necessary for self-esteem and mastery motivation, or the control of negative feelings and the development of prosocial ones that promote good peer relationships.

THE DEVELOPMENT OF RELATIONSHIPS

While the behaviour of a placed child is undoubtedly a significant feature in unsuccessful placements, it is clear from the work of those who have interviewed new parents that there is an interplay between behaviour and relationships. There will always be a point at which behaviour becomes intolerable, but that point appears to vary for different families (Hodges & Tizard, 1989b). It is likely that a number of factors influence the 'critical point', including the parents' own expectations about children's behaviour, their ability to manage the behaviour, and their mechanisms for containing their own feelings about it. Another very important factor must be concern that the behaviours may be harming other children in the family. However, the investigations by Tizard and her colleagues led them to conclude that it was primarily the strength of the relationship between parent and child that determined the level of parent satisfaction. When a good relationship had developed, quite significant behavioural difficulties could be tolerated.

Permanent Placement and Attachment Theory

In trying to understand the mechanism by which early adverse experiences may affect the development, in particular social development, of late placed children and the manner in which these problems may impact on placement security, academics and practitioners have drawn especially on attachment theory (e.g. Fahlberg, 1981; Howe, 1997). This approach hypothesises that disturbances in the initial attachment relationship of abused or maltreated youngsters affect their later relationships through their internal representations, or working models, of caregivers. Such processes may be particularly important in the case of substitute placement because a child's ability to respond to the new parents may be crucial to the security of the placement in the longer term (Nelson, 1985; Hodges & Tizard, 1989b).

Attachment theory has provided a structure for categorising the security of the relationship between young children and their caregivers (usually the mother). The quality of these early relationships is held to be carried forward into later ones via the child's representations, or internal working models of relationships. The immediate and short-term effects of abusive parenting on children's attachment behaviour were outlined earlier, but it is still unclear how persistent these effects are if there is a positive change in the caring environment. The impact of multiple changes of relationship on children's internal models of caregivers is also unclear.

In late permanent placements, there is a coming together of children with complex attachment histories and parents who, of course, have attachment histories of their own. All the children will, at a minimum, have been separated from birth parents and been placed with foster parents or relatives. Some will retain strong attachments, even in combination with maltreatment, and many will have experienced a pattern of broken, restored and re-broken relationships. They may carry multiple mental representations of attachment figures prior to the placement including their birth parents, relatives, previous foster parents and social network members. In addition, there may be many memories of brief attachments both positive and negative. Little is known on whether representations of brief attachments endure, but if relationships with caregivers persistently fail to meet children's need for stability and predictability, they may be wary of, or be unable to make, any new attachments. It is also important to consider non-parental figures who may have provided an alternative source of security and stability.

It is also crucial to examine whether new permanent placements are able to effect changes in representations and behaviours. Does security and stability allow the children to relearn or reconstruct their models of adult caregiving? If this does not take place or takes place very slowly, what impedes it? For example, Lynch and Cicchetti (1991) distinguish between global and specific models of relationships. The maltreated child may have generalised the poor relationship with the primary caregiver to all relationships and the model may be very resistant to change, at least until adolescence when cognitive maturation allows new information to be accommodated. Progress in understanding these processes will require longitudinal studies of carefully selected and representative samples with good measurement of these relationship patterns over time. For late placed children, a concept like 'good enough attachment' might better convey what might be expected.

THEORIES OF PARENTING AND THEIR RELATION TO PERMANENT PLACEMENT

The other key factor in the stability of late permanent family placements concerns the parenting skills, perceptions and experience of the new parents. How parents respond to a child's arrival in their home will be affected not only by the child's behaviour but also by their own expectations and beliefs.

Belsky (1984) has drawn attention to the multiply determined nature of parenting. These determinants include: the developmental histories of the parents; their personalities and psychological resources; the quality of their own relationship; and the contextual sources of stress and support. Abidin (1992) has argued for the inclusion of social and environmental factors. Such influences will also affect substitute parents, although the selection process should exclude those whose personal histories and current circumstances and relationships are a risk to parenting.

Just as parenting is multiply determined, so it also encompasses a wider range of activities and behaviours apart from basic physical care and nurturance, including: management and control strategies; warmth, responsiveness and the fostering of relationships; inputs to cognitive and intellectual development; and the provision of security and stability. The optimum approach involves first sensitive and responsive interactions that foster emotional security, attachment and exploration (Baumrind, 1971; Parker *et al.*, 1979), and second, consistent, non-aggressive but firm control that sets boundaries but also fosters mastery and a sense of control (Patterson, 1982). The more parenting departs from this, the more it is insensitive, inconsistent, confrontational and aggressive, the more problematic children's emotional, behavioural and intellectual development tends to be.

These characteristics are well summarised in Maccoby and Martin's (1983) classification of parenting patterns (Table 1.1). In this scheme the authoritative/reciprocal pattern has been associated with greater competence, social responsibility and independence in children.

In applying this scheme to parenting unrelated, disturbed older children, parents who have been specifically recruited, adequately assessed and prepared are likely to fall into the authoritative/reciprocal category

Table 1.1: Maccoby and Martin's two-dimensional classification of parenting (Maccoby & Martin, 1983)

	Responsive Child-centred	Unresponsive Parent-centred
Demanding, controlling	Authoritative– reciprocal	Authoritarian Power assertive
Undemanding, low in control attempts	Indulgent	Neglecting, ignoring, indifferent, uninvolved

and should have the capacity to offer warm, accepting, sensitive parenting and to manage challenging discipline problems. However, as Quinton and Rutter (1988) stress, these are not fixed within-the-parent attributes but are manifested in relation to two-way interactions in specific parent/child relationships. Thus, the authoritative/reciprocal pattern arises not only because of the parents' control style, but also from the child's level of compliance: an important influence in late permanent placements because of the children's emotional and behavioural problems. If the relationship develops badly, there may be a switch from a positive to a negative parenting pattern, probably of the authoritarian/power assertive type. The new parents may reduce their commitment, withdraw warmth, become more authoritarian or perhaps become increasingly avoidant.

Theories of Late Placements

Ever since Kirk (1964) first raised the question of the difference between adoptive and birth parenting there has been a debate on the nature of this difference and the conditions that allow adoptive parents to feel entitled to parent. Of course, in many respects, substitute parenting is similar to parenting birth children: carers can be subject to the same adverse and unexpected circumstances such as job losses, financial problems, bereavements and difficulties in their own relationships. However, there are features of parenting children in late permanent placements that are different from the parenting task that confronts birth parents, apart from issues around the sense of entitlement. These involve: recognising the implications of the child's previous parenting history; acknowledging the child's prior experiences and relationships and concern with identity and loss; interpreting disturbed and seemingly incomprehensible behaviour; managing behavioural problems; adjusting to the strategies the placed child has learned for dealing with intense feelings. In addition, new parents will be concerned with maintaining pre-existing family relationships, managing their own feelings towards birth parents (particularly if there has been abuse) and imparting the new family routines and culture.

There have been some attempts to theorise about the progress of late placements over time in terms of family relationship formation and family readjustment. Pinderhughes (1995) has proposed a four stage model, progressing via anticipation and accommodation to resistance and resolution. Five domains of family functioning are specified as important – cognitions, resources, stressors, coping and relationship representations – but with different levels of salience as the family moves through the stages. Pinderhughes is currently conducting a small-scale, process-oriented, longitudinal study to examine the sequence of stages and to take measures in each domain. If the theory is useful it should be able to predict which combinations of child and family will adapt and assimilate most quickly and which will be slow to adapt or unsuccessful.

A theory of late placement should also include models for the integration of two sibling sub-systems, when children are placed in families with birth children. The analogy with step-families is often made. Visher and Visher (1996) stress the amount of time it takes for new relationships to grow, the normal lack of confidence and entitlement in parenting new children and differing expectations based on prior parent/child relationships.

The new parent's own nurturance history may shape adoptive parenting and the growth of relationships, although little is known about this at present. Adults' models of attachment prior to the birth of a child predict the quality of the infant–parent relationship at a year in birth families (Fonagy et al., 1991), but it is not known whether similar processes apply to relationships between adoptive parents and their new children (Main, 1996).

SUMMARY

We introduced this chapter with a presentation of the challenges of complex placement decisions for older children and the related organisational and resource factors. The review of theoretical and empirical work revealed that while difficult behaviour and older age at placement continue to feature in relation to poorer outcome, it is now known that the propensity for the development of meaningful and mutual relationships is crucial to parental satisfaction with, and the stability of, the placement. There has been a growing awareness of the complexity of the interplay between the previous experiences of parents and children and the way in which these may affect the expectations that each party has of the permanent placement.

Although research has shown positive outcomes for the majority of late placements, findings have been hard to aggregate because studies differ in many ways, including sample characteristics, length of follow-up period and measures of the psychological status of the children. For this reason, there was a need for much more detailed documentation to answer questions not just about disruptions, but also about the type and intensity of problems these children experience; which problems are likely to remit more quickly and which will be persistent; which parenting approaches provide the greatest pay-off; and what aspects of the social work role are significant in setting up and supporting placements. Our attempt to answer some of these questions can now be presented.

2

AIMS, DESIGN, SAMPLING AND METHODOLOGY

In designing this study we were eager to capture a wide range of possible difficulties and adaptations relevant to the developmental progress of the children. For this reason, our choice of measures covered the many emotional, behavioural and social difficulties, at home and at school, that the children might have. The selection of areas was influenced by the theoretical literature and existing empirical studies of maltreated and permanently placed children. Comprehensive and systematic data of this kind are an essential basis for examining which factors in the children's backgrounds and placement experiences are related to the problems they have, as well as determining which problems persist, which attenuate and why.

AIMS OF THE STUDY

The main aims of the study were:

1. To document one year placement outcomes, including rates of disruption.
2. To investigate the impact of pre-placement experiences on placement outcome at the end of the first year.
3. To establish the pattern of change in psychosocial difficulties over this time.
4. To discover whether differences in the parenting style of the new parents were associated with outcome.
5. To establish how the new parents regarded the social work support and whether the quantity and quality of professional input, before and after placement, was associated with outcome at a year.

DESIGN

The study used a prospective, repeated measures design in which the type and severity of the children's problems and the parents' responses to these were assessed shortly after the placement, again after six months, and finally at the end of the first year. This design was chosen, not only to document the level of difficulties the children were showing, but also to see whether parenting styles and social worker support were related to the children's recovery. In addition, it offers a sound basis for longer-term follow-up.

A comparison group was not included because the main focus was on differences in outcome *within* a group of children who had all experienced inadequate early parenting, rather than on a comparison of the level of problems *between* such a group and children within the normal range of rearing experiences. In addition, the identification of a comparable group of maltreated children who were *not* permanently placed would have been very difficult. However, in order to provide some indication of the level of difficulties in these children, we used a number of standard measures for which general population data are available: the Rutter A2 Scale for parents (Rutter *et al.*, 1975) and measures of verbal and non-verbal intelligence for the children. Teachers completed the Rutter B2 Scale (Rutter *et al.*, 1975) on the emotional and behavioural adjustment of the children in school and of one control child of the same age and sex from the same school class.

SAMPLING CRITERIA

The sample was restricted to children placed between the ages of five and nine inclusive. This age range was chosen for two reasons: first because children in middle childhood form a large proportion of those 'looked after' children who require permanent substitute families and secondly because disruption rates for permanent placements had been shown to rise over this period (Thoburn & Rowe, 1988). We expected this group to be more challenging than children placed earlier in life and therefore to have more of the problems associated with disruption. Resources did not allow the upward extension of the age range. Moreover, a study that included adolescents would have raised a number of additional issues, especially the effects of the onset of puberty, that could not have been dealt with adequately in a sample of this size.

When children were placed with siblings who were within the age group, one child from the group was randomly selected for intensive study. Placements that involved children with severe learning difficulties or profound physical handicaps were excluded because these problems present fundamentally different challenges to new parents

(Harris & McHale, 1989) and because the proposed sample size would not have provided groups large enough for adequate analyses. The sample criteria were very similar to those used in our previous study of late placed boys (Rushton *et al.*, 1988), so that we could make some comparisons with them. The main difference between the samples was that this study included girls, so that gender differences in outcome could be examined.

Participating Authorities

The sampling was restricted to local authorities. Independent agencies were not used as referral sources because they did not hold statutory responsibility for the children. However, children placed with families who were recruited via independent agencies were included. Twenty-seven social services departments in and around the London area were approached and invited to take part. Twenty-three authorities agreed in principle. Four refused because of pressure of work or departmental reorganisation. Inner London Boroughs were the most likely to refuse. In the end, 18 of the 23 authorities that agreed to participate made referrals (8 urban boroughs and 10 counties). The number of 'looked after' children in the referring authorities varied between 2 and 13 per 1000 of the population under 18 years. Seven authorities provided 69% of the cases.

Referral Procedure

Our original hope had been to include a representative sample of permanent foster placements as well as placements made with a plan for adoption. However, our study design meant that we had to see families within about one month of placement and it proved impossible to identify most permanent foster placements this quickly. There turned out to be many ways of embarking on permanent foster care and in most authorities the decision-making process was not accessible to the researchers, or the decision for permanence occurred in the context of already existing placements. It was simpler for authorities to identify children for whom adoption was intended, largely because of the use of adoption panels for decision-making and the more formal nature of adoption planning. In the end, the sample did include 12 placements where long-term fostering was intended (four of these children were placed with a view to adoption later), but we cannot be sure that these are representative of all long-term fostering arrangements.

We identified cases by asking authorities to inform us of children meeting the criteria at the time that a 'match' was found between them and a new family. The social worker was then asked to help us make contact with the new parents. No details were passed to the research team until the consent of the family had been obtained. Ensuring that all eligible cases were referred required substantial effort and involved regular and time-consuming liaison with nominated contacts in each authority. Referrals to the study were received over a 21 month period in the early 1990s.

The Sample

A total of 84 eligible placements were reported but 23 of these did not become part of the study. In six cases, social workers said that they were too overburdened to help, or that they judged it unwise to approach the family at this point. In five cases, the court or those with wardship responsibilities refused permission even though the new families were willing. Finally, 12 families declined to take part: 15% of the new parents who were approached by their social workers. The final sample, therefore, comprised 61 families, that is 73% of the eligible cases.

Given the perennial pressures on local authority social services departments and the known difficulties associated with collecting samples such as this, we were very pleased with both the referral and the participation rate. These social workers and families were asked to take part in our research at a time when their lives were being turned upside down by the practicalities and anxieties of introductions and impending placement.

Missing Cases

Cases not referred

Every attempt was made to ensure that authorities notified us of eligible children, but we became aware that cases were sometimes missed. There was usually no administrative mechanism through which we could check on the numbers of these. We were not aware of any selection biases in this process – for example through social workers selectively referring easier or more difficult children – but it was not possible to know how many missing cases there were nor whether these losses introduced biases of other kinds.

Biases through refusal

An assessment of possible sampling bias was possible for those cases where families declined to take part or where professionals refused access. Anonymised information was obtained from social workers on all these cases. The refusal group and the research sample were compared on six variables: gender, age at placement, placement type, outcome at one year, pre-placement changes of environment and the children's previous parenting experience. There were some differences between the groups. These are listed in Table 2.1. Participating parents were significantly more likely than refusing families to have children of their own. There was also a tendency for refusing families to have more than one child placed with them. These two factors are not unrelated since the majority of experienced parents will still have children at home and probably only have room for a single child. There was a significantly higher rate of disruption among the refusal group and it may be that the reason for refusal in some cases was that the placement was already in difficulty.

The implication of these differences between participating and refusing cases will be discussed in Chapter 14.

DATA COLLECTION

We collected data for this study in three ways: through *interviews* with social workers and parents, through *questionnaires* completed by parents and teachers, and through *direct assessments* of the children. The data collection plan is given in Table 2.2 and the content of the instruments described briefly below. Where appropriate a more detailed description of the instruments used is provided in the relevant chapters.

Interviews

All the interviews in this study were conducted by one of the authors and a research colleague and followed an investigator-based approach (Brown, 1983). This approach is best described as a 'conversation with a purpose' (Richardson *et al.*, 1965). It provides for the systematic, but flexible coverage of topics of interest, using predefined codings. It is not limited by either the vagaries of the free-form interview or the constraints of the structured instrument.

Table 2.1: Comparison of participating and non-participating cases

	Refusals ($n = 23$)	Participants ($n = 61$)	$p =$
Singly placed child	44%	64%	0.074[a]
Foster placement	4%	13%	NS
Index child male	64%	53%	NS
Previous parenting – mother	36%	69%	<0.01
Previous parenting – father	32%	72%	<0.001
Mean age of index child	85 months	89 months	NS
Mean no. of placements	6.7	5.4	NS
Placement disrupted by 1 year	26%	5%	0.024[a]

[a] Fisher's exact test. NS: not significant.

Table 2.2: Timetable of data collection

Type of measure	1 month	6 months	12 months
Interviews			
Child's social worker	•		•
Family's social worker	•		•
New parents	•	•	•
Questionnaires			
Rutter A2 Scale (new parents)	•	•	•
Rutter B2 Scale (teachers)	•	•	•
Expression of feelings	•	•	•
Direct assessment of the children			
Continuous performance	•		•
Matching Familiar Figures	•		•
Raven's Progressive Matrices		•	
British Picture Vocabulary Scale		•	
Tester ratings of behaviour	•		

Interviews with social workers

The child and family social workers (CSW and FSW) took part in a face-to-face interview at their place of work, lasting for one to one and a half hours, at one month after placement and again at a year.

The *one month* interview with CSWs allowed the interviewers to build up a picture of the children's experiences. The information included the child's pre-placement history and psychosocial difficulties and the preparatory work conducted with the child. The interview with the FSW covered the characteristics and preparation of the new family. Both

CSWs and FSWs were asked about their prediction for the success of the placement and the post-placement support plans offered by them or other professionals. Information was also collected from all social workers on their training and experience of family placement work, and the supervision and consultation available for this work within their authority.

The social worker interviews at 12 *months* focused on their perceptions of the progress of the placement over the year, the amount of social work support required, their interventions and the liaison between the CSW and FSW.

Interviews with new parents

Interviews with the new parents were conducted in their own homes and lasted around two and a half hours. Fathers' as well as mothers' contributions were considered essential and so interviews were arranged with both parents, wherever possible. There were three women heading one parent families and one man.

The parent interviews were based on instruments devised for previous studies of parenting (Quinton & Rutter, 1988), and developed for use with substitute parents of older children in the pilot study (Rushton *et al.*, 1988). This instrument was augmented by standard assessments of children's psychosocial functioning used in the Isle of Wight/Inner London Comparative study (IoW) (Rutter *et al.*, 1975), and the Parental Account of Child Symptoms (PACS) (Taylor *et al.*, 1986).

The areas covered in the interview were: demographic characteristics; the new parents' views on the assessment and pre-placement period; the placement type and structure; the placed child's psychosocial functioning; the parents' methods of handling problems; the child's place in family routines and activities; the parents' assessment of the progress of the placement; the child's school experience; peer relationships; contact between the child and birth parents or other significant people from the past; the stresses felt by the new parents and the support they were receiving and their wishes and views in regard to services.

At six months the parents gave an account of the progress of the placement, reviewed the difficulties the children were showing at one month and discussed any new problems that had arisen.

At one year the progress of the placement was again reviewed and the systematic assessment of the children's psychosocial functioning repeated. In addition, data were collected on contact arrangements and their impact, as well as on the parents' perception of social work services and support.

Questionnaires

The Expression of Feelings Questionnaire (EFQ) (see Appendix A)

At the time of data collection, we were unable to find any attachment measures that had been devised for this age group and so we developed a 48 item questionnaire to be completed by the parents which assessed the development of open, secure and affectionate behaviour by the child towards the new parents. These aspects of the relationship are related to features of secure or insecure attachment but we have avoided calling this a measure of 'attachment' because it was not possible to evaluate it against attachment measures that would be acceptable to the academic community. The questionnaire covers the child's emotional closeness to the parents, his/her openness in expressing feelings and willingness to share distress, and the seeking and accepting of affection. It was completed independently by mothers and fathers at 1, 6 and 12 months into placement. Comparison data were collected on children in the same age group from 54 birth parents with children attending two primary schools in the south of England.

Rutter A and B Scales

Rutter A2 Scales were completed by parents at each data collection point. The A2 Scale is a 31 item questionnaire with an established cut-off that distinguishes children with clinically significant emotional and behavioural problems from those without, and which yields sub-scales measuring emotional and conduct problems and hyperactivity. Where parents gave permission, the children's teachers completed the parallel 26 item teachers' scale on the index child at 1 and 12 months, and also on one unidentified classmate of the same age and sex.

Direct Assessment of the Child

It was not considered appropriate, by either the research team or the social service departments, to question the children directly about their new families during their first year of placement. However, it was possible to collect some measures of the children's cognitive and behavioural functioning in the majority of cases (Table 2.3). All of the direct assessments were conducted in the children's new homes, mostly in the early evening.

Measures of attention and impulsivity

Parents in the pilot study had reported problems in attention and impulsivity much more frequently in late placed children than is the case in general population samples (Rushton *et al.*, 1988). An association was also found in other studies of children in care (Yule & Raynes, 1972) and of adopted children (Andresen, 1992). These problems proved to be among the most persistent for the pilot study children (Rushton *et al.*, 1995) and have implications for scholastic progress and for peer relationships. Therefore, it seemed important to assess attention and impulsivity more directly. The Continuous Performance Test (Corkum & Seigal, 1993) is a computer-based game of 'snap' designed to measure attention and Matching Familiar Figures is a card matching test (Cairns & Cammock, 1978). These were used to assess impulsivity and both were administered at 1 and 12 months after placement.

Intellectual development

Recently, attention has been drawn to the much neglected issue of the intellectual development of children in foster care (Heath *et al.*, 1994) with the general finding of a disappointing lack of progress for these children. As yet, little is known about the intellectual development of children late placed in permanent substitute families nor whether the level of development has implications for improvements in psychosocial functioning. For these reasons measures of verbal and non-verbal IQ were included in the assessments and administered at six months. This point was chosen because the load on them would have been too great if the measures had been added to the attentional ones at the 1 or 12 month point. Verbal ability was assessed using the British Picture Vocabulary Scale (Short Form) (Dunn *et al.*, 1982). Spatial ability was assessed using Raven's Progressive Matrices (Raven, 1958). The direct assessment sessions were used as an opportunity to rate the children's behaviour under conditions of mild stress and in the presence of an adult stranger. The Tester's Ratings of Infant Behaviour (TRIB) (Wolke, 1986) was adapted for this age group.

Table 2.3: Summary of available data

Type of measure	1 month	6 months	12 months
Interviews			
Child's social worker	61		53
Family's social worker	61		55
New parents	61	60	58
Questionnaires			
Rutter A2 Scale (new parents)	52	46	49
Rutter B2 Scale (teachers)	49		49
Expression of feelings (new mothers)	51		38
Direct assessment of the children			
Continuous performance	47		45
Matching Familiar Figures	32		43
Raven's Progressive Matrices		47	
British Picture Vocabulary Scale		47	
Tester ratings of behaviour	43	39	38

SUMMARY OF AVAILABLE DATA

Although it was possible to collect complete sets of data on the majority of cases, there were, inevitably, some missing data. This arose most commonly because parents did not agree to the testing of the children or were too busy to complete all the questionnaires. In addition, there are variations in the numbers of cases between the first and the 12 month interview because of placement disruptions. A summary of available data is given in Table 2.3.

COMMENT ON THE ANALYSIS

In presenting the study findings we decided to omit analyses using the six month data, apart from the cognitive tests. This was primarily because the changes between one and six months were slight and their inclusion complicated the presentation without adding significantly new information.

In all the analyses, small variations in sample size across tables are not commented on unless the reasons for the missing data are germane to the analysis. Where appropriate, checks for any differences in results because of data variations have been applied. We have attempted to combine statistical rigour with a feeling for the individual cases and to reflect the statistical findings in qualitative material. We have used statistical procedures which take into account the repeated measures nature of our data wherever appropriate. For continuous measures we have usually used repeated measures analysis of variance, paired t-tests or related techniques. The McNemar test was used as the alternative to χ^2 for repeated measures categorical data. However, the analyses are necessarily complex and the balance of the presentation is towards highlighting those statistically reliable results that we can present with confidence.

Although we frequently report the full results of statistical analyses, to avoid too much repetition we have sometimes omitted the detail. The reader should assume that any association described as significant indicates a relationship beyond the 5% level of probability.

3

OUTCOMES AFTER ONE YEAR IN PLACEMENT

If the avowed aim of placement is to provide the child with a permanent home then the disruption rate is an incontestable indicator of placement outcome. However, there are many intermediate stages on the way to disruption or permanence and our interest was more in examining these stages than in documenting predictors of breakdown. By the end of the first year, just 3 of the 61 cases in the study had disrupted. We were able, therefore, to focus the analyses almost entirely on differences in outcome among the surviving placements. It is important to describe how these were assessed. The chapter begins with a discussion of the definition and measurement issues related to placement outcome, followed by a description of the measures we have chosen to use and the outcome groupings in the study sample.

WHAT IS AN OUTCOME?

The selection of outcome measures in family placement research is frequently acknowledged to be problematic and no system is without its limitations. There are several factors that need to be considered. Firstly, the term 'success and failure' is a judgement that is value-laden and does not lend itself to universally agreed definitions. Secondly, such a judgement may vary according to whom is being consulted and the expectations they hold concerning the aims of the placement and how likely it is that these can be achieved. Thirdly, the level of problems may fluctuate and the degree of stability of a placement may vary over time. Fourthly, the most reliable assessment of the outcome of a late placement may not be adequately assessed until beyond adolescence and into early adulthood.

We were very aware of these challenges to outcome measurement. Nevertheless, even at a year, differences between placements were evident. The majority of families and children had settled well together and were realising each other's hopes and expectations to a greater or lesser extent, but there were some families who were struggling with disappointment, frustration, concern and sometimes despair. While we would not wish to suggest that these groupings are unchangeable, it seemed important to learn whether there were any clear factors that might account for this difference. Although a year is a relatively short time, examining the status of the placements at this point does have implications for the preparation of parents and children and for post-placement support.

WHOSE PERSPECTIVE?

There are several parties involved in making permanent placements, and each will have a view on whether the chosen course was the right one for the child in question. In common with much adoption research, our main source of information on the placement outcome was the parents' report given during interview. While we felt that the children's views were of major importance, their ages and the newness of their placements deterred us from consulting them. The views of the children's social workers and family placement workers were also available to us and their views were often phrased more objectively than those of the parents, but, in practice, the parent and social work reports were for the most part very similar. Some discrepancies were noted but these tended to occur where there was an element of conflict between parents and workers. This is discussed in more detail in Chapter 12.

The birth parents, often excluded from adoption research, may have been able to contribute an important perspective. However, a check showed that many birth parents had not had contact with their children for many years and, in many cases social services did not have current addresses for them. This would have made them a difficult group to trace. We estimated the likely success rate and decided that it would not be possible to trace a representative sample of birth parents.

OUR MEASURES OF OUTCOME

In order to simplify the presentation of a large amount of information, drawn from different sources, we have chosen to restrict ourselves to two major outcome measures, which will feature throughout the book. The first describes *placement stability* at a year and the second indicates the *direction of change* in the children's problems.

Assessing Placement Stability

One of our major interests in selecting outcome measures was to group the placements according to how stable they were at a year. After careful consideration we chose to use the parents' reports as the major source of information on which to base our assessment of placement stability. We reasoned that, with children of this age, it is the views and wishes of the parents that are likely to determine the continuity of the placement. As the social work judgements tended to be very closely related to the parent reports, and were probably a reflection of them, we have not reported these in detail.

Our examination of the parent reports suggested that two aspects of their response to the placement by one year were important in assessing its stability. These were the level of the parents' satisfaction with the placement and the development of an attached relationship with the child. Therefore a binary summary variable, which took account of both of these elements, was computed. A clear account from the parents of either the development of a positive relationship between them and the child or their satisfaction with the placement was sufficient for the placement to be categorised as 'more stable'. Thus, placements described as 'less stable' showed little sign of a good relationship developing with either parent and low levels of parent satisfaction.

Placement Stability at 12 months

According to this assessment of placement stability, 72% of the place-ments were working out well and appeared fairly stable at the one year point. They were not without difficulties, but the family felt that they were able to manage the problems and that relationships were develop-ing satisfactorily. These families were able to describe positive features of their children's behaviour and personalities as well as acknowledging their problems, and were happy that the child had become a member of the family.

While only 3 of the 61 placements (5%) disrupted in the course of the first year, there were an additional 14 instances (23%) where placements were not going so well. There were strong signs that the child's presence in the family was a source of strain and 60% of these families reported significant crises during the year as opposed to just 14% in the more stable group. These parents were less likely to balance criticism of the child with positive descriptions; they were disappointed by a lack of relationship development with the children; they voiced reservations about the wisdom of accepting the placement and of the support provided both before and after the child came to them.

Assessing the Developmental Progress
of the Children

In addition to the parents' overall perspective, we were keen to have a systematic measure of the children's emotional and behavioural problems and of changes in these over the course of the year. Our starting point, which shaped the choice of measures on the children, was that late placed children are likely to show a multiplicity of problems across a range of psychosocial domains.

The parental interview contained detailed questions on the extent and type of the children's emotional and behavioural difficulties. Parents were taken systematically through a list of problems and asked to give detailed descriptions of how these were shown and of their frequency and severity. These data were rated by the interviewers according to clear criteria and cross-checked to ensure comparability of rating thresholds and data quality.

The interviews provided a wealth of detail about the children's specific emotional and behavioural difficulties, each rated on four-point scales, and allowed summary scores to be derived at both interview points. The individual scales were dichotomised at a point indicating a definite problem and then combined to form the summary scale. Thus, each point on the summary scale indicated the presence of one distinct problem. For example, persistent bed-wetting or frequent aggressive outbursts would each add one to the scale.

The difference between the 1 month and the 12 month score provided an indication of *direction* of any overall change in the children's behaviour, that is improvement, deterioration or stability over time. The direction of change was, not surprisingly, closely related to our placement stability variable but was not identical.

In their raw form these 'recovery' scores range from negative through positive. They are used in this form in some analyses and in categorical form in others. The categorical form was used to group children according to the extent to which their problems changed, relative to the level of change in the group as a whole. The categorical grouping of

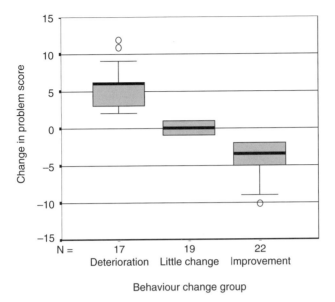

Figure 3.1: Change in problem score according to behaviour change groups. NB. Three cases are missing from deteriorated group due to disruption prior to one year interview

direction of change was defined in terms of 1.5 or more standard deviation units (Z scores) above or below the mean symptom level for the group as a whole. In practice, this was an increase or a decrease of two or more symptoms over the year.

This procedure divided the sample into three similarly sized groups showing:

(a) an increase in problem behaviours – behaviour deteriorated ($n = 17$);
(b) little change in problem behaviours ($n = 19$);
(c) a decrease in problem behaviours – behaviour improved ($n = 22$).

A change of just two or more problems may seem slight, but, for the most part the changes in the number of behaviour problems was more substantial. The means and ranges for all three groups are illustrated in Figure 3.1. This shows that children in the 'improved' category showed an average decrease of around four behaviour problems (although one child managed to drop 10 points). Children whose behaviour was classified as deteriorating were, on average, exhibiting an increase of five problems at 12 months over their score at the start of placement.

We wanted to categorise the children in this manner because we were interested to see how problems changed over time and how the direction of change might relate to other pre-placement or within-placement factors.

COMPARISONS BETWEEN THE TWO OUTCOME MEASURES

We were very aware that these two main outcome measures – the security of the placement and changes in the children's behaviour – could interact. The children's behaviour could affect the parents' view of them and how they related to each other. Conversely, the child's behaviour might be a response to the parents' attitudes. Some models for the direction of these effects are given in Chapter 14.

Table 3.1 shows the overlap between the assessment of placement stability and the behavioural change categories. These two factors are significantly correlated with each other (Kendall's tau-b = 0.307, $p < 0.005$). However, these two measures are clearly not simply reflections of the same thing. This is shown by the seven families where the children were showing increasing difficulties but where the parents nevertheless remained positive about their child and committed to the placement.

Table 3.1: The overlap between placement stability and direction of change in children's problems

Change in problems	Less stable	More stable	Totals
Deteriorated	13	7	20
Little change	4	15	19
Improved	0	22	22
Totals	17	44	61

Group differences significant (χ^2 = 22.7, d.f. = 3, $p < 0.001$).

SUMMARY

In this chapter we have acknowledged some of the difficulties associated with measuring 'outcome' for permanent placements, and presented the rationale and the process by which we arrived at our summary measures of good or poorer outcome. Two specific outcomes were identified: first the degree of stability of the placement at the 12 month interview point and secondly the direction of change in the children's behavioural problems. Although these two factors were shown to be closely related to each other, they are sufficiently distinct to warrant separate treatment in some contexts. Both of these groupings are used in the analyses that follow, although placement stability is considered the primary descriptor of outcome.

4

THE CHILDREN'S BACKGROUNDS, HEALTH AND BEHAVIOUR

Permanent placement for older children frequently follows a considerable period of being 'looked after', often as a consequence of abusive or inadequate parenting. The introductory chapter outlined the problems that can result from such adverse experiences in early life and it is important, therefore, to consider the histories of this group of children before exploring placement outcomes. In this chapter we describe the children's backgrounds and experiences up to the time of their permanent placement.

The data on the children's backgrounds were compiled through detailed direct interviews with the children's social workers. In these interviews the social workers and the researchers worked through the agency records in order to arrive at a comprehensive history of the children's experiences. This was not just a summary of the types of pre-placement care but also a complete history of placement changes, the reasons for moves and the quality of care in each.

As is to be expected for a group of children permanently placed in alternative families at this age, the social work records showed that the great majority of them had experienced marked adversity. This included family disruption, parental marital difficulties and psychiatric disorder, physical and sexual abuse, neglect and a serious lack of adequate parenting. This level of adversity was set against better experiences in foster or other substitute care but in nearly all cases the children's early experiences posed a challenge to normal development.

THE BIRTH PARENTS' PROBLEMS

The birth parents' own problems are summarised in Table 4.1. The overlap of problems is a familiar one for parents who are not able to continue

Table 4.1: Characteristics of the children's birth families

	Birth mother	Birth father	Birth family
Parental presence	(*n* = 61)	(*n* = 61)	
Always there	90%	31%	
Completely absent	2%	41%	
Any step-parenting	3%	29%	
Parental characteristics	(*n* = 60)	(*n* = 31)	
Poor relationship with child	44%	38%	
Unable to cope with parenting	80%	65%	
Chronic physical illness	10%	10%	
Psychiatric illness	22%	13%	
Alcoholism/drug problem	22%	43%	
Parental death	5%	8%	
Family circumstances			(*n* = 56–58)
Marital discord			57%
Poor circumstances			62%
Financial hardship			62%

with the upbringing of their children. Four-fifths of birth mothers and 65% of birth fathers were assessed as having difficulty in coping with parenting, and over half of the mothers and fathers had poor relationships with their children. These parenting difficulties went along with a range of other psychosocial problems such as major psychiatric disorder, in 22% of mothers and 13% of fathers, and substance abuse, in 22% of mothers and 43% of fathers. Indeed, when intermittent alcohol or drug misuse was included, 38% of mothers and 53% of fathers were rated as having difficulties and, when intermittent psychiatric problems were considered as well, 47% of mothers and 57% of fathers were suffering from mental disorder or having personality difficulties of some kind. Marital discord was evident in over half of the families, as were poor living conditions and financial hardship.

It is likely that these figures greatly underestimate the level of some psychosocial difficulties. Systematic interview assessments of parents with less severe parenting difficulties than the parents in this study have shown the great majority of parents to be suffering from mental or personality disorders at the time that their children were taken into care (Quinton & Rutter, 1984). The above figures are more in line with the rates of disorder that have received treatment than with the true level of mental illness or distress.

Despite these problems the great majority of children continued to live at home with their birth mothers until their parenting finally ended, apart from those times when they were temporarily away in placements outside the family. The picture was very different for birth fathers. For 41% of children the birth fathers were entirely absent from their lives and only intermittently present for a further 28%. As would be expected given this picture, step-mothering was a rare occurrence but 29% of children had step-fathers at some time.

THE HISTORY OF ABUSE AND NEGLECT

Given these high levels of family difficulties and the fact that it was finally considered necessary to find permanent alternative families for these children, it is not surprising that abuse of various kinds was very frequent. These data were taken from the social workers' accounts of the children's histories where all experiences of physical or emotional maltreatment, sexual abuse and neglect were recorded. In the case of physical abuse, sexual abuse and neglect, the figures reported here refer to confirmed incidents of abuse. In the case of emotional abuse the figures include cases where there was a strong suspicion of emotional maltreatment having taken place. This is because of the difficulty involved in identifying and 'proving' emotional abuse.

Because of the complexity of the children's experiences we have chosen to present the data on emotional maltreatment separately, although the overlap between emotional and other types of maltreatment is discussed later in the chapter.

Neglect, Physical and Sexual Abuse

Dealing first with poor *physical* care, we found that neglect was by far the most common form, with 46% of children reported as suffering neglect. Experiences of physical and sexual abuse were less common but were still recorded in 31% and 21% of cases respectively (Table 4.2). A number of children were described as having been abused in more than one manner. When the overlap between neglect, physical and sexual abuse was considered the majority of children were rated in one category only (57%), but 18% experienced two kinds of abuse and 2% more than this.

The pattern of sexual and physical abuse showed some difference between the sexes. Boys were more likely to have been physically abused than girls (38% v. 27%) and girls to have been sexually abused than boys (31% v. 9%), although neither of these differences was statistically

Table 4.2: The overlap of types of maltreatment
(confirmed abuse only)

Type of maltreatment	n	%
Adequate physical care	14	23
Neglect only	17	27
Physical only	14	23
Physical and neglect	3	5
Sexual only	4	7
Sexual and neglect	7	11
Sexual and physical	1	2
All types	1	2

significant. The three sexually abused boys were all abused by birth parents whereas over half of the girls (5/9) were abused by step-fathers or other adults. This gender difference did not hold for physical abuse where about half of the abused boys and girls were maltreated by step-parents or others.

The children's history of abuse, as recorded on the social work records, divides the sample into four fairly equal groups: (i) Those with no confirmed history of abuse ($n = 14$); (ii) those with neglect only ($n = 17$); (iii) those with physical abuse, but without any known sexual component ($n = 17$); and (iv) those who were sexually abused, whether or not they were also physically abused in other ways ($n = 13$).

Emotional Maltreatment:
Scapegoated and Rejected Children

In the course of collecting the background data from social workers, it became apparent that, in addition to these abusive or neglectful experiences, many of the children had experienced emotionally abusive parenting. For a proportion of these children this treatment occurred in the context of other abusive experiences, like the threats commonly used by sexual abusers to ensure a child's silence (four cases). For others this abuse accompanied physical neglect and was part of a more general lack of interest or inappropriate care from parents who sought to have the child provide for their emotional needs (four cases). In one case emotional abuse coexisted with physical maltreatment. These forms of emotional abuse tended to be meted out to all the children in the family.

However, there were a total of 22 children who appeared to have been either singled out from siblings for negative treatment or rejected by their birth families. This parenting problem was not part of our initial systematic check on the children's earlier experiences, but when the importance of this experience became apparent to us, we checked through the histories taken from social workers and recorded where rejection or singling out had been mentioned in the description of the child's experiences. Since the social work interview contained no specific questions concerning the extent of scapegoating or rejection, the figures reported here should be regarded as an estimate only.

Sixteen children were rated as having been emotionally rejected by their birth mothers. All of these children had siblings who were not rejected and who, in many cases, remained with their birth parent/s. A further six children appeared to have been singled out for markedly differential treatment within their birth families. The social work descriptions suggested that these children were frequently made scapegoats for family problems, punished for misdemeanours they were not responsible for and often blamed for the parent/s' own circumstances or state of mind.

Apparent reasons for rejection

The 22 children who experienced some form of 'singling out' or 'rejection' by birth parents are considered as one 'rejected' group. There was no recorded 'reason' for the rejection in 30% of the cases, but for the remainder a variety of factors appeared to come into play, including being of undesired gender (8%), having a physical or intellectual deficit (8%) or following the death of a sibling (4%). In the majority of cases, however, the rejection involved a choice between the child and adult relationships (50%). Many of these children were the product of failed short-term relationships and the rejection was often precipitated by the advent of a new partner. Some mothers found the child to be a reminder of a hated 'ex-boyfriend', or compared the child unfavourably with a subsequent 'love child'. It is possible that this feature is a marker for some unattractive behavioural or physical characteristic of the child, but this kind of information was not available to the study.

The overlap between emotional maltreatment and other forms of abuse

When the overlap between the forms of abuse or neglect, outlined earlier, and emotional maltreatment is considered (Figure 4.1), we found that scapegoated and rejected children were significantly more likely than others to have been physically abused (Fisher's exact test $p = 0.034$),

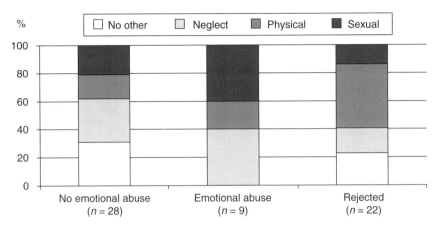

Figure 4.1: The overlap between emotional abuse and other types of maltreatment

while they were somewhat less likely to have suffered neglect or sexual abuse. There were no differences between boys and girls in terms of likelihood of scapegoating or rejection. Once emotional abuse is taken into account, along with other forms of abuse, only nine of the sample children were described as not abused.

PLACEMENT HISTORY

It is not surprising, given the frequency of abuse and neglect and parental inability to cope, that the sample children had complex care histories as well. For some children there were repeated attempts at rehabilitation; others experienced a multiplicity of placement changes while being looked after, sometimes as a result of their own difficulties. However, the placement patterns showed considerable variety, as is shown in Table 4.3.

The average age at first admission was just over three years (38.5 months), with approximately one-third of the children first admitted to care under the age of two. Direct problems with parenting were by far the most common reasons for the first admission (neglect, emotional abuse, not coping or abandonment 49%; physical or sexual abuse of the child or a sibling 28%). In the remaining cases admission was precipitated by a range of parental personal or circumstantial factors (physical illness or death of parent 10%; psychiatric disorder or addiction 10%; and childbirth 3%).

Table 4.3: History of admissions

Admissions	
Mean age at first admission (months)	38.5 (s.d. 25.0)
Mean number of admissions	5.4 (s.d. 3.7)
First admission < 2 years	30%
4 or more admissions	67%
Returns home	
Mean number of returns home	1.2 (s.d. 1.5)
No returns home	44%
1–2 returns home	36%
3 or more returns home	20%

No statistically significant differences between boys and girls. s.d.: standard deviation.

The number of placements and returns home made in this process was very variable, and more so for boys than girls, but nearly two-thirds of children had four or more moves prior to their permanent placement. These moves reflected the often persistent attempts to work with the families and/or rehabilitate the children. Figure 4.2 illustrates the differences in the mean number of placement changes according to the primary reason for first admission.

The range for number of placement changes was from 1 to 19, and the number of changes after the last period with the birth family was from 1 to 8. A more comprehensive description of these placement sequences, which we call chains, is provided in Appendix B.

There were a number of notable features in these data concerning placement changes. Firstly, some of these chains were extremely long, both when rehabilitation with the birth parents was still being attempted and after the last return home. Secondly, the number of placements was significantly different depending on the reason for first admission. Chains were shortest when those reasons involved sexual or physical abuse and longest when the initial reasons were contextual problems, such as temporary care whilst the mother had a baby. In general the chains were longer when the initial reasons did not directly suggest parenting problems although, of course, nearly all cases involved difficulties in parenting in the end.

Thirdly, there were considerable variations in the number of times the children went back to live with a birth parent or parents. Return home was rare when the first admission was for physical or sexual abuse. Only 10% (3/30) of these children ever went home and, in each case, on one occasion only. When the initial problems involved other kinds of

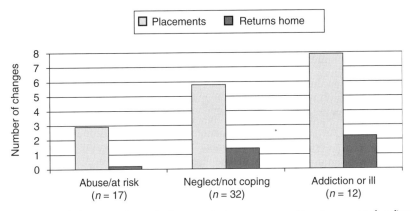

Figure 4.2: Mean number of placement changes according to reason for first admission ($n = 61$). Differences in number of placements $F = 8.24$, $p < 0.001$; returns home $F = 9.56$, $p < 0.001$

parenting difficulty, 63% of children went home at least once. Not surprisingly, the average number of returns home for each group was different simply because the average length of chains was different. Once these differences in the lengths of chains were taken into account, the variation between the groups was not statistically significant. That is to say, when children had chains of similar lengths, return home was not more commonly part of the chain in one group than in another.

Placements After the Last Time at Home

Some children appeared to have an extended number of placements after their last time with their own parents (see Appendix B), and this raised the question of whether this was related to the original reason for admission, to less effective social work, or to the children's behaviour. The first of these possibilities was examined by comparing the length of these 'end chains' for each group. In fact, differences were very small, and this suggested that the move to permanence occurred at a comparable speed for all groups, once it was decided that rehabilitation was not possible.

Nevertheless, some of the end-chains appeared excessively long. The information on each placement recorded whether its end was the result of planning or was a consequence of unexpected disruptions caused by the child, the family, other people or unforeseen circumstances. This information was used to examine the other two possibilities – that longer end-chains were the result of either indecisiveness on the part of social workers or, alternatively, problems in the child. This was done by checking the *reasons* for placement changes and seeing whether these were related to a lack of planning or to problems in the child's behaviour.

Although it appeared that unplanned changes occurred more frequently as the number of moves increased, when the total number of moves was taken into account, unplanned moves were not disproportionately concentrated in the longer sequences. That is, the data did not support the possibility that long end-chains were the result of indecisive social work. On the other hand, there *was* a strong association between longer end-chains and disruptions associated with the children's behaviour during their placement careers, even when the total number of moves was controlled.

We can conclude from this analysis that the particularly long end-chains were more a function of difficult behaviour on the part of the child, than of dilatory social work. However, a lack of social work planning up to this point might itself have contributed to the level of disturbance in the children.

Comment on the Placement Histories

The above analyses have concerned the reasons for the first admission and the placement chains that followed from them. However, it should be remembered that the reason for the first admission did not reflect continuing differences between the groups in the children's experiences in the long run. Although the reasons for first admission differed, the proportion of children suffering abuse or neglect at some point was very high so that subsequent careers of those whose first admissions were for reasons *other* than sexual or physical abuse often included these adversities in the end. Thus 37% (11/30) of those first admitted through other kinds of parenting problems were subsequently found to have been abused physically or sexually, as were half of those first admitted because of parental psychiatric disorder or addiction (3/6), and both of those first admitted because of their mother's confinement. The only group where sexual or physical abuse did not occur was that where admission was precipitated by physical illness, but half (3/6) of these children experienced emotional abuse or neglect.

We should emphasise that the analyses of placement chains presented here does *not* necessarily reflect the typical history of all children first admitted for these various reasons. Our sample reflected the careers of those whose parents were, eventually, considered unable to parent adequately, that is, it was defined on *outcome*. If the sample had been defined on the reasons for first placement rather than on the outcome, the chains might have looked very different. For example, it would seem unlikely that first admissions because a mother was having another child would normally lead to long placement chains ending in permanent alternative care.

Parenting Experiences in Alternative Care

The study collected data, wherever it was available, on the social workers' perceptions of the quality of parenting provided in each of the children's previous placements and the nature of the relationship between the child and carer. In the majority of cases the quality of care was judged to be at least adequate and most of the children showed signs of developing reasonable relationships with their carers. Table 4.4 shows the proportion of the sample that had experienced poor quality care or difficult relationships in any of their previous foster placements. A small number of children had more than one placement that was less than ideal.

Table 4.4: Parenting and relationships in previous out of home placements

	Quality of care	Carer–child relationships
61 sample children	Adequate in all – 88% Poor in 1 – 10% Poor in 2 – 2%	Satisfactory in all – 75% Poor in 1 – 13% Poor in 2 – 12%
Of 127 medium-term placements	Satisfactory – 93% Unsatisfactory – 7%	Satisfactory – 79% Unsatisfactory – 21%

Between them, the 61 sample children experienced 127 earlier placements, each with different carers, that lasted for more than three months. As is clear from the table, while the quality of care was judged by social workers to be satisfactory in most cases, the carer–child relationship had been of some concern in 20% of placements.

By contrast, quality of care during periods when the children returned to birth parents was rarely described positively. Of the 27 children who returned home, only 7 were described as ever receiving appropriate care and for only 1 of these 7 children was the care consistently good during all returns home. Further analysis showed that the experience of good parenting was inversely related to the proportion of their lives spent with birth parents. Despite their views on the birth parents' inability to provide adequate parenting, the social workers felt that the majority of children showed at least some signs of attachment to the birth parent.

SUMMARY OF PRIOR EXPERIENCES

The extent of adversities in the backgrounds of the children is striking. The family background for the majority included parental marital problems, mental illness or personality disorders, poverty and poor circumstances. The children's parenting experiences were very poor. Very few of their birth parents provided an adequate developmental environment and, indeed, the great majority of the children had been subject to abuse or neglect. Over two-thirds had experienced four or more placement changes. The proportion of their lives in which they had received adequate parenting was inversely related to the length of time they spent with their parents, but only 8% (five children) had been adequately parented for more than half of their lives. It is not surprising that their social work records document a whole range of health, emotional and behavioural difficulties. These problems are outlined in the next section.

HEALTH AND BEHAVIOUR PRIOR TO CURRENT PLACEMENT

The social workers' accounts provided information on the children's health and behaviour prior to their move into their current family, and gave an estimate of those problems that the social workers thought would pose difficulty for the new parents.

Physical Health

Our sampling criteria excluded children with marked physical or intellectual disabilities, but nevertheless a number of them entered their new families with health or developmental problems that needed to be taken into account. Indeed, the number of children with potentially troublesome health problems was striking. The majority of these problems were amenable to treatment, but nevertheless, coping with them

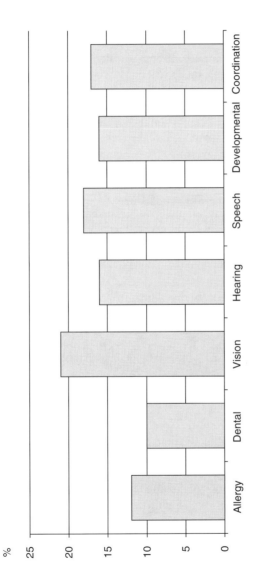

Figure 4.3: The prevalence of health problems

must have provided an additional burden for both the children and the new parents. The data allowed for only a broad description of health problems, because they were based on social workers' records and not on direct assessments. Figure 4.3 illustrates the frequency with which different health problems were found among the sample children.

The eight children who had allergy problems suffered from asthma or had eczema that required medication. However, none of the problems in this group of disorders was considered handicapping. Eight children were thought to have an immediate need for dental work due primarily to poor diet and neglect of dental hygiene. In two cases there was concern about dental development in the long term, with the anticipation of possible bone grafting for one child. Fourteen children had problems with their vision, but in only two cases were the deficits said to be pronounced. One child arrived wearing spectacles that were found not to be needed! Eight children had problems with hearing or had been treated for such problems in the past. In all cases the problems had been attributed to infections. Three children had grommets fitted, and three had minor hearing loss. There were two cases of 20% or more hearing loss.

Nine children had speech problems or delays. Two had cleft palate repairs and, in all, five had been treated by speech therapists. Six of these nine children had continuing problems with delayed speech at the time of placement. Apart from the speech problems discussed above, seven children were said to be showing general developmental delays, and eight children were considered to be clumsy or poorly coordinated to varying degrees.

The overlap of health and developmental problems was examined. Thirty-one children came to their new families with no recorded difficulties and a further 12 had mild correctable eyesight or dental problems only. The physical impediments for 18 children (30%) were rather more significant. In order to give some idea of the level of difficulty the physical problems of these 18 children were grouped according to the extent to which they currently interfered with the children's lives. The *mild* group (11 children) had detectable and persisting problems but ones that did not interfere with their lives or appear to warrant continuing treatment. The six children in the *moderate* group had problems that interfered with their social lives to some extent and required some continuing attention, but were not seen as a serious impediment to their developmental recovery. For example, one boy in this group had poor eyesight, considerable hearing loss and noticeable clumsiness, including a tendency to fall over things. One child had more *serious* difficulties needing significant dental work, had poor eyesight and a heart murmur. He was in a special school because of these problems as well as behavioural difficulties.

Behaviour

Views on the children's behaviour were available from the social workers for both the family and the children. The agreement between them on these problems was very high. Therefore, in order to simplify presentation, only the information taken from the child's social worker is used in the following account.

As is clear from Figure 4.4, the most common problems involved conduct difficulties such as disobedience, defiance, temper and similar behaviours, or emotional difficulties involving worries, fears and anxieties. Just under half (48%) of the children were seen as having moderate or severe conduct problems and 49% emotional problems. Overactivity occurred at a moderate or marked level for nearly one-quarter (23%), with nearly two-fifths showing some problems of this kind. Fewer children were said to have developmentally abnormal habits such as bed-wetting or soiling (17%), although a further 12% had mild difficulties of these kinds. We should stress that these assessments were not based on systematic data or on clinical criteria. Nevertheless they represent the views social workers had on the kinds of problems the children were showing that might lead to problems for the new parents or compromise the placement.

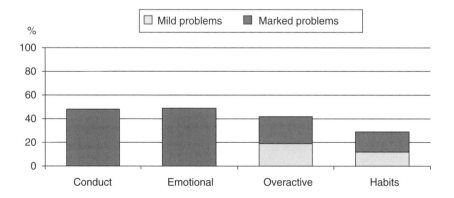

Figure 4.4: The prevalence of behaviour problems

Table 4.5: Features of the previous placement

	n = 61
Mean time in previous placement (months)	18.8 (s.d. 12)
Placed from:	
Relative care	3%
Foster care	87%
Therapeutic setting	6%
Children's home	3%
placed with any siblings	38%

No statistically significant differences between boys and girls.

THE KIND AND QUALITY OF THE PLACEMENT PRIOR TO PERMANENCE

The final set of circumstances likely to affect the children's behaviour in the early weeks of their new permanent placements concern the length and quality of the placement immediately before they joined their new family. It is not easy to predict in which ways such influences might work. For example, a child moved from a long-standing placement in which there was attachment to the previous carers might show more disturbance in the new placement than a child moving from a brief or unhappy placement into a more secure and loving one. This is a matter for further empirical investigation in which the characteristics of the placement prior to the transfer to a permanent family are directly assessed. Such information was not available in this study as the assessment of the quality of the previous placement relied on the social workers' reports.

The sample children had spent widely differing amounts of time in their previous placement, as is shown in Table 4.5. They had, on average, been in that placement for over a year and a half, but this varied from one month to five and a half years. The great majority of children (87%) moved to their new families from foster care, but two children had been living with relatives and six were in therapeutic facilities or children's homes.

The social workers' views on the quality of parenting in these placements and the extent to which the children were attached to carers there are given in Table 4.6. The 53 children in foster care had high quality parenting in all but 6 cases and were said to be attached to their carers in

Table 4.6: Quality of parenting and attachment in the previous placement

	n	Good quality parenting (%)	Attachment in previous placement (%)
Relative care	2	100	50
Foster care	53	87	41
Therapeutic setting	4	75	0
Children's home	2	50	0

No statistically significant differences between boys and girls.

only 43% of cases. The 2 boys living with relatives both had good parenting and were attached to their carers. In contrast, none of the 6 children in residential therapeutic facilities were said to be attached to any carers and 2 were also said to have less good parenting. The lack of attachment is likely to have been partly a function of the emotional/behavioural problems that occasioned the referral for therapy, but it is worrying that the care was not good in some cases.

SUMMARY

This chapter has documented the very poor early experiences of these children. They came from families with a multiplicity of psychosocial problems including learning difficulties, major mental disorders, problems with physical health and problems in interpersonal relationships. In the great majority of cases the children had been abused, neglected or rejected. Many had experienced multiple moves in care before their final permanent placement and many arrived in their new families with health and behavioural problems.

The experience of rejection, uncovered as part of the history for a significant proportion of the children, may prove especially damaging to their capacity to form attachments to new parents. Such experiences may require a great deal of expert help if they are to be ameliorated. If children have learned to assume responsibility for almost anything that goes wrong, it is likely that they will blame themselves for the failure of their relationship with their birth parents and may seek to reproduce the rejection as affirmation of their 'world view', a process described for emotionally abused children by Iwaniec (1995). The importance of this particular feature of early experiences will be discussed when we turn to consider the factors associated with better and poorer outcomes.

There is no doubt that this was a group of children desperately in need of warmth and stability in their lives. It was also clear that they needed other kinds of help as well: in their emotional and behavioural development, and their family and social relationships. How well the children and families were prepared for the task ahead, what kinds of help they received and what factors were associated with recovery or with continuing problems will be discussed as the placement story unfolds.

5

NEW FAMILY CHARACTERISTICS AND PLACEMENT ARRANGEMENTS

In any discussion of placement outcomes for older children, it is necessary to take the context in which the children were placed into account. There are several features of placements that are important in matching children and families. Some of these – for example, adoption versus fostering, contact with the birth family and matching on grounds of ethnicity – arouse strong opinions. There is, in addition, a cluster of new family characteristics that appears to be associated with poorer progress. In the fostering field, some researchers have found that placements with mothers over the age of 40 tend to be more successful than placement with younger parents (Trasler, 1960; Parker, 1966; Berridge & Cleaver, 1987; Triseliotis, 1989). Barth and Berry (1988) also found disruption to be associated with higher educational level of the new mother, a finding not replicated elsewhere. A number of researchers have reported higher disruption rates when there are birth children close in age to the placed child (Parker, 1966; Wedge & Mantle, 1991). Findings with respect to the advantages and disadvantages of sibling placements are less consistent. Some researchers have found that children placed on their own have more successful foster placements (George, 1970; Napier, 1972) but others have found placements to be more successful if siblings are placed together (Festinger, 1986; Berridge & Cleaver, 1987).

SIBLINGS.

This chapter describes the demographic characteristics of our sample of new families and the new family constellations created by the placement. The matching features for which we had information included ethnicity, sibling versus singleton placement, plan for adoption versus permanent fostering and child-free versus established new families. 'Child-free' refers to those families who had no children resident in the home at the time of placement. Conversely, 'established' families are those who already had children under 18 years of age living at home.

DEMOGRAPHIC CHARACTERISTICS OF THE NEW FAMILIES

Almost all of the 61 new families were couples. Only 4 families were lone parents: 3 mothers and one father. Couples had been living together for an average of 14 years (range 3–25). The average age of new mothers and fathers was 39 and 41 years respectively (range 27–56; 31–59) and was similar for the parents in child-free families and those who had children at home. The only difference related to age was a tendency for parents to be older if one of them had parented before.

There were some differences in the children's pre-placement history according to the age of the new mother. Those placed with older mothers were likely to have had more moves while in care, a greater number of unplanned moves and more returns home than those placed with younger mothers. However, there was no association between children's behaviour problems and mothers' age nor did parental age relate to outcome at the end of the year.

Educational Status of New Parents

The new parents had a variety of educational and occupational back-grounds. Nearly half of new mothers (40%) and a quarter of new fathers (24%) had left school at 15 or 16 and entered the employment market immediately. Two-thirds of mothers and around half the fathers had taken up opportunities in further education and vocational training. An equal number of mothers and fathers (18%) had higher educational qualifications.

More mothers in the 'higher education' group were child-free at the time of placement and more had sibling groups rather than single children placed with them, but there were no differences in terms of the number of previous placements, returns home or prior maltreatment. Maternal education was not related to outcome at a year.

Employment Status of New Parents

The occupations represented included landscape gardeners, car park attendants, teachers, social workers and scientists. The majority of the new families (60%) were classified as social class I, II or III non-manual (Registrar General's classification) but a substantial minority were employed in skilled or unskilled manual jobs. There were no significant differences in any of the outcome measures according to the social class of the new families.

These families had a traditional work pattern: almost all of the fathers were employed full-time away from home, although 13 worked flexible hours. Two were engaged in full-time education, but this still took them out of the home for much of the day. One father worked from home. In contrast, mothers made more use of part-time, home-working and flexi-time opportunities. Only 15 mothers were employed full-time and 7 of these worked flexi-time in order that the children could be cared for. Twenty-one (35%) mothers were not engaged in paid work. The remaining 24 mothers fitted occasional or part-time work around their child care commitments. There were no differences in placement outcomes between mothers in paid work and those who stayed at home.

ETHNIC AND CULTURAL BACKGROUNDS OF THE CHILDREN AND FAMILIES

Most of the new parents were white and of UK origin (54), as were most of the placed children, but 10 of the 61 children had at least one birth parent or grandparent from an ethnic minority.

It is now generally accepted that growing up in a family of similar heritage offers benefits to children. Indeed the Children Act (1989) places a requirement on practitioners to take the cultural, religious and racial needs of children into account when planning for their care. Our classification of minority ethnic status included all children whose records indicated minority ethnic heritage, including that of their great-grandparents. Using this classification, half of the 10 ethnic minority children were placed with ethnically matched families. Table 5.1 outlines the ethnic background of these 10 children and of the new families with whom they were placed. Of particular note is the fact that the majority of the children who had at least one African-Caribbean (A/C) parent were placed with ethnically similar families. The one child from this group who was placed trans-racially moved with his white siblings. In contrast,

Table 5.1: The parentage of minority ethnic children and the ethnicity of their new families

Child's parentage	Placed with	Matched
2 A/C parents	2 A/C parents	Yes
2 A/C parents	2 A/C parents	Yes
1 A/C parent	A/C mother/white father	Yes
1 A/C parent	A/C mother	Yes
1 A/C great grandparent	2 white UK parents	No
1 Asian grandparent	2 white UK parents	No
1 Asian grandparent	2 white UK parents	No
2 part Asian parents	2 white UK parents	No
1 S. European parent	White UK mother, European father	Yes
1 Middle Eastern parent	European mother, white UK father	No

A/C: African-Caribbean.

of the five children of Asian, Middle Eastern or southern European origin, only one was placed with a new family with similar ethnic characteristics.

There are two possible explanations for this disparity between children with African-Caribbean heritage and other minority children. In recent years many agencies have made the need to find African-Caribbean families a major focus of their home finding work. As a consequence, African-Caribbean parents may be more aware than those from other cultures of the need for alternative families and make themselves more available to placement agencies.

An alternative explanation may be that, within our sample, the children not matched for ethnicity were usually more than one generation removed from their minority ethnic origins. Many of these children, despite their biological inheritance, had been born to white mothers and had grown up in a predominantly white culture. These children were often unaware of their fathers' ethnicity and in some cases social workers were unable to be specific about paternity. Therefore it is possible that social workers placed greater emphasis on ethnic matching where ethnic status seemed more salient to the child.

The interviews with social workers revealed that, despite the trans-racial and trans-cultural nature of some of these placements, consideration had been given to the child's ethnic background in making the placement. Even where a fully matched placement had not proved possible, efforts had been made to ensure that the new families had some knowledge of, or connection with, the children's cultural backgrounds.

There were no significant differences between children from ethnic minority backgrounds and white children in terms of their pre-placement experiences, but only 2 of the 10 children who had ethnic minority backgrounds were placed with siblings, compared with 20 of the 51 white children. There were, similarly, few differences between white and ethnic minority children in placement characteristics. All 10 ethnic minority children had been placed for adoption. The only major difference between these groups was a significant tendency for children from ethnic minority backgrounds to be placed in larger families. This was particularly true for children moving into unmatched placements. All five of the children who were ethnically matched were placed on their own, leading to families of one to three children. However, the placements of the five children who were not matched were into larger families (three of these five families had seven children at home after placement). There were no significant differences in outcome at a year according to whether or not the placement was strictly matched for ethnicity. Neither was there any evidence that children with a minority ethnic background had to wait any longer for placement.

PLACEMENT PLAN: ADOPTION OR FOSTERING

The majority of the children (49) were placed with a definite plan for adoption. Four children were placed under fostering regulations but with a view to adoption and eight children were placed for long-term fostering. All those with an eventual plan for adoption were grouped together when comparing fostering and adoptive placements. The fostering group is too small to allow statistical testing, but there were some interesting differences.

All of the children who had been sexually abused, and all but one of those who had been physically abused, were placed with some plan for adoption. However, children placed with the primary intention of long-term fostering, rather than adoption, tended to have experienced more moves in their care history and more returns home. Of the eight children for whom the plan was for fostering, five (62%) had experienced being singled out or rejected by their birth families, while this was true for only 32% of the adoptive placements. We found no significant differences between adoptive and foster placements in relation to either behavioural change over the year or placement stability.

The only strongly significant difference to emerge between those children placed for fostering and those placed for adoption concerned birth parent contact (Figure 5.1). Seven of the eight foster children had seen

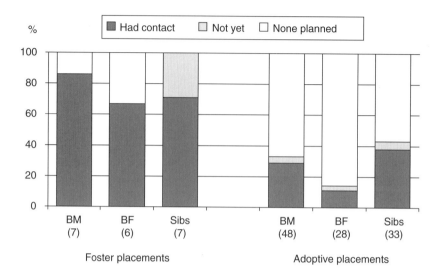

Figure 5.1: Contact with birth family members in first year for adoptive and foster placements. Group differences for all three contact figures: birth mother (BM) $\chi^2 = 10.2$, d.f. $= 2$, $p < 0.01$; birth father (BF) $\chi^2 = 9.5$, d.f. $= 2$, $p < 0.01$; siblings $\chi^2 = 5.8$, d.f. $= 2$, $p < 0.054$

their birth mothers and siblings in the course of the first year of placement, and most had seen their birth fathers. This was true for only a minority of children placed for adoption, even in the case of sibling contact. Thus the primary reason for selecting a fostering arrangement, rather than an adoptive placement, seemed to be that face-to-face contact with birth parents was to continue. There are, of course, a number of factors that might determine whether face-to-face contact continues during the placement and we shall deal with this later.

The Status of Adoptive Placements at One Year

Of the 53 placements where adoption was the eventual aim, 50 were still intact at one year. Of these, 13 families had completed the adoption process, 23 had started the application procedure and in 14 cases the new parents had not begun to file the application. The behaviour of the child appeared to have a strong impact on whether the application to adopt was made. Behaviour scores were higher, indicating more problems, at both 1 month and 12 months after placement if the application had not been lodged, although the differences were only significant at 12 months ($F = 4.3$, degrees of freedom (d.f.) $= 1,48$, $p < 0.05$).

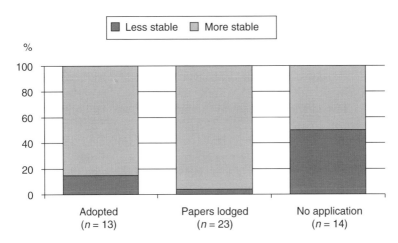

Figure 5.2: The stability of adoptive placements at one year and progress of the adoption application. Group differences are significant $\chi^2 = 11.6$, d.f. $= 2$, $p < 0.005$

The parents who had not made applications were more likely to be having parenting difficulties at a year, especially in showing warmth and sensitivity towards the child and managing their aggression (see Chapter 13). Lack of maternal attachment and satisfaction with the child and poorer placement stability were all associated with no request for adoption. A larger proportion of the children in the 'no adoption' group were described as not having attached to the new family, and there was a greater likelihood of difficulties between the placed child and a new sibling.

All of these associations were statistically significant, with the exception of attachment to the new family. These data suggest that, for most of the 14 families, the lack of progress in the adoption process reflected uncertainties about finalising the adoption rather than other possible barriers. A number of parents who had moved forward with the adoption did, however, talk about their frustration at the slowness of the bureaucracy and administrative aspects of the adoption, even where there were no legal obstacles. The timely completion of the social worker's report to the court could be a bone of contention.

Contested Placements

A total of 13 placements (12 adoptive and 1 foster) had either been through, or were engaged in, legal challenges at the one year point. Most commonly the children's birth families were contesting the adoption (10 cases), or the contact arrangements (7 cases). In 2 cases the entire placement and the plan was being contested.

Of the 13 children whose birth families were challenging some aspect of the plans, 6 were not aware that this was the case, 3 were unconcerned about it, 3 showed some distress at the problems, and considerable upset was reported in 1 case. Two of the 13 new parents were unconcerned and 5 reported only a moderate level of distress, doubtless reassured by practitioners' opinions that the placement decisions would be upheld by the courts. However, considerable anxiety was experienced by 6 families. Despite the distress which could be caused by these difficult circum-stances, there was no evidence that legal processes had any deleterious effect on placement outcomes.

CONTACT WITH BIRTH FAMILY

According to social worker reports, only 22 of the placed children had seen their birth mother in the year prior to placement. For 13 of these children the meetings were regular and their birth mothers were reliable in attending meetings. Nevertheless, the social workers felt that the meetings were predominantly positive for only 6 of the children. The factor that seemed to play the biggest part in governing levels of contact prior to permanent placement was the birth mother's involvement in physical (10 cases) or sexual (6 cases) abuse of the child. Contact occurred in only one such case and there the mother's involvement in the abuse was suspected rather than confirmed.

Other characteristics of the mothers, such as physical or psychiatric illness, substance misuse, neglect of the child or poor relationship with the child, did not discriminate between those who had contact and those who did not.

The most striking feature of the data for birth fathers was their absence. Social workers were only able to tell us about 37 birth fathers at the start of the placement, including 3 who had died. Only 12 children had seen their birth fathers in the last year, but when they did they tended to see them regularly and many of the fathers were considered reliable. This contact was described positively for over half of the 8 children for whom data were available. As with birth mothers, birth fathers who were perpetrators of physical or sexual abuse were less likely to have had contact with their child in the year prior to placement. Fathers who were

Table 5.2: Plans and realities of contact with birth family members

Social work plan and outcome	Birth mother	Birth father	Siblings
None planned – no contact	31	24	10
Plans unclear – no contact	6	2	9
Contact planned – no contact	0	1	6
None planned – had contact	8	1	3
Plans unclear but had contact	4	0	2
Contact planned – had contact	6	6	10
	55	34	40

mentally ill were also unlikely to have seen their child. A brief review of the case notes suggested that, while mentally ill mothers suffered from depressive symptoms, most of the fathers had personality problems, being unpredictable and sometimes violent.

Continuity of Contact into the Permanent Placement

Table 5.2 shows the contact plans at the time of placement and the extent to which they were adhered to. The numbers vary a little because some birth mothers had died; there were no data at all from social workers for a large number of birth fathers (21); and some children had no siblings. Three cases are missing because of disruptions. The figures include both face-to-face contact and contact by letter or exchange of information (Table 5.3). It is clear that for over half the sample the placement plan did not include an expectation of contact with either parent. In total, 21 children had some contact with at least one birth parent, but in only 16 cases was this face-to-face: 9 with the birth mother, 4 with the birth father and 3 with both.

Generally, when contact with birth parents was planned it went ahead according to the plans. The picture was different for contact with siblings where planning was often less clear or not followed through even when clear plans existed. This is surprising since none of the new parents said they were uncomfortable with the idea of sibling contact. Plans may not have been implemented either because of difficulties in engaging both sets of carers at the same time or because of problems in finding the right time for all the children. Where both sets of children were with substitute families, the new parents were frequently left to organise the contact on their own. While such an arrangement may feel

Table 5.3: Type of contact with birth family members

Type of contact	Birth mother	Birth father	Siblings
None	37	27	25
Letters/information	5	1	5
Meetings	13	6	10
Not applicable	3	24	21
Total	55	34	40

more 'normal' when it works, it is clear that these contacts may not be arranged routinely in the first year.

The Parents' View of the Impact of Contact

Analysis of the impact of contact proved extremely difficult. Not only were the numbers of children who had contact relatively low, there was also a wide variety of contact arrangements, ranging from an hour spent under the supervision of a social worker, to an agreement whereby one child periodically stayed overnight with her birth family. In some cases meetings or letters had been arranged as a 'one off' happening, perhaps as a means of saying goodbye, while other children were seeing family members on a very regular basis throughout the year.

Despite the low numbers, some features deserve comment. There was no relationship at all between contact and level of behaviour problems but, when we compared those children who had any face-to-face meetings, a higher proportion of children with direct contact were in the 'less stable' group at the end of the first year of placement. However, this association was complicated by the differential rates of contact between those in foster and prospective adoptive placements. Thus, while 88% of foster children had contact with birth parents during the first year, this was true for only 18% of children placed for adoption ($\chi^2 = 16.7$, d.f. = 1, $p < 0.001$). Once the type of placement was taken into account there was no association between birth parent contact and placement stability. The low numbers did not allow us to test whether contact or the placement type was the more important factor.

New parents whose children were in contact with birth parents had views and observations of the arrangements. The new parents reported that contact visits with and, on occasions, information from birth parents could be unsettling for the children. This was said to occur with 70% of

Table 5.4: The effect of birth family contact on the placement according to new parents

	Birth mothers (n = 18)	Birth fathers (n = 7)	Siblings (n = 14)
Predominantly helpful	1 (6%)	1 (14%)	3 (23%)
Helpful and unhelpful aspects or neutral in impact	13 (72%)	4 (57%)	10 (70%)
Predominantly unhelpful	4 (22%)	2 (29%)	1 (7%)

birth father and 45% of birth mother contacts. This unsettling occurred before or after a visit and showed itself as anxiety or over-excitement. In most cases it diminished fairly rapidly.

Not all of the new parents attended the contact meetings, but where they did so they described the interaction between the child and birth parent as minimal in about 25–30% of cases. The majority of new parents reported contact to be either helpful to the placement or neutral in effect. As is clear from Table 5.4, in the majority of cases parents felt that birth family contact had either little impact on the placement or offered a balance between aspects that were helpful and those that hindered the progress of the placement. It was clear from the data that parents' views on whether or not contact was affecting either the children or the place-ment generally changed over time, at least partially in response to the character of the most recent visit or letter. These changes could go in either direction, with parents coming to view contact with more reser-vations where preceding interaction had been questionable or with more openness when they could see that the birth parents were reliable and responsible in their dealings with the children. Where children had seen or heard from their relatives on several occasions in the course of the year, we have presented the latest or most significant parental view in Table 5.4.

Contact was perceived as unhelpful when parents felt that the children received mixed or inappropriate messages from birth parents. For example, one family reported the confusion engendered in the child when visits to the birth mother were full of promises that she would return home for good one day. Another family described how their child had recounted his father's instructions never to let social workers or the new family know what he was thinking. Some of the parents who were happy with the way contact was going thus far still had some concerns about how it would work out in the longer term. In a few cases parents talked with some concern about the distress of children who did not receive anticipated birthday cards or visits.

Table 5.5: Parenting experience of new parents

Parenting experience	Child-free families (21)	Established families (36)	Lone parents (4)
None at all	9	–	2
One parent only	12	–	–
Own birth children	–	23	2
Previously adopted	–	5	–
Previously fostered	–	8	–

Although parent attitudes toward sibling contact were positive, about one-third of the children were described as unsettled by meeting siblings and there were one or two cases where parents thought that the contact was unhelpful to the placement. In some 40% of cases the new parents were surprised by the lack of positive interaction between the children during these meetings.

FAMILY CONSTELLATIONS

Previous Parenting Experience of New Families

Just over one-third of couples (21) embarked on the placement with no significant shared experience of parenting children of this age but, in over half of these cases, either the mother or father had experience of parenting in a previous relationship (12 cases). Of the remaining 36 couples, 23 had children of their own, 3 had previously adopted an infant, 2 had adopted an older child, and 8 had gained all of their experience through fostering. Of the 4 lone parents in the sample, 2 had no previous parenting experience although both had considerable experience of children professionally, and 2 had children of their own (Table 5.5).

There was no tendency for more problematic children to be placed with experienced parents but there were differences in *outcomes* according to previous experience, with experienced parents apparently having more difficulties. However, these difficulties were associated with other differences between experienced and inexperienced parents, including the presence of other children and features of the children's earlier lives. These influences are analysed in more detail later. First, we examine the structure of the families created by the placements.

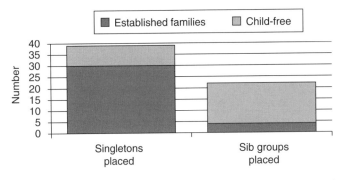

Figure 5.3: New family constellations: placement groups by new family type

Family Constellations After Placement

Thirty-nine of the 61 placements were of children who joined their new families on their own (Figure 5.3). Nine became 'only children' in previously child-free families but the majority (30) entered homes where there were children already resident. These resident children were usually the new parents' own birth children, but occasionally were fostered or adopted children. All but three of the singly placed children had siblings being cared for elsewhere.

The remainder of the sample consisted of 22 sibling groups: 17 groups of two; 4 groups of three; and 1 group of four children. All but 4 of these sibling groups moved to families who did not have children living at home at the time of placement. In most cases the eventual family sizes were small to average: a one-child family in 9 cases; two children in 26 cases; three children in 14 families and four children in 8 families. Four families had between six and eight children living at home after the placement.

Singleton versus Sibling Placement

One important question was whether singleton and sibling placements differed in their outcomes. There were no significant differences in the level of behaviour problems between children in singleton and sibling placements at one month, according to the parents' reports. However, there was a tendency for those placed alone to show less behavioural improvement than those placed with siblings ($\chi^2 = 6.6$, d.f. = 1, $p < 0.05$). Similarly, although there were no differences in parental satisfaction

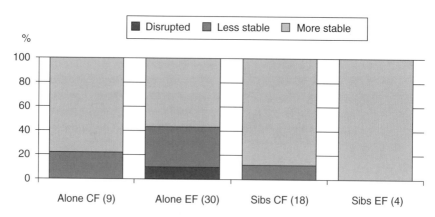

Figure 5.4: Placement stability at a year according to new family constellation. EF: established family; CF: child-free family

between children in singleton and sibling group placements at one month, parents of children placed singly were reporting significantly more reservations by the end of the first year than those who had sibling groups placed with them ($\chi^2 = 5.20$, d.f. $= 1$, $p < 0.05$). Placements of single children were significantly less likely to be categorised as stable (Figure 5.4).

It would be easy to conclude from this analysis that being placed with siblings is a protective factor and that being placed alone increases the risk of poorer progress. However, the picture is more complicated because the majority of less stable singleton placements occurred among those placed in established families. All three disruptions occurred within this last group. That this association is not simply evidence that established families necessarily have more difficulties is clear from the fact that all four of the placements where sibling groups joined established families went well. Possible explanations of these complex associations between the type and structure of placements and outcome are discussed in Chapter 14. Some preliminary issues are discussed below.

Placing Single Children with Established Families

It has long been recognised, by both researchers and practitioners, that placing children into established families can increase the risk of poorer outcomes under certain circumstances. In particular, too small a gap in age between a placed child and the birth children increases the chance of disruption. Earlier findings suggested that this was the case when the

Table 5.6: Outcomes for singly placed children according to age difference between placed and resident children

	Placement stable at a year	Behaviour not deteriorating	n
Eldest or middle	37%	37%	8
Younger by 0–36 months	57%	57%	7
Younger by 37 or more months	67%	51%	15

child was within five years-of-age of the nearest birth child (Trasler, 1960; Parker, 1966; Berridge & Cleaver, 1987). More recently, Wedge and Mantle (1991) argued, on the basis of their research, that the placed child should be the youngest by at least three years. In our study, of the 30 instances where single children were placed with an established family, the placed children usually became the youngest but there were 6 situations in which the placed child became a middle child and 3 cases where he or she became the eldest in the family.

Table 5.6 gives the outcome on placement stability and behaviour changes according to the singleton children's position in the new sib group. There was a tendency for placement stability to be higher when the children were the youngest by more than 36 months and for behaviour to show less deterioration when the children were the youngest. Neither of these findings reached statistical significance but the stability figures are in line with the findings from other studies quoted earlier. However, as Table 5.6 shows, a larger age gap did not offer absolute protection against an association with poorer placement outcome: one-third of the placements where there was more than three years age difference were in the less stable group at a year. It may be that the relationship between a resident child and an incoming child influences the parent's response to the placement even when the resident child is some years older. While interaction problems with new siblings may put extra stress on the placement and reduce the harmony of family life, it is plausible that the threat to placement continuity is less where there is a larger age gap, since resident 'teenage' children may be less dependent on the family and likely to be less distressed by difficult relationships with the incoming child.

Two factors were strongly associated with the poorer outcomes for single children placed into established families. Firstly, half of these children placed (15/30) were in the group that had been singled out or rejected by their birth families. Secondly, poorer outcomes were more common where the placed child had developed a poor relationship with a 'new' sibling. These two factors are associated, such that of the 15 rejected children in this group, 9 had a poor relationship with a new sibling. It seems likely that the experience of rejection may be particularly associated with problems in making and sustaining relationships. The analysis of these influences is taken further in Chapters 9 and 14.

PRACTICE IMPLICATIONS

The implications that can be drawn from these analyses are that the family constellations created by the placements and the relationships that develop within them are important considerations for placement practice. Relationships between birth children and incoming children may present difficulties even when there are large age gaps and it should not be assumed that finding new siblings for the placed children is always a good thing.

Contact issues were not always handled well in this sample. In particular, contact with birth siblings was often left entirely to the parents. This could work happily but, on occasions, new parents may have needed help and encouragement to ensure that contact was maintained when this was important to the child. Furthermore, comments from the new parents indicated that problems could arise where birth parents acted inappropriately at contact meetings. Clearly these encounters need to be sensitively managed by the social worker in the interests of the children. Finally, it is important that the legal and administrative aspects of the placement are efficiently organised at the point when the new parents wish to proceed to adoption.

SUMMARY

In this chapter we have described the new family structures into which the children were placed and the associations between these features and placement outcomes at one year. None of the demographic factors were found to affect the progress of the placements. On the other hand, placements expected to remain as long-term foster care were less stable than intended adoptions. The adoption process was less likely to be underway where behavioural problems remained high and when the new parents and the children had not formed attached relationships.

Only a minority of children had contact with birth parents in the year prior to placement, often because of a history of abuse. However, when contact arrangements had been put in place these were usually carried through. In addition, contact with family members often occurred even when it was not part of a plan. Contact was much higher in foster placements and was associated with somewhat lower placement stability, although it was not possible to disentangle these overlapping associations. Nevertheless, fewer than half the sample had any contact at all with birth parents and only about a quarter had met with their birth parents in the course of the year. There had been surprisingly little exchange of information, perhaps because this is often an annual event and a longer follow-up may be needed for it to occur.

The final section of this chapter examined the bringing together of placed children and new families and explored the associations between the new family constellations and placement progress. Particularly striking was the association between the placement of single children into established families and less security in the placements by the end of the year. The findings broadly supported previous findings about the risks associated with too narrow an age gap between placed and birth children but this effect was not strong. Placement in established families appeared to be a more risky option but this conclusion was complicated by the success of the small sample of sibling groups placed this way. We try to disentangle these complicated relationships between family con-stellation, children's characteristics and outcome in Chapter 14.

6

PREPARATION OF THE CHILD

We did not address preparation for placement in the introductory chapter and so we take this opportunity to present the rationale for, and discuss the practice of, direct work with children. There has been an increasing requirement for adequate professional intervention when placing children with new families. The Houghton Report (DHSS, 1972) expressed concern about the number of children who were being placed for adoption without social work help and recognised the major significance of the placing process both for the child and for the adoptive parent. Section 1 of the Adoption Act (1976) specifies the services to children and adopters that the local authority should aim to provide. The placement of older children in particular has raised the profile of pre- and post-placement services.

Clearly the most vital function of placement agencies is to bring together those children in need of placement with a properly selected, assessed and prepared substitute family. Although the current study is mostly concerned with developments subsequent to placement, the preparation process for the child and new parents is regarded as essential to assist the child to accept and be accepted by the new family. Preparation should help the child to develop a meaningful attachment to the new family and it should alert the new family to the more predictable challenges of substitute parenting. In this chapter we examine the preparation of the child and in Chapter 7, the preparation of the new family.

THE SOCIAL WORK ROLE IN PREPARING THE CHILD FOR PLACEMENT

The broad responsibilities of the child's social worker (CSW) are to involve the child or children in the planning and preparation for the move, and then to organise the smooth transition of the child to the new parents' home. Thoburn (1988, p. 85), in writing about the principles and practice of the CSW's role, has highlighted the 'close and complex relationship' that is likely to arise in helping a child towards the decision to move to a new family. In earlier periods of placement practice, perhaps more stress would have been laid on preparing and educating the new parents and less attention was paid to the needs and wishes of the child (Curtis, 1983).

Theory, Skills and Method in Preparing the Older Child for Permanent Placement

Sawbridge and Carriline (1978) see the essence of the CSW's task as helping older children to grasp the meaning of what is happening to them and preparing them for forming an attachment to the new parents. Practice texts have become more insistent on the need for pre-placement preparation for the child. In the words of one commentator:

> It is argued that the skill and commitment of substitute parents should not be considered sufficient to help children who remain confused and angry about what has happened to them or who perceive themselves as bad, blameworthy, destructive and unlovable because of previous experiences. If permanent placements are intended to safeguard a child's future, it is negligent to allow children to move into new families without adequate preparation (Smith, 1984, p. 70).

Direct work with individual children in transition has been developed by practitioners and organisations in the UK (Batty, 1986; Aldgate & Simmonds, 1988; Sainsbury, 1994) and practice has often been heavily influenced by the views of American child psychotherapists and adoption specialists such as Claudia Jewett Jarratt (1978), Kay Donley (1984) and Vera Fahlberg (1994). The emphasis in their work has been on helping children to recover from loss by attending to the process of grieving, by helping them to leave the adults to whom they may be attached and to begin the process of making a fresh attachment to new parents.

These approaches have been concerned with children's emotional lives and these authors have emphasised the need to find methods to help children bring their concerns to the surface and to come to terms with painful feelings from the past. These developments have contrasted with previous beliefs that children would be best served by not reviving memories of previous losses or ill-treatment ('Least said, soonest mended'). There is still much to be learned, however, about what it is that children can remember, how accessible it is via verbal means and whether they should always be encouraged to remember a painful past.

A more comprehensive structure to guide social workers involved in child preparation has been proposed by Corrigan and Floud (1990) and includes a phase of intervention which they call 'in-depth repair work'. This shades into the domain of child psychotherapy, demands highly skilled practice and raises the question of whether these professional skills are available within social work, whether they should be considered part of the social work task and to what extent they can be obtained from local resources.

However, little empirical evaluation of the effectiveness of this direct, pre-placement work has been undertaken. The practice literature, much of it centred on Life Story Work, puts forward claims for a whole range of benefits for the child, such as enhanced self-esteem, a positive sense of identity and less need to 'act out' conflicts. Some of these claims for direct work will be addressed here.

INTERVIEWS WITH THE CHILDREN'S SOCIAL WORKERS

The CSWs were interviewed twice: at 1 month and 12 months following the new placement. Most of the information used in this chapter is drawn from the initial CSW interviews. Information was gathered on 58 placements at one month and 58 a year later; this included three post-disruption interviews. Data were missing on three cases at each point.

The social workers were interviewed at their workplace and they could refer to their own case files for specific information. All the respondents were asked the same questions, their replies were coded numerically, and detailed notes were kept and referred to later when presenting case illustrations. Data were gathered on the details of the child's history and the social workers' own planned and actual pre-placement interventions as well as any additional therapy provided.

SPECIALIST PSYCHOLOGICAL HELP

The majority of the direct work was done by the CSWs. However, a significant element of their role was, in addition, to recruit specialist therapeutic intervention as necessary. Of the 58 cases, there were 18 children who had at some time received therapy and a further 9 cases

Conduct
problems
22%

Emotional
problems
15%

Bereavement
11%

Sexual
abuse
33%

Advice
19%

Figure 6.1: Reason for specialist referral

where the social worker or carer had sought specialist consultation. Referral was usually to psychologists and child psychotherapists. The problems prompting the referral are given in Figure 6.1. Requests for advice were mainly to child psychiatrists asking whether contact with birth parents was advisable or whether certain problem behaviours were to be expected in the circumstances.

THE RATIONALE OF LIFE STORY WORK

Life Story Work has been advanced as a tool for helping children to deal with gaps, confusions and distortions in their remembrance of the past that may, if not resolved, inhibit development. The theory proposes that children can carry such unresolved emotions into new placements and behave in ways that put the placement at risk. Ryan and Walker (1993) are strong advocates of the use of Life Story Work and see it as providing a structure for talking to children and helping them to accept the past as well as a means of responding to their entitlement to accurate knowledge about their history so that the children can make informed decisions.

Making the Life Story Book

The Life Story Book itself is a means of making a lasting physical record of the child's life based on photographs, drawings and writing. However, it has been stressed that the Life Story Book should be more than merely a collection of memorabilia and should not be hastily collated with very little involvement of the child. In 90% of cases there was a Life Story Book. Forty per cent of the books were said to be up to date and the other 50% were in the process of being completed. The absence of a Life Story Book in 10% of cases was due to the child being either difficult to engage or very articulate so that it was seen to be less necessary. However, half of these children had access to other objects related to the past such as photographs, documents, drawings, a history sheet or a family tree.

It was encouraging to know that this work was being undertaken for most of the children although, without access to the Life Story Book itself, it was not possible to say how full a picture of the child's life it was, how much the child had been involved or how sensitively or therapeutically it had been used. Occasionally the CSWs in the study prepared the Life Story Book themselves and gave it to the child rather than compiling it jointly. Others used it as a therapeutic tool for the better understanding and resolution of past unhappiness. It was apparent in the interview with CSWs that the amount of time and expertise devoted to the Life Story Book varied according to the individual practitioner's skill and, significantly, whether they held pressing child protection cases.

The Life Story Work in the study was carried out by the CSW in 89% of cases and the remainder by the family social worker (3%) or other staff (8%). Where others carried out the work this was because the CSW was too pressured so that the task was contracted out to another social worker, or because more specific expertise was required, or because the child would not tolerate the allocated social worker doing this work. The Life Story Work was not necessarily started immediately prior to the adoptive placement, or by the CSW, for in many cases it was started on first reception into care and augmented throughout the child's care history.

THE SOCIAL WORKERS' CHARACTERISTICS AND THEIR DIRECT WORK WITH THE CHILD

The social workers who carried out the direct pre-placement work with the child were predominantly child care workers carrying child protection responsibilities. Most of them had known the children for some years. These CSWs were all qualified social workers, although only a small minority said they had specific training for direct work in relation to establishing permanent placements. In three instances the child's case

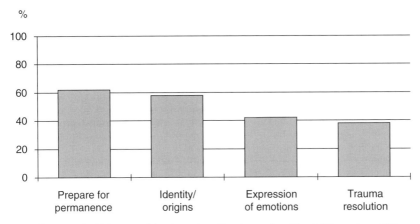

Figure 6.2: Primary objectives for direct work with children (n = 59)

had been reallocated to a specialist, freelance social worker. In a further five cases, some or all of the preparatory work was undertaken by child therapists.

The preparatory work was mostly done in the foster homes from where the majority of children (87%) were transferred. Otherwise, work was done in therapeutic centres or children's homes. A number of the foster carers were described as contributing to the preparation process although they often did so less formally, as part of everyday family life, and through talking to the child about future plans and encouraging a positive view of the move.

A substantial amount of social work time was devoted to this work immediately prior to placement. Seventy-nine per cent of CSWs said that they saw the children on a weekly or fortnightly basis in the transition period and 9% saw them more frequently. The sessions lasted for an hour or more for three quarters of the cases and under an hour for the remainder. However, in a small minority of cases (12%) direct work was undertaken monthly or even less frequently.

The CSWs were asked to identify their primary reason for conducting direct work prior to placement (Figure 6.2). The most frequent reason given (63%) was to prepare the child for a permanent new home. This involved the basic task of informing the children of the placement plans, helping them to understand why they could not return home or stay in their current environment and why it was decided to move them to a permanent new family. A slightly smaller proportion (58%) gave 'identity work' as a focus. Here they helped the children to have an accurate and positive picture of who they were and to acknowledge what had happened to them. In one case a black social work student was allocated to a case for a limited number of sessions to help the child understand her racial origins and identity. Less frequently (43%) they had more therapeutic aims such as helping the children to express their feelings more openly and honestly. The smallest proportion (37%) aimed to conduct work that shares much in common with child psychotherapy and the CSWs used terms such as 'in-depth work' involving the 're-working of past trauma'. This was explained as attempting to achieve some measure of resolution of painful emotions relating to loss or abuse so that these were not 'acted out' in the new placement, possibly jeopardising its stability. It should be remembered that these were intentions and not actual records of the work as implemented.

The majority of children (86%) were said to be active and enthusiastic in the direct work sessions although the remainder were more difficult to work with, being described as passive, withdrawn or hostile. It could be said that these children were defending themselves against the remembrance of painful experiences. Indeed when some CSWs encouraged the children to 're-process' their previous losses and traumas, this evoked uncooperativeness, hostility or poor concentration, which were extremely difficult to manage.

The Use of Specific Techniques in Direct Work

There have been attempts to provide aids to communication with children that do not rely entirely on verbal ability and are intended to have a more powerful impact (e.g. Catholic Children's Society, 1983; Alton, 1987). Many simple techniques are available to social workers: happy–sad face, feeling cards, unfinished sentences, glove puppets, doll figures, imaginary telephone conversations, chairs, Fahlberg's Three Parents, Ecomaps, the candles ritual, the moving calendar and ways of dealing with questions of identity with black and mixed parentage children.

The use of specific techniques was taken in this study to indicate the ability of CSWs to work more appropriately through play and symbols rather than through words alone. Despite developments in these methods of communicating with children, it appeared that the use of specific techniques was not very widespread and CSWs still relied in the main on direct interviews. In six cases the CSW thought the child was communicating well verbally and there was no need to use other methods. Of those cases where Life Story Work had recently been attempted ($n = 48$)

45% said they used no specific techniques, 42% used a single technique and 13% said they used several techniques. Toy telephones and puppets were used most frequently. Many social workers encouraged children to make drawings or plasticine figures alongside talking with them, although they did not tend to think of these as specific techniques.

Evaluating Direct Work

We examined the impact of the direct work by the CSW on progress in the first year of placement. This was not a test of a perfected model of direct work conducted in a specialist agency, but an enquiry into its routine application in a social services context. The social workers were not chosen for their special expertise in placement work. In fact most of their other work was 'investigative' and for them the permanent placement of older children was a fairly infrequent occurrence. Unlike a controlled trial, comparing one approach with another, the research team were not specifying the content of the direct work nor selecting or training the practitioners. This evaluation resembles, therefore, a field experiment with child preparation in the hands of the social workers who happened to be allocated to the cases.

The CSWs were generally optimistic about the value of their preparatory work. Fifty-two per cent thought the direct work sessions were very beneficial to the child, 30% moderately beneficial, but 18% thought the objective of preparing the child for placement had not been adequately realised and the level of understanding achieved by the child in connection with the move was thought to be superficial. In such cases the CSWs described the difficulty of having to decide whether to continue with the preparation work in the hope of progress or to go ahead with the placement because further delay would be undesirable.

Describing and Classifying the Quality of Direct Work

While it was clear from the interviews that the CSWs varied considerably in the level of expertise they brought to the work, there was no standard method for measuring the quality of preparation work. Clearly, counting the number of visits made or time spent with the children provides useful information, but it is not an adequate marker by itself for quality of work. The level of the direct work was therefore assessed by examining the replies the CSWs gave and the researchers' detailed notes. A summary rating, blind to outcome, was then made. Judgements about

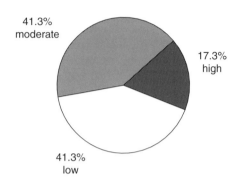

Figure 6.3: Level of direct pre-placement CSW work

quality of work were based on information about their aims and achievements, the extent to which the work addressed specific issues of concern to the child, the range of skills employed and familiarity with theory and current practice in placement work.

From careful assessment and discussions within the research team, the level of social work input was divided into three categories (Figure 6.3). Clearly these are judgements and, as such, are open to challenge with regard to the number of categories chosen, the naming and content of the categories and the risk of misclassification. We have reasonable confidence in our groupings given that they were based on detailed and systematically collected evidence and we present here the basis for the categorisation.

Low level (n = 24, 41.3%)

In these cases CSWs were supportive to the child and assisted with practical plans for the transfer to a new home, but little time was spent individually with the child and the work was superficial and the aims were unfocused. They did not engage with the children's feelings about the past and said they were too inexperienced, under-trained, lacking in confidence, over-stretched and unsupervised to carry out more intensive direct work.

Moderate level (n = 24, 41.3%)

In these cases, more thorough and confident work was carried out with more frequent individual contact. The CSWs described their attempts to help the children achieve an accurate view of their history and a positive sense of identity and self-worth. They attempted more 'in-depth' work, such as helping the child to acknowledge painful emotions relating to loss or abuse on the grounds that these feelings would not then be 'acted out' in the new placement. On occasion, they encountered resistance or hostility from the children and some CSWs found this discomforting and felt challenged beyond their competence, particularly when professional practice supervision was lacking. Life Story Books were sometimes begun but left incomplete.

High level (n = 10, 17.3%)

In these cases, time was taken to develop the trust of the children and to engage with their painful emotions. The work was conducted in a suitable place free from interruption. It was structured and time limited and the CSWs were able to list their specific aims. They were articulate about theories on the needs of children in transition and used a range of appropriate communication techniques. They completed the work, including the Life Story Book, and achieved their own aims before the placement was made. In the majority of these cases the preparation was done by local authority social workers who had a special interest in developing direct work. In the other cases specialist psychotherapists were recruited in addition to, or largely replacing, the CSW role.

Common activities of these social workers involved recovering and unravelling past history, reinforcing the good memories and recalling the painful ones and exploring feelings towards birth parents (especially where a child had idealised fantasies of a mother–child relationship). These workers used a range of techniques including play therapy, the interpretation of the child's drawings and anatomical dolls as an aid to understanding and communication. One CSW helped the child to build a model airport out of paper as a means of symbolically representing the departures and arrivals in the child's complicated life. The direct work sometimes had a more active component like taking a child to visit her mother's grave in one instance and a father in prison in another.

This more therapeutically oriented work was attempted when children had severe problems and there was a need to attend to their psychological problems in order to make a move to a permanent family placement possible. There could be formidable problems involved in struggling to relate to children who could not settle in the sessions, who resisted attempts to encourage them to express or reflect on their past or who could only express their feelings in violent outbursts.

RELATING PREPARATORY WORK TO OUTCOME

The most obvious outcome measure is 'disruption', but given that only three placements ended by a year (5%), there are not enough cases on which to test the differential impact of three levels of work. Furthermore, dividing outcome into disruption versus continuing placements does not adequately represent the number of difficult but continuing placements. Most of the practice literature suggests that the preparatory work will show itself in positive changes in behaviour and emotional problems. There was no doubt that many of the children were highly disturbed when placed (see Chapter 8).

The impact of preparatory work was first assessed against the two main summary measures of the security of placement and the direction of change in emotional and behavioural difficulties. Further summary measures and case examples are used in order to explore reasons for the impact of preparatory work or its lack.

First we examined whether low level input was related to poorer outcomes. In order to do this the 'moderate' and 'high' level input groups were collapsed into a category termed 'higher level' ($n = 34$). The results were disappointing. By the end of the *first year* in placement, the level of CSW direct work appeared to make no difference to the stability of the placement, or to the improvement or deterioration in problem levels, or whether the child made attachments to the new parents. These findings are in keeping with other research into late placements where links have not so far been demonstrated between 'service variables' and outcome (Barth & Berry, 1988; Borland *et al.*, 1991).

One possible explanation was that the best preparatory work might have been targeted on the most difficult cases. If this was the case then clearly positive effects might not be expected after only one year in the placement. This proved not to be the case. The quality of work was not related to the children's overt emotional or behavioural problems. Nor was it related to the children's pre-placement care careers, including their experiences with birth parents, the number of moves they had made, or prior disruptions. Only two factors in the child's background were significantly associated with the level of CSW input: age at placement and abuse history. The higher level of input was given to older children (F = 4.1, d.f. = 1,56, $p < 0.05$) and to children who had been physically and sexually abused rather than neglected (χ^2 = 8.27, d.f. = 3, $p < 0.04$). These are separate factors: age at placement and type of abuse were not correlated. We cannot tell whether these differences in the level of service are based on theories and beliefs about who needs more input or are simply chance associations that would not be repeated in another sample.

Nevertheless it seemed valuable to explore further whether we could identify any factors that worked against direct work being effective in the short term. One possible candidate was overactive and restless behaviour in the children. Our previous work and that of others had shown this to be common and persistent amongst children with experiences like those in our sample. This, indeed, appeared to be an important factor in this study also. The higher CSW input was found to be related to improvement at one year for children who were not overactive and restless at one month (Fisher's exact test $p = 0.007$) but to have no impact on adjustment or attachment in the presence of overactive/ restless behaviour. In fact, 13 out of 16 overactive children receiving higher input were found in the 'many problems' group at a year. The implication of this finding is that it may only be when children are able to remain calm and to concentrate that preparatory work can have an effect on outcome in the short term.

We next explored whether there were any reasons why even a high level of intervention appeared ineffective overall. For this we returned to the original threefold classification of the levels of CSW preparation work in order to relate this to progress during the year. For this analysis we chose a measure of change in the level of problems defined as above or below the 25th percentile on the total behaviour problem score at one month. The bar chart (Figure 6.4) shows the proportion of children with many or fewer problems at one month and one year in relation to low, moderate and high levels of direct work. There were no statistically significant differences in behaviour difficulties between any of the groups at either point in time. Half of the children with high level preparation still had multiple problems at 12 months.

Of course, it is possible that our choice of measure missed important features of the children's lives or behaviour which could have both led to the differential levels of preparation and reduced any immediate benefit of the high quality work. In order to explore this possibility we examined the case notes of the 10 children who had received high level

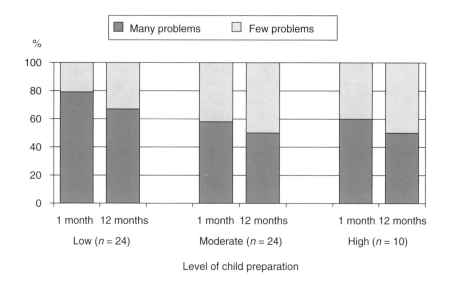

Figure 6.4: Problems at one and twelve months according to levels of child preparation

work to see whether there might be individual circumstances that worked against the preparation being effective. These two case examples illustrate the complexity of the issue.

Mary and Karen were similar in age; each had been sexually abused in their early years and been removed from home before starting school. Both children received high levels of work to help them understand their past experiences and anticipate the new placement. Both girls joined families who already had children at home, neither was free from difficulties when they were placed, and both sets of parents reported some difficulty in developing warm feelings for their child but, by the end of the year, Mary was much more settled than Karen. When we looked at their case histories we found that, while there was much in common between the two, there were also a number of differences, particularly in relation to ongoing events in their lives.

Mary had received a good deal of her early care from her extended family and was not thought to be attached to her mother. After being removed from her birth family, leaving two half siblings behind, she never returned home and received little information about her family. Her previous carers had reinforced the work done by the social worker in an appropriate manner and the move to the new placement went relatively smoothly.

Karen, in contrast, was an only child and had an intense relationship with her mother, although this was inappropriate in many ways. In addition to the loss of this relationship, Karen also had, over time, to deal with news of two or three very upsetting events in her birth family. In addition, her foster parents, to whom she was very attached, were finding it difficult to let go and to encourage her impending move. Although the person conducting the direct work with her was very skilled and experienced, she reported great difficulty in engaging Karen in the task and felt that the work could not be completed until Karen was more settled in a permanent placement.

For Mary, it is plausible that the preparatory work contributed to her settling with her new family. Karen's experiences emphasise the point that direct work does not happen in isolation and various factors, which may counteract any immediate benefits arising from preparatory work, can intervene at any stage

Reasons for a Lack of Association

Why is there a lack of a consistent association between quality of work and outcome? A variety of reasons can be suggested. *First* it is possible that, overall, the CSW work was not sufficiently thorough or skilled to make a measurable difference to problem levels in the children. However, the lack of measurable impact of even highly skilled input indicates that there is more to it than this. The *second* possibility is that older children with high levels of disturbance such as these need much more sustained work before preparation will show benefits. One test would be to see whether the lack of effect holds for younger children who have been less exposed to adversity. *Third*, the children most in need of pre-placement help may not have received the highest level of work, although this did not seem to be a clear feature in our sample. A poor match of expertise to level of difficulty will contribute to the lack of overall beneficial effect. *Fourth*, it is possible that the premises on which this work is currently based are wrong.

This may apply to all aspects of the process or specific elements. For example, it may be mistaken to assume that the work is best done at this time. Children will vary on when and in what way they are ready for it, as Karen's case showed. In addition, theoretical assumptions are made about the need for attention to various factors, such as loss, but this may or may not be what the child needs immediate help with. Further, the level of input may be affected by assumptions about the importance of particular experiences such as sexual abuse, to the relative neglect of issues such as the quality of relationships, under the untested assumption that the experiences are the key to the behaviour.

Differences in level of work may also arise because some children are easier to work with or their experiences provide a clearer focus for the work. For example, less work may have been done with younger children because CSWs expected them to respond well to permanent placement or because they were harder to communicate with, being less articulate. Similarly, the CSWs may have thought that physically and sexually abused children had a greater need for help or they may have found it easier to respond to the consequences of 'tangible' abuse rather than absence of adequate parenting.

These factors were certainly related to the level of preparatory work, whereas the level of emotional and behavioural difficulty the children were showing was not. As the allocation of levels of work was not entirely random, differences in outcome will not be influenced by the CSWs' work alone but also by the factors leading to differential service quality.

PRACTICE IMPLICATIONS

It is dispiriting to have to report that much of the child preparation work was under-developed and the aims and methods poorly formulated. Clearly, if the work is to be undertaken by mainstream child care workers, they need better training and supervision, legitimation of the task, protection from other demands and proper allocation of time to do it.

The recommendations of child care specialists about the importance of preparation of the child do not appear to be finding very full expression in social service settings. Admittedly it is hard to transfer psychological techniques developed in more sequestered clinical environments to social services departments and methods are frequently practised tentatively or in diluted form. Training schemes resulting in accreditation to do permanent placement work will help to clarify expectations, set agreed standards for appropriate knowledge and skill and disseminate expertise.

It appeared that child protection responsibilities and permanent placement work were often not mutually compatible and that in some cases it may have been better for another worker to become engaged earlier and to take on the child preparation work. Some family placement teams now take over all placement work once the decision is made to place permanently.

It is of interest that, in the absence of overactive/restless behaviour, there was a positive association between intervention and outcome. The practice implication to be drawn from this finding is that proper psychological assessment of overactivity should be conducted when making choices about the aims and intensity of preparatory work. If the overactivity inhibits the chance of achieving a positive effect, resources may need to be shifted to preparing the new parents specifically to acquire effective techniques for handling this problem. In some cases medication in combination with psychological intervention may be advisable. In our earlier follow-up study (Rushton *et al.*, 1995) overactivity/restlessness remained an enduring problem even at eight years after placement.

What is being demanded from the social work service in relation to the placement of older children is a skilled, knowledgeable and sensitive workforce, theoretically well equipped and trained in the use of a range of specific techniques. This touches on the continuing debate as to how far focused, specific, therapeutically oriented methods, usually developed in clinical settings, can be applied in the frequently over-stretched social services context. In many cases the methods were used tentatively and in diluted form and were applied unevenly across the sample. If the effectiveness of practice is to improve, skilled intervention needs to be focused on those least likely to make a good initial adjustment and most likely to retain their difficulties in placement.

SUMMARY

This chapter has given an account of the professional social work service provided for the children in the period leading up to placement. Intensive visiting took place in many cases to prepare the child for the move, but there was wide variation in the quality and volume. We found no associations between the level of direct work and our measures of placement progress. There were indications that overactivity in the child may be an impediment to effective intervention.

The discussion of the findings and practice implications have raised a number of questions and it is important to be clear about the conclusions and implications that may be drawn from the data we have presented. In addition, the data suggest that there may be an interplay between the complexity of children's previous and continuing experiences and any impact of direct work. Future research therefore needs to focus on what work needs to be done with which children, at what point in time, in which circumstances, and by whom.

7

PRE-PLACEMENT WORK WITH NEW FAMILIES

This chapter deals with pre-placement work, including all the aspects of selecting families and matching them with a suitable child, preparing parents for their new role, providing information about the child's medical and developmental status and background and finally placing the child or children in the new family. Much of this chapter is drawn from the parents' own accounts, one month into placement, of this process. Other information comes from the initial interviews with the family social workers (FSW) in which they described the preparation service they provided.

Of course, these families are the successful applicants who were approved to have a particular child or children placed with them. The findings are therefore not representative of the experiences of all applicants, some of whom will have withdrawn and others who will not have been selected. Selection and preparation has been developed by practitioners to become a more collaborative, discussion-based exercise which has been modified considerably since the professionally led 'vetting' procedures that were once used (Dubois, 1987).

PREPARATION OF PROSPECTIVE PARENTS

Group Sessions

For most of the new parents the preparation was a two-stage process: meetings in the applicant's home combining assessment and information-giving along with an expectation that they would attend a preparation group to learn more about becoming new parents. A typical programme involved several group meetings or a day-long training event. As well as the opportunities to meet other applicants, these sessions were likely to cover: the kinds of children available for permanent placement;

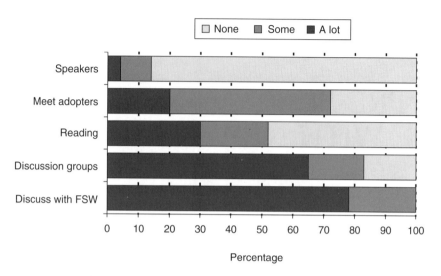

Figure 7.1: Frequency of preparation methods used

information-giving about adoption and fostering procedures; and the agency's support structures. There were presentations and discussions on topics such as: the effects of abuse and neglect; attachment and re-attachment; separation and loss; and attitudes to contact with the birth parents. Book lists were distributed and 'homework' was sometimes required. Figure 7.1 shows the extent to which these methods were used. New parents received little information on what kind of post-placement services they could expect, what form they would take or what other resources might be provided if the need arose.

It was surprising that reading material was so little used, given the increase in literature designed to help applicants think about special needs children. It was also striking that the sessions were nearly all social work led. Rarely did a psychologist, child psychiatrist or teacher speak to the groups.

The Usefulness of the Preparation Groups

The majority of prospective parents said they had benefited from the preparation sessions offered by the agency (42% found it somewhat and 42% very useful). It gave them opportunities to think about what kind and number of children they would be willing to take, to reflect on their own strengths and weaknesses and the added complications of taking an older child. However, the remaining 16% found the preparation groups of no value and it was the experienced parents who were more likely to be dissatisfied (χ^2 = 7.3, d.f. = 2, $p < 0.05$). The dissatisfied group consisted entirely of parents with previous child care experience and represented just under a third (10/35) of the experienced parents. None of the inexperienced parents shared this negative view. The most disgruntled attender stated unequivocally: 'the course was a total waste of time and the person running it was useless!'

Many social workers had made a point of interviewing all family members individually as part of the home assessment, but the possible impact on the families' own children was a major concern for some parents and they felt insufficient attention was paid to this in the group preparation sessions. Some objected that the presentation of children awaiting a family struck the wrong balance of 'pleasures and problems' and tended only to emphasise the challenging behaviours. Occasionally the coverage was found to be too global and failed to meet specific needs. The aspects of the preparation with which experienced parents expressed most dissatisfaction were the sessions on assuming responsibility for children for the first time and developing parenting skills.

The most appreciated aspect of preparation tended to be the opportunity to meet people who had already had children placed. Furthermore, the applicants much preferred hearing from experienced substitute parents about taking older children than from social workers as it helped them to think more realistically about potential changes to their lives.

Individual Sessions

The group meetings were accompanied by a number of individual sessions with the FSW to discuss more specific expectations and prospects and what they thought they could and could not cope with. Kaniuk (1992) stresses the importance of developing positive relationships between the new parents and the FSW at this stage to build a foundation for 'containment and support' should difficulties arise post-placement. Some of the individual work with the FSWs concerned painful recollections about the discovery of infertility and the search for its origin, the problems and stresses of infertility treatment and the process of deciding whether to remain childless or to take on an older, unrelated and probably disturbed child (Houghton & Houghton, 1984; Brebner *et al.*, 1985). Prospective parents were encouraged to anticipate specific problems in the child or to consider their reactions to aspects of the child's background such as parental mental illness. The FSWs discussed the possible effects that placement may have on the marital relationship and lifestyle, especially in the case of children moving to child-free homes. Sometimes circumstances needed closer attention, such as grief following the death of a child, or perhaps where parents had experienced earlier marriage difficulties. Complications could also arise if investigation revealed evidence prejudicial to the application. Some parents had had fraught experiences with previous foster children and even disrupted placements that had left them feeling guilty or disappointed.

The main mode of agency practice was to conduct an assessment of the applicants' suitability and to give approval as foster carers or potential adopters independently of particular children. In only five cases was the assessment conducted with a specific child in mind. In most cases (77%) the FSW who had conducted the assessment remained allocated to the family to provide post-placement support. In the remaining cases the support was provided by a colleague in the same agency (21%) and only once by a worker from another agency. It was unusual for the FSWs to have any contact with the children prior to placement, although they may have introduced themselves during the linking process.

The majority of new families were applying to adopt or foster for the first time and this is reflected in the length of time the FSWs had been working with them. At the time of the research interview (one month into placement), the FSW had known the new families for an average of 5 months with a range of 1–15 months. The initial meetings with the FSW focused on the suitability of the applicants and an exploration of what kinds of children they were hoping for. Attempts to anticipate future difficulties also featured in these sessions.

Disquiet has often been expressed by prospective adopters and permanent foster parents at the length of the assessment process. This concern was registered in the SSI report (DoH/SSI, 1993). According to the social work records, the assessment of the applicants in this study took between 2 and 21 months with a mean of 8.7 months (s.d. 13.7). Seventy-nine per cent took between 2 and 11 months but for 21% the process lasted between 12 and 21 months. In the cases where the FSWs acknowledged that there had been an unwelcome delay ($n = 20$), 9 of these were explained as due to the need for aspects of the new family to be addressed more fully before approval could take place and 11 to lack of staff available to process the assessments.

CHARACTERISTICS OF THE FAMILIES' SOCIAL WORKERS

In all of the referring authorities, policy dictated that adoption and permanent fostering work was done by qualified staff. Sixty-three per cent of the social workers supporting the placements worked in local or central adoption and fostering units (also called family placement or family finding teams). The remainder (27%) worked in the adoption or permanent placement units of independent child care agencies. In a few cases (10%), support for the new parents was undertaken by social workers carrying a broad range of child care responsibilities. All but three of the FSWs interviewed were white, the remainder were African-Caribbean, and all but two were female. The time spent in their current post ranged between 2 months and 20 years (38% had spent under 2 years; 28% between 2 and 4 years; and 33% had spent more than 4 years).

ASSESSING THE ACCEPTABILITY OF THE PLACEMENT PLAN TO OTHER CHILDREN IN THE FAMILIES

The formation of the new family, especially when other children are already present in the household, is a significant feature in modern adoption practice. Thirty-two new families in the sample already had at least one resident child and most of these were birth children. The FSW had a considerable amount of direct discussion with these children about the placement plans in 18 of these families (55%), but in 15 cases (45%) discussion was said to have been minimal. Instead, social workers had arranged the placement with only the new parents' views in mind, despite the influence these new sibling relationships might have on the placement. In only one case did the social worker think the placed children would not be easily accepted by the birth siblings. She was proceeding with the placement in the hope that positive relationships would develop in time.

INFORMATION ABOUT THE CHILD TO BE PLACED

New parents need information about the child or children they are taking on which is both thorough and reliable in order to decide whether they can rise to the specific challenges in caring for and understanding the child. In general, the better the quality and accuracy of information, the easier the parental adjustment to the child should be.

Difficulties that emerge later in parent/child relationships may be related to misconceptions, false expectations and ignorance about the child to be placed.

The initial information about the children was usually given to the new parents via their own social worker with the help of the Form E produced by the British Agencies for Adoption and Fostering and followed up by a visit from the child's social worker. The next source of information was from the previous carers. Some of this would be passed on before matching and some after. In some cases parents would also meet school teachers and therapists before the children were placed. New parents found meeting people who had been involved with the children in the past particularly helpful.

The new parents were asked how satisfied they were with the information they were given in four areas: medical history, the child's background and experiences, the child's emotional and behavioural profile and familiar daily routines.

Information on Current Health and Medical History

Although the agency has an obligation to inform the new parents about the mental and physical health of the child to be placed and whether there are any special health needs, the medical and developmental reports shown to the parents varied considerably in detail. In 66% of cases the medical information was said to be either absent or inadequate. This is a matter of concern because 'in care' populations often have significant rates of both diagnosed and undiagnosed medical problems (Wolkind, 1979). Some long-standing medical problems only came to light later in the placement. The discovery of such problems can adversely affect the child's development and parents feel misled about the poor state of health of many of the children.

A third of the new parents (34%) were satisfied with the amount and accuracy of the information given about the child to be placed. The 66% who were dissatisfied were made up of 12% who said they had been given no medical information and knew nothing about the history of childhood illnesses and immunisation status. One of these families complained that they had no idea their child had a heart murmur until they had to take her for her regular hospital appointment. At the time of the interview new parents were trying to register the child with their GP, hoping to receive more information when the medical records were passed on. The other 54% were not so strongly dissatisfied but thought the medical information given was inadequate and lacked detail in some areas. For instance, there was concern to know about mental illness in the birth family and the genetic risks. One set of parents were very embarrassed when they were unable to tell the dentist whether their child was allergic to penicillin. Three families later found the medical information to be incorrect or not entirely accurate. Of those who made an effort to gain more information ($n = 27$, 44%), 17 of these (63%) were frustrated in these attempts, as promised information was not forthcoming.

Information on the Children's Background History and Experience

Most of the children had complicated biographies which required careful reviewing of the case files in order to extract the salient information. In fact, almost half (44%) of the new parents thought the level of detail was inadequate. This caused difficulty when the child began to talk about the past and to reveal prior fostering breakdowns or periods of residential care of which the new parents had not been aware.

Fifteen per cent pressed, unsuccessfully, for more information. One couple complained that the child social worker (CSW) would not support their request for further background information when they were trying to understand the child's worrying sexual behaviour. It was hard for parents to judge whether the records were indeed faithful accounts of the child's past, but 10% had discovered inaccuracies.

The child's Life Story Book was an important source of background information. One parent said she was amazed at how many relatives the child had and realised how they must all be wondering about her. However, these varied in the amount of detail they held about people and events in the child's history.

Information about the Child's Behaviour and Emotions

When the new parents first discussed taking a particular child they received details of behaviour to assist their decision. Some were shown videos of the child in a foster home and they also gleaned some information from previous carers when visiting them. Over half (55%) said they were given a great deal of information about the child's behavioural and emotional status but 41% were given little or no information. Five per cent of these were explained by placements that were arranged in a hurry with promises of information to follow.

Seventy per cent of parents found the information about behaviour and emotions of considerable use to them but the remainder found it inadequate. Parents who pressed for further information were rewarded with satisfactory information in a quarter of the cases. However, half (49%) found the descriptions they were given to be inaccurate once the children had arrived. One mother said:

> There was a horrendous Form E about this naughty, aggressive little girl – and she isn't any of those things.

This feeling of being misinformed clearly perturbed the new parents and it is important to consider how this situation might have arisen. One possibility is that the Form E was completed some time ago and had not been recently revised. It is possible that the children had, in fact, behaved very differently in the previous home in contrast to the picture the new parents were seeing once placed. Furthermore, certain aspects of the child's behaviour may have been either exaggerated or minimised by the social workers in order to make the child more appealing to the new parents. It is also possible that the new parents had in some way mis-remembered the original information. Further research is necessary to establish whether some or all of these processes lead to inaccurate information on the child's history.

Information about the Child's Daily Routines

It is very important in the early months of the placement to preserve some consistency in routines concerning meal times, bedtime rituals and the special preferences of the child. Although 44% of parents said a considerable amount of information was given, 21% said nothing was passed on about routines in the previous home and the remainder only received a little. Although new parents found this information of considerable help when it was available, they tended not to press for further information about routines. Those who did, found it was easy to obtain by checking with the previous carers. However, many new parents made the point that whilst it was useful to know what had been expected of the children in the past, they had their own 'house rules' to which the children had to adapt.

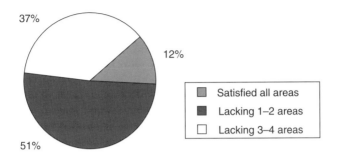

Figure 7.2: Adequacy of information-giving according to new parents

The Consequences of Poor Quality Information

Similar levels of inadequate information were found for each of the four areas investigated. This ranged from 42% of new parents finding information on behaviour to be inadequate to 66% of parents in relation to medical information. The overlap in levels of information-giving in these four areas was then examined (see Figure 7.2). Twelve per cent of new parents were satisfied with the information given in all four areas, 51% reported inadequate information in two or three of the areas and 37% were dissatisfied in three or four of the areas. For this latter, very dissatisfied group, the social work service was also regarded as inadequate. Sixty-five per cent (15/23) of those given very poor information complained that their CSW had provided no support. A significant amount of poor practice is revealed here and this is a concern that has been voiced before in other older child placement research (Barth & Berry, 1988).

Poor information-giving was then examined to see if there were any discernible effects on the placement. Although the lack of information was of concern to the new parents and they frequently had to press for more, there was no significant association with any measures from our parent interviews like parental stress levels, satisfaction with the child at one month and a year, or overall satisfaction with the placement over the first year. That is, those given very poor information were no more likely than those with better information to be dissatisfied with the child or the placement. The new parents appeared, for the most part, to develop positive feelings about the child and general satisfaction with the placement despite the serious lack of information.

There is room for improvement in the quantity and reliability of information passed to the new parents. The difficulty in gaining access to reliable information clearly depends on efficient record systems in the agencies and the need to protect professional time to update and summarise files and to give time to passing on the information to the new parents. Reliable information is crucial to help the parents understand the child's behaviour and to develop appropriate expectations of the child and to prepare them to help the child deal with the past.

PARENTS' VIEWS ON THE LENGTH OF INTRODUCTIONS

Planning the length of introductions, assessing the 'readiness' of the child and family for the transition and deciding on precisely when to make the final move are all key aspects of the placement process. The pace of events is clearly a matter of judgement in order to make the transfer as smooth as possible and to lay the strongest foundations for a secure placement.

Five per cent of placements were made extremely rapidly, within a week of introductions. Some families found the speed of transfer was extremely difficult, whereas others accommodated it remarkably easily. Thirty-two per cent of the children were placed within 4 weeks of first meeting, nearly half (43%) were placed between 4 to 8 weeks, 8% between 8 to 12 weeks and 17% after more than 3 months. The majority of new parents (70%) were satisfied with the length of the introduction period. More parents (20%) found introductions too long, than found them too short (10%). One father said: 'It was a very long drawn-out process that needs speeding up'. However, the parental frustration has to be set against the need to proceed at the right pace in order to complete the children's preparation work.

There was no statistically significant association between the duration of the introduction period and the parents' opinion of the waiting period. The group of 41 parents who found the duration acceptable included the majority (6/10) of those where the placement process was lengthy, that is more than three months after introductions.

PRACTICE IMPLICATIONS

The dissatisfaction of experienced parents with aspects of the preparation process, suggests that social workers need to acknowledge the skills of these parents, whilst helping them to understand that these children may pose new or different parenting challenges. It is also important that children living in the home are adequately prepared for the major changes that a new sibling may bring to their family life.

The shortcomings of the information-giving included both omissions and inaccuracies. In order to address these problems, it is clear that improvements are needed in the initial gathering of information as well as its collation, updating and retrieval. The appropriate use of the 'Looking After Children' forms (Parker *et al.*, 1991) should result in significant improvements in collection and storage of key information.

The imparting of information about children, which may be highly charged, is a complex process and social workers need to be alert to both the extent to which it is received and the way in which it is interpreted by parents. Information should be imparted in written form as well as verbally, in order that parents can return to it at a later stage.

SUMMARY

This chapter has given an account of the parents' experiences of preparation for placement. There was a marked difference between experienced and inexperienced parents in their satisfaction with the group-based preparation courses, with those who had parented before complaining of a service that was not geared to their specific needs.

Serious problems with information-giving were revealed. This has often been the subject of complaint in the past and it is troubling to have to record continuing omissions. Crucial information was not being passed on and too frequently it was sketchy, inaccurate or out of date. This applied in particular to information about the child's medical history and pre-placement experience, responsibility for which must rest with the placing agency. In contrast, the passage of information from the previous carers to the new parents was particularly important and useful.

8

THE CHILDREN'S ADJUSTMENT AT HOME

The children in our study had had very poor and unstable early experiences and could be expected to have significant emotional and behavioural problems. One of the main purposes of seeking permanent families for them was to provide the stability that might allow these problems to diminish. However, as outlined in Chapter 1, research has repeatedly found behavioural difficulties to be associated with placement disruption and, not surprisingly, with less parental satisfaction. Of course, emotional and behavioural problems have implications for the children, not just regarding the extent to which placements are successful, but also in affecting their chances of achieving happiness in other areas of life.

If persistent, the long-term costs of these difficulties can be extremely high, both to the children and to society. Notions that the children are 'acting-out' or 'testing' their new parents are not an adequate explanation for all problems. Nor is it correct to expect problems to go away of their own accord if a stable and loving environment is provided. If placements are to succeed it is essential that social workers and prospective parents have a clear idea of what challenges the children will present and how easy or difficult it may be to change them.

In this chapter we deal with the parents' accounts of the children's behaviour and how they expressed their worries, anxieties and distress. The complementary data from other sources is discussed in Chapter 10, where we examine the children's school experiences and look at behaviour in different contexts, and in Chapter 14, where we examine the relationships between behaviour and other aspects of placement. This chapter focuses on the challenges the children presented to their new parents, but it should not be forgotten that the children also provided them with many rewards as well.

ASSESSMENT OF THE CHILDREN'S ADJUSTMENT

The parents' view of the children's behaviour was assessed in three ways: first they gave their own free account of the behaviours they found most challenging. This provided their first-hand perspective on which types of difficulty were most problematic and stressful for them. They were then taken through a comprehensive list of 50 symptomatic behaviours that were used to assess whether the children were showing clinically significant levels of difficulty. The areas covered included conduct, emotional and relationship difficulties as well as overactivity. This approach ensured that the same information was obtained for all children and allowed us to classify the children's problems according to modern diagnostic criteria. Finally the parents completed a standardised self-completion questionnaire, the Rutter A2 Scale. Scores of 13 or above on this scale have been shown reliably to distinguish children with psychiatric difficulties from those without and the scale also yields sub-scores on conduct, emotional and hyperactive problems. This scale was used in addition to the parents' verbal accounts because of the sub-stantial amount of general population data available on it. This was important because our study did not include a general population comparison group.

The Parents' Free Accounts of Challenging Behaviours

The parents were first asked to say what had struck them most about the children when they first arrived and, in particular, what kinds of behaviours had caused the greatest problems in the first month of the placement. They were asked to give descriptions of up to three *different* kinds of difficulties. Only three parents said they had not faced any particular challenges at this time. The other 58 described a total of 140 difficulties shown by the children. We recorded the difficulties they described in two ways: first, by broadly categorising the elements of the incidents – for example, whether they merely involved oppositional behaviour or whether the children were also tearful and distressed at the same time – and secondly, by rating the frequency and severity of the episode.

The majority of the incidents were both 'serious' and 'frequent' (Table 8.1). Some problems, by their nature, although also serious, were more episodic. This applied especially to sexualised behaviour, a problem that was of considerable concern to the parents, regardless of its frequency.

Table 8.1: Frequency and seriousness of behaviour problems recounted by parents

Problem category	Mild infrequent	Mild frequent	Serious infrequent	Serious frequent	Total
Conduct	1	18	9	55	83
Emotional	–	4	1	20	25
Relationships				5	5
Activity level	–	–	–	7	7
Sexualised behaviour	1	–	3	3	7
Habitual and other	–	4		9	13
Total	2	26	13	99	140

The 99 serious and frequent episodes occurred in 50 of the 61 placements: 20 parents described just one serious problem, 11 two and 19 three problems. Twenty parents reported only oppositional, aggressive or defiant behaviour in their children and three others only distress, unhappiness or withdrawal. Only one child was seen as overactive and restless, without any other problem. The remaining 26 children showed a mixture of difficulties. However, although a number of different behaviours could have been described in any episode, in practice the parents tended to report the predominant features only. Thus just 21% of episodes of conduct problems included elements of unhappiness and distress, and 9% descriptions of overactivity. The type or number of problems was not related either to features of the placement or to the age, gender or previous experiences of the children, although there was a tendency for overactive behaviour to be described more often for boys.

The Nature of the Problems

Defiance, disobedience and displays of temper were well ahead in the league of behaviours directed at parents during the first year of placement. Many children put up a good deal of resistance to their new parents, sometimes resorting to verbal or even physical abuse in order to avoid complying with instructions. Lying in order to avoid trouble was common.

Emotional problems included anxiety, worrying and fears. Several children were severely frightened of the dark when they were first placed, others worried about being left alone or about intruders. Some were extremely anxious whenever they encountered a new person or situation.

In the course of the year, sexualised behaviour was described for 12 children, a problem these parents found particularly hard to deal with. Some children masturbated in public, others used sexually precocious language, and, in some instances, directed precocious behaviour at the parents themselves. Such interactions brought to the surface a range of strong emotions in the parents, from anger at what the children had experienced to their own personal discomfort. Interestingly, sexual abuse was known or suspected in only 8 of these 12 cases. Fourteen children who were known or suspected to have been sexually abused did not show sexualised behaviour, but some parents were anxious about how their children might respond to the onset of puberty.

Problems associated with the children's activity level or habitual behaviours were less frequently mentioned by parents spontaneously. The overactivity described by parents, in this context, tended to involve difficulties with gaining the children's attention sufficiently long to accomplish daily tasks such as eating or dressing. Behaviours categorised under 'habitual' or 'other' included things like bed-wetting, soiling and problems with eating such as extreme fussiness or, alternatively, gorging of food.

Changes in the Parents' Free Account over the Year

A comparison between the parents' free accounts at 1 and 12 months presents a complicated and fluctuating picture, with some problems being resolved but with new ones arising as well. Two children were described by their parents as problem-free throughout the year and eight managed to resolve all of their difficulties. Twenty-one resolved at least one of their original problems, 27 maintained all of them to some degree and serious new problems arose during the course of the year for over half the sample (36 children). As at one month, these problems primarily concerned misbehaviour and defiance, although there were several examples of emotional and other difficulties developing as well. In many cases these new difficulties were in addition to existing problems, and thus some parents came to face notable additional challenges with their child.

Some of the problems that appeared to arise during the year may have been present from the beginning but only gradually recognised. These included stealing or hoarding of food and lying, a common problem and one that parents found particularly hard to tolerate. Sometimes the new problems were seen as positive, for example, where timid or passive children became more assertive, even though the new behaviour may have been hard to handle.

Parents naturally attributed positive and negative changes to different factors. The reduction in problems was most often attributed to the security given by the placement (14%) or to their own handling of specific problems (32%) and, indeed, there were many examples of positive changes occurring as parents understood the children better and found ways of avoiding needless confrontations. Increasing problems, on the other hand, were often seen to be due to the child's immaturity, insecurity or personality. In some of these cases some parents felt that the children were clearly unhappy, that they 'really knew how to get to them', and that they wanted the placement to end and engaged in behaviours that might bring that about.

Stress Associated with Freely Reported Problems

Examining the reports across the year, we found that mothers were more likely than fathers to find these difficulties distressing. This was probably a reflection of the time spent looking after the children. It was the severity of the incidents, rather than their frequency, that stressed the parents. Figure 8.1 illustrates how most of the serious problems led to considerable concern or distress for at least one parent. These data are based on problems reported at one month but are indicative of similar patterns in relation to different types of problems as they occurred throughout the year. The degree of stress arising from conduct, relationship and overactivity problems is not surprising, but the lack of concern about emotional problems might be interpreted as alarming and deserves some comment. As described above, the problems that were rated as 'emotional' tended to be fears or worries rather than persistent difficulties with mood of the sort associated with depressive disorders. Thus, while the parents were aware of and described these difficulties for the children, in terms of the impact on day-to-day life and challenge to parenting these problems were less pressing than others.

Parental Free Accounts and Placement Outcome

These accounts of problems at the start of placement and arising through the year were strongly related to less secure placements at one year

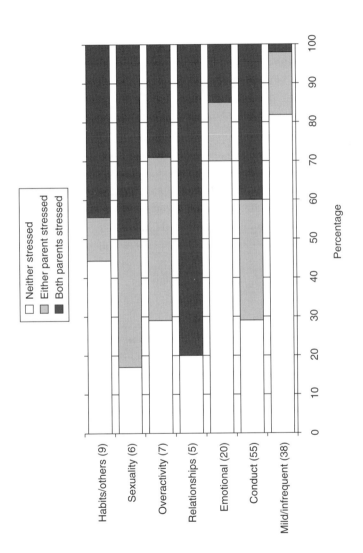

Figure 8.1: Parents' free accounts of difficulties: type of problem and associated stress at one month

Table 8.2: Mean numbers of free account problems according to placement stability at a year

	Mean	S.D.	Significance
Problems at 1 month			
less stable	2.06	1.0	$F = 3.8$ (1,59) $p = 0.057$
more stable	1.45	1.1	
Problems arising in year			
less stable	1.67	1.2	$F = 9.3$ (1,57) $p = < 0.005$
more stable	0.77	0.91	
Total number of problems			
less stable	3.93	1.4	$F = 14.9$ (1,57) $p < 0.001$
more stable	2.22	1.5	

(Table 8.2). This is not surprising, since the parents' perceptions of difficulties and the stress associated with them must have been a major element in the lack of satisfaction with the placement, which was part of the rating of instability.

There are, however, reasons for concluding that such open accounts of problems, despite their force and vividness, are not necessarily specific enough to provide a basis for a closer analysis of the behaviours that caused difficulties to the placement. The correlation between the number of serious problems described in the free accounts and the scores derived from the systematic interview (see below) was significant but modest at the one month point (Kendall's tau = 0.316 (61), $p < 0.005$) although it became much stronger by one year (tau = 0.695 (58), $p < 0.01$). Even at this point, 30% of those not described as problematic on the free account had rateable difficulties on the systematic interview, and 38% of those described as problematic did not.

Two features of these free descriptions deserve comment. First, although the idea was to allow the parents to describe whatever struck them most, unbiased by questions prompting for particular problems, in practice they described incidents in a way that was easily translated into modern clinical categories. Secondly, it was clear that the parents were mostly worried by defiant, uncooperative or aggressive behaviour. This is not surprising since they had been asked to focus on what they found particularly challenging or worrying. On the other hand, this may have led them not to include episodes that seemed less bothersome or in pressing need of action. Thus, they focused on unhappiness and distress much less frequently than on conduct problems and they rarely picked out overactive and restless behaviour, even though this is one of the most persistent difficulties in this group of children, and one that affects most aspects of their lives from progress at school to their relationships with the family and the development of friendships.

Because of the vagaries of the free accounts, we confine the remainder of the analysis to the systematic data provided by the symptom checklist and the Rutter A2 Scale.

THE SYSTEMATIC PARENTAL ACCOUNT OF SYMPTOMATIC BEHAVIOURS

The Incidence of Specific Behavioural and Emotional Problems

If associations between previous experiences, current experiences and placement outcome are to be understood, it is important to ensure that comparable information is obtained on all the children. In order to ensure this, parents were taken systematically through a list of emotional and behavioural difficulties. For a problem to be rated as present, it had to be outside the usual range of behaviour for children of this age and to interfere with their social and emotional development.

The frequency of occurrence of the individual items at both 1 and 12 months is given in Table 8.3 and grouped according to type of behaviours. The comparisons omit from the one month sample the children whose placements had broken down by the end of the year. As can be seen, the children showed a multiplicity of difficulties. In over two-fifths of cases the children's relationships with their new parents at the start of the placement were marked by irritability, defiance, temper or sulkiness. In addition to these problems, a quarter of the children were poor or fussy eaters and a substantial number ate or chewed inedible objects ('pica'). There were problems with wetting and soiling for 20%. A third had specific fears and anxieties and 40% worried persistently.

The systematic questioning revealed much higher levels of overactive behaviour than was reported in the free accounts. Nearly half of the children were overactive, restless and had difficulty with concentrating or settling to activities, even those that they chose for themselves. In addition, a substantial proportion of the children were either aggressive, teasing and bullying in their relationships with other children (28%) or were teased, bullied and lonely themselves (28%). If these problems with

Table 8.3: Frequency of specific symptoms for boys and girls at 1 and 12 months

	Boys (n = 30)		Girls (n = 28)		Total (n = 58)	
	month (%)	year (%)	month (%)	year (%)	month (%)	year (%)
Eating problems	27	23	18	11	28	17
Pica	23	17	4	11	17	14
Bed-wetting	14	10	10	7	12	9
Daytime wetting	7	3	15	7	11	5
Sleep problems	7	7	7	0	7	3
Stomach aches	3	0	11	0	7	0
Soiling	3	10	7	4	5	7
Headaches	0	0	7	0	3	0
Fears						
General worries	30	40	7	28	19	35
Health worries	3	0	0	4	2	2
Misery/depression	0	0	0	0	0	0
Teased	24	30	22	36	23	33
Bullied	14	10	7	0	11	5
Loneliness	3	0	7	7	0	4
Teases	24	10	15	18	20	14
Aggressive	20	4	11	11	16	7
Bullies	4	3	0	11	2	7
Lying	27	47	43	54	35	50
Defiance parents	47	40	32	32	40	36
Irritability	45	23	21	36	32	29
Sulkiness	17	27	25	25	21	26
Fantasising	17	17	7	18	13	17
Tantrums	17	7	18	7	17	7
Defiance others	4	7	4	7	4	7
Feels people against him/her	7	7	0	11	3	9
Stealing	0	13	0	4	0	9
Destructive (family)	13	0	4	0	9	0
Destructive (own)	7	13	0	11	3	12
Cruelty to animals (now)	3	10	4	11	3	10
Firesetting	0	3	0	0	0	2
Fiddling	47	53	39	29	43	41
Restless (home)	50	40	43	46	47	43
Restless (elsewhere)	30	17	11	18	21	17
Overactive (home)	33	30	43	25	39	28
Overactive (elsewhere)	23	23	15	25	20	24
Poor attention (adult directed)	54	58	56	54	55	56
Poor attention (chosen activity)	37	20	46	39	41	29
Poor attention (school)	44	55	39	43	42	49
Social disinhibition	23	13	46	39	36	26
Disinhibition (others)	7	10	7	18	7	14

peer aggression and isolation are taken together, 43% had notable difficulties in their relationships with other children.

There were very few differences between boys and girls in these patterns, although boys were significantly more restless outside the home than the girls and also worried more.

Changes in Specific Symptoms over the Year

Some of the changes in the levels of specific symptoms over the year appear quite large but none of the changes over the year for either boys or girls reached statistical significance (McNemar test). Indeed, the only score that changed significantly was the total score on lying, which increased over the year ($p = 0.035$), probably partly as parents became more accustomed to the children and knew their ways better. Nevertheless, some changes were quite large. For example, worrying in girls increased fourfold, while tantrums reduced considerably. While the overactive behaviour of girls within the home diminished, their overactivity in other situations increased. The number of boys who were having difficulty in maintaining attention at their own chosen activities decreased between 1 and 12 months.

There are no obvious reasons why these changes might have occurred and caution is necessary in drawing conclusions from the data. In the first place, variations in reporting at each point in time for different behaviours and according to gender may have caused these differences. Secondly, the statistical tests show that these differences may have arisen by chance. Even the one significant difference may be a chance finding, given the number of comparisons that were made.

PATTERNS OF BEHAVIOUR IN RELATION TO STANDARD CLASSIFICATIONS

Another way to assess the level of the children's difficulties is to see how the behaviours described above are patterned and how they relate to standard psychiatric classifications of difficulties: that is, to ask how the children's behaviour compares with accepted research and clinical definitions of disturbed emotional and behavioural development. Of course, single items of difficulty may need help from parents and others even if they do not suggest a more serious pattern of disturbance.

The first analysis examined the patterns of disturbance according to DSM-IV criteria – the most recent diagnostic classification from the American Psychiatric Association (1994). Not all symptoms relevant to DSM-IV were collected but the areas covered by the interview were adequate for this purpose. Symptoms included in each diagnosis are described below. The data on the grouping of items under this scheme are presented in Table 8.4. This analysis is confined to the common childhood disorders: conduct problems, emotional difficulties and hyperactivity/attention deficit disorders.

Conduct Problems

Standard classifications of conduct problems now divide these difficulties into oppositional-defiant and conduct disorders. The former are characterised, as the title suggests, by a persistent pattern of negative, defiant, disobedient and hostile behaviour towards authority figures and the latter by a repeated and persistent pattern of behaviour in which the basic rights of others are violated. These disorders are strongly age related, conduct problems in younger children being usually of the oppositional/defiant type. We used two sets of individual symptoms to make ratings on these dimensions. The *oppositional/defiant* scale included the following items: irritability, sulkiness, temper tantrums, lying, defiance to parents and other adults and teasing or irritating other people. The *conduct disorder* scale included: aggressiveness, destructiveness at home and elsewhere (two items), cruelty to animals, truanting, bullying and fire setting.

As was clear from the individual items (Table 8.3) and from the parents' free accounts, the oppositional/defiant group of difficulties was the one giving most trouble to the parents at one month. Although no children reached the standard research criterion for conduct disorder, 16% of boys and 10% of girls showed four or more of the oppositional behaviours, an indication of definite disorder.

These classifications of disorder hardly do justice to the general level of difficulty the parents were facing, since 44% of boys and 48% of girls were rated as showing two or more of these problems. When the conduct disorder items were added to this oppositional list, and four or more problems taken as indicating disorder, 25% of boys and 10% of girls showed oppositional/conduct problems. In the course of the year there was some decline in these problems in the boys, although this change did not reach statistical significance.

Table 8.4: Standard classifications of behaviour for boys and girls at 1 and 12 months

	Girls 1 month (%)	Girls 12 months (%)	Boys 1 month (%)	Boys 12 months (%)	Total 1 month (%)	Total 12 months (%)
Conduct						
Oppositional-defiant	10	11	16	3	13	7
Conduct disorder	0	0	0	0	0	0
Emotional						
Anxiety[a]	3	7	19	13	12	10
Fear	28	29	41	33	34	31
School refusal	33	29	26	27	29	28
Childhood depression	0	3	0	3	0	3
Overall emotional rating	24	21	41	27	33	24
Overactive/attention						
Poor attention	46	50	41	43	43	47
Overactive[b]	39	29	41	30	40	29
Pervasive overactive/attention rating	14	29	34	13	25	21

[a] Boys significantly higher than girls $\chi^2 = 6.1$, d.f. = 1, $p < 0.05$.
[b] Boys higher than girls $\chi^2 = 3.5$, d.f. = 1, $p < 0.06$ at 1 month and boys higher at 1 than 12 months $\chi^2 = 5.25$, d.f. = 1, $p < 0.03$.

Emotional Problems

The children showed high levels of anxious and fearful behaviour. A rating of generalised anxiety disorder was made for children who were persistent worriers and also showed persistent sleep disturbance and/or irritability. Nineteen per cent of boys but only 3% of girls had this kind of generalised anxiety disorder, a statistically significant difference. Fears were common for both sexes, and a quarter of the boys and a third of the girls had refused to go to school on at least two occasions in the first month. Interestingly, no children were described by the parents as persistently sad, depressed or chronically unhappy. This may have been because such problems, if they existed, were swamped by the more obvious and active difficulties.

The various items indicating emotional difficulties were combined to form an overall scale of emotional problems. The items were: school refusal, eating problems, sleeping problems, worrying, fears, chronic unhappiness and depression (two items), and obsessional behaviour (although this was not rated as present at either point in time). Forty-one per cent of boys and 24% of girls scored on two or more items on this scale, a sizeable but non-significant difference.

The general level of anxious and fearful behaviour on the specific symptom categories was similar at both points in time, but the overall level of emotional/anxious symptomatology declined, especially for the boys. This suggests that there was some improvement in the children's affective state, even though the level of problems remained high. One boy and one girl showing symptoms of childhood depression are included in the scale because they were rated as showing chronic unhappiness, even though the parents did not report their mood as clinically depressed.

Overactivity and Attentional Problems

The relevant symptoms rated from the parental accounts were divided into firstly, those measuring *attention* (an ability to settle to or concentrate on activities chosen by the child, by parents or by teachers); and secondly, problems of *overactivity* or restlessness (as indicated by excessive fiddling with objects, inappropriate activity, squirminess and fidgetiness at home and elsewhere, and marked disinhibition).

Over two-fifths of both boys and girls had difficulties with attention and similar proportions were overactive and restless. Definitions of hyperactive disorder require that these behaviours are not only shown to an excessive degree but also that they occur in more than one context – for example, at home and at school. When this criterion was added to the rating, a third of boys still showed rateable disorder, but this was true for only 14% of girls, a substantial but non-significant difference.

In the course of the year there was some decline in overactive or restless behaviour for both boys and girls, but the most striking change was in pervasive attentional/overactive problems. Thus, whilst the parents reported the children as remaining notably overactive, restless and lacking concentration in the home, the extent to which this behaviour also occurred in other environments declined quite markedly for the boys, but increased for the girls, which accounts for the increase over the year in the proportion of girls classified as pervasively overactive. As we have suggested previously, in relation to other aspects of behaviour, it is possible that in the early weeks of placement, parents had only had limited opportunity to observe the children in other environments or receive feedback from other people.

The Overlap of Disorders

It is necessary, finally, to consider how many children showed more than one of these areas of difficulty and how many were substantially symptom free or had only minor problems. These data are given in Table 8.5.

It is striking that over half of the children showed one of these psychiatric disorders. It is also clear that the disorders showed considerable overlap, although this was different according to the type of disorder. Emotional problems occurred most commonly on their own (60%), but overactivity overlapped with other disorders over half of the time (53%).

Table 8.5: Overlap of disorders

Type of disorder	% of sample
No disorder	45
Emotional only	20
Overactive only	12
Oppositional only	7
Emotional + overactive	5
Emotional + oppositional	3
Overactive + oppositional	3
All three	5
	100

Oppositional problems occurred together with other disorders on nearly two-thirds (64%) of occasions.

It should be clear from the data presented already that the 45% of children who did not meet formal criteria for disorder were not necessarily problem free. If the total number of symptomatic behaviours are taken together and summed, the average number of problems experienced by the 'no disorder' children was still substantial (mean 6.1, s.d. 4.9 versus mean 14.6, s.d. 7.3 for those with disorder; ($F = 27.3$, d.f. = 1,59, $p < 0.001$)), with 45% of children in the former group still showing four or more problems one month into placements.

QUESTIONNAIRE MEASURES FOR COMPARISON WITH OTHER POPULATIONS

In the absence of up-to-date epidemiological-based interview data, we compared the parents' accounts of the levels of difficulty within our group of children with the general population using the Rutter A2 questionnaire. This instrument produces a total score and a series of three sub-scores (for conduct, emotional and hyperactive problems). Total scores of 13 or above have been shown reliably to discriminate children with clinically significant levels of problems from those without. Data were available for 52 children at one month. The parents of the remaining 9 were unwilling to complete these ratings at this time. The findings are given in Table 8.6, which shows that over half of the boys and girls in our sample rated above the cut-off of 13 for emotional and behavioural problems. The majority of problems for both sexes involved conduct difficulties, although girls were more likely to be rated as showing emotional problems.

These rates of disorder are markedly higher than those found in other research. General population studies have found that around 15% of boys and 8% of girls rated at or above the cut-off of 13 (Rutter et al., 1970, p. 413).

Even when studies of children in care are considered, the level of disturbance in our sample is substantially higher. Rowe and her colleagues (1984) found that 29% of children in long-term foster care between the ages of 5 and 15 scored at, or above, the cut-off. Unlike our sample, those children had been settled in placement for some years, and their behaviour may have become less problematic as a result. In an unpublished 1984 study, Holbrook found a similar level of disturbance (25%) in foster children aged 10–13, as did Yule and Raynes (1972) for

Table 8.6: Proportion of boys and girls scoring 13 or more on Rutter A2 Scale at one month

	Boys (%)	Girls (%)
Score of 13 or more	54	58
Emotional sub-score	11	21
Conduct sub-score	43	37

n: boys = 28, girls = 24.

Table 8.7: Changes in parent questionnaire score. Moves into and out of disorder groupings between 1 and 12 months

Never scored above the cut-off	31%
Above cut-off at 1 month, below at 12 months	14%
Below cut-off at 1 month, above at 12 months	12%
Always above the cut-off	43%

The cut-off for the parent questionnaire is a score of 13 or more.

children in group cottage children's homes (26%). It therefore appears that the level of disturbance in our sample, as rated by the new parents one month into the placements, was substantially higher than that of other children, even those in family or residential care.

Changes on the Parents' Questionnaire

Parents' questionnaires were available on 42 children at both 1 and 12 months. As Table 8.7 shows, the picture according to the parents' scale was largely static, with most of those children who were rated below the threshold at one month remaining well and the majority of those rated above the threshold remaining problematic. A small proportion of children changed category, with equal numbers moving in either direction.

The patterns of association over the year were similar for boys and girls and, as far as could be ascertained given the low frequencies, applied in a similar way to all types of problem. The small amount of change should be treated with caution, since this might reflect chance variations in the rating of the scales, a factor taken into account by the test statistics.

A similar picture emerges if the total scores on the parent questionnaire are used, rather than the scores based on the categorical cut-off. As Table 8.8 shows, there was little change in the average level of difficulties

Table 8.8: Changes in parent questionnaire scores. Mean scores at 1 and 12 months for boys and girls

	1 month mean score (s.d.)	12 months mean score (s.d.)
Boys	13.65 (7.7)	14.58 (9.4)
Girls	14.01 (7.6)	14.01 (10.0)

Difference between 1 and 12 months not significant.

rated. There were no differences between the boys and the girls in the average level of disturbance at one month, and for neither did the level of problems change significantly.

CONSTRUCTING A CHANGE CATEGORISATION

The above analyses show that the amount of change in emotional and behavioural problems over the year in the group as a whole was dis- couragingly small. Our main conclusion from the statistical analysis of the data was that there was little change in the level of difficulties: a striking difference from the findings from the pilot study (Rushton *et al.*, 1988). However, the interviewers' impressions of the patterns of change over the year were not entirely in accord with this view. In particular, there was a feeling of substantial improvements for some children and substantial decline for others. These changes applied only to sub-groups of children, groups that were too small to affect the overall statistical picture, even when the appropriate repeated measures analyses were performed.

However, in order further to explore possible changes in sub-groups of children we divided the sample into three roughly equal 'outcome' groups based on the total symptom scores from the systematic inter- views with the parents – the most detailed and thorough of the assess- ments. We decided not to base this measure of outcome on categorical measures of disorder because we were interested in detecting changes *within* a group of children with an initially high level of difficulties, rather than in movements in and out of formal diagnostic categories. Instead, the outcome groups were defined in terms of a *change* in symptom level (up or down) of 1.5 or more standard deviation units (Z scores) above or below the mean symptom level for the group as a whole. In practice, this was an increase or a decrease of two or more symptoms over the year.

Table 8.9: Average changes in total item score and subtype scores for children whose behaviour improved or deteriorated

Change in	Improved group (22)		Deteriorated group (17)		Significance
	Mean	S.D.	Mean	S.D.	
Overall score	−4.4	2.6	+5.6	3.0	$F = 86$, $(2,55)$ $p = 0.000$
Conduct score	−0.6	1.0	+1.6	1.7	$F = 3.8$, $(2,55)$ $p = 0.027$
Emotional score	−0.3	0.7	+0.5	1.1	$F = 15$, $(2,55)$ $p = 0.000$
Hyperactive score	−1.8	2.3	+1.6	2.8	$F = 11$, $(2,55)$ $p = 0.000$

This analysis produced three groups: (a) 22 children who showed improvement over the year, (b) 18 children who showed similar symptom levels at both points, and (c) 21 children who showed more problems. Although a two symptom change may seem somewhat small, in practice the average level of change in groups (a) and (c) was substantial. Thus those in group (a) improved by an average of four symptoms and those in group (c) got worse by an average of six. We also checked the sub-score changes for conduct, emotional and hyperactive problems between 1 and 12 months and found that there were significant differences between groups (a) and (c) in the changes in these subscores in line with the direction of overall change (Table 8.9).

It must be emphasised, however, that these ratings of change are simply differences with respect to the level of problems in the group as a whole. Thus, *improvement* should not be read as *recovery* or a return to normal levels of functioning. The main reason for devising this rating was to see whether any factors in the children's earlier histories or in the nature and qualities of the placements might be predictive of changes in their levels of adjustment.

Not surprisingly we found these change groups and indeed the children's total scores on the interview measures to be highly related to placement stability. However, there were also associations with other aspects of the placement arrangements and some features of the children's earlier experiences. These associations are discussed further in Chapter 14.

PRACTICE IMPLICATIONS

The high level of behavioural difficulties reported by new parents would probably be expected by most of those involved with 'looked after' children. However, on the basis of the data from this sample, it is important to note that, while many children show some improvements in their behaviour over time, a rapid and complete resolution of difficulties should not be expected for the majority of late placed children. Most families will need to be prepared to deal with at least some defiant, overactive or deceitful behaviour and be equipped, before placement, with appropriate strategies for dealing with these and with mechanisms for coping with their own feelings and responses.

Sexualised behaviour does not appear to be restricted to those children who are known to have suffered sexual abuse, which would suggest that this possibility should always be addressed thoroughly during preparation.

SUMMARY

It is clear from the above examination of the children's behaviour at home that the placed children came to their new families with a multiplicity of emotional and behavioural difficulties. Parents' free accounts of serious behavioural problems that had occurred repeatedly indicated a high level of conduct and other difficulties, which could cause a good deal of anguish and frustration. These accounts emphasised the dynamic nature of children's behaviour with many of the original problems resolving only to lead to the emergence of some new difficulty in more than half the sample. Parents also rated over half of both boys and girls above the cut-off on the Rutter A2 Scale and indicated conduct problems much more commonly than emotional difficulties, although both of these were much higher than in comparison data.

A striking difference between the parents' free accounts and the systematic interviewing was that the former emphasised problems that led to stress and to difficulties in control, especially oppositional behaviour. The systematic interviewing, on the other hand, highlighted the very high levels of distress, anxiety and worrying and also of inattentive and restless behaviour. Only about a sixth of children were rated as having oppositional or conduct disorders, whilst two-fifths had problems associated with fears and anxiety. Both types of measure confirmed the findings from the pilot study of very high levels of pervasively restless and inattentive behaviour. This means that accounts of problems in the first year of placements that are based only on parents' free accounts are likely to miss difficulties that may eventually prove more persistent and problematic.

As a group there was little change in the children's emotional and behavioural adjustment over the year. The picture was similar whether the parents' free descriptions, the systematic accounts or the parents' ratings on the Rutter A2 Scale, were analysed. The children tended to remain oppositional or defiant and with high levels of restless and inattentive behaviour. In addition, the levels of fearfulness and anxiety remained high. On the other hand, there were some signs of positive change, with some decline in difficult and disobedient behaviour, in the level of emotional problems and in pervasive problems of restlessness and inattention. Moreover, the overall lack of change concealed some more substantial changes for a minority of children. For some these were very positive, for others, negative.

9

THE DEVELOPMENT OF NEW RELATIONSHIPS

In our review of adoption-related topics in Chapter 1, it was clear that only modest progress has been made in conceptualising the process of relationship formation in late placements. In the first place, transposing the language of bonding and attachment from terminology originally devised to describe infant/carer interactions to the formation of relationships in late placement may involve a considerable change of register. Nevertheless, we need to advance our knowledge on the quality of relationships that can reasonably be expected to develop, on how long this may take and on the factors that promote or prevent the satisfactory development of all relationships in the new family.

It is worth rehearsing some of the distinguishing features of these new relationships. Some children may have developed secure previous attachments but many will have had problematic ones in the past and all will have experienced broken relationships. The growth of new relationships needs, therefore, to be understood as a process of re-attachment for the children. Coupled with this, the children may have other emotional and behavioural difficulties, which are a challenge to the parents and may impede the development of satisfying relationships from both the parents' and the child's side. In addition, the new mothers and fathers may have differing expectations of the attachment process based on their experiences with previous birth and foster children. Finally, the children's own relationships with their birth parents or siblings, or with other children in the new home, may impinge on the development of mutual attachment with their new parents. Where the re-attachment process is slow, or fails to develop, we need to learn whether there are particular experiences in the children's past that may hinder the process and whether the difficulty is specific to the relationship with their new parents or part of a more general problem.

Since nearly all of our sample had experienced neglect or abuse, as well as multiple moves, it could be expected that a proportion of them would only slowly or partially develop trusting new relationships. In this study, we did not routinely have access to information about the children's experiences with their birth parents, and so were unable to assess their earliest attachments. However, we were usually able to obtain some information about the way in which the children had attached to substitute carers and the feelings they expressed about their birth parents. These factors, combined with their present responses to their new parents, enabled us to make a qualified interpretation of their capacity to form new relationships with significant adults.

DATA COLLECTION ON RELATIONSHIPS

Most of the information on relationships derives from the interviews with new parents at 1 and 12 months into placement. Further data are taken from maternal responses to the EFQ (Expression of Feelings Questionnaire), whilst the responses of teachers on the Rutter B2 Scale are used as one of the indicators of the quality of peer relationships.

When we began this study, we could find no recognised method of directly assessing attachment in older children placed for permanence that seemed appropriate or acceptable for this particular sample. Therefore we developed the Expression of Feelings Questionnaire to record key features of the new relationship. We focused on behaviours that other studies suggested might be related to the development of attachments, for example, the extent to which the children expressed their feelings openly; how they behaved towards their parents when they were angry, upset or seeking attention; how they shared feelings or accepted comfort; and the extent to which the parents felt the child trusted or cared about them. Because the instrument was new, we collected data from a group of 54 parents from the general population recruited through two schools in a socio-economically mixed area.

The questionnaire contains 48 individual items related to the appropriateness and frequency of emotional expression. Only a minority of children scored on any individual item, but the sum of difficulties distinguished the groups more sharply. Comparisons between the sample responses and a general population control group suggested that a high score on this questionnaire (exceeding 83) was indicative of problems in social interactions and a difficulty with expression of feelings. Details on the content of the questionnaire, its scoring, and the differences between the groups are given in Appendix A.

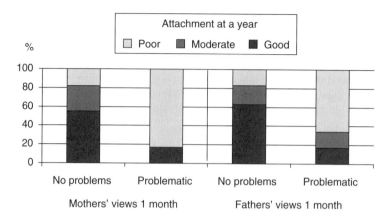

Figure 9.1: Parents' perceptions of relationship difficulties at one month and attachment groupings at a year. Group differences significant for mothers and fathers ($\chi^2 = 19.2$, d.f. = 2, $p < 0.001$; $\chi^2 = 11.5$, d.f. = 2, $p < 0.005$)

RELATIONSHIPS WITH NEW PARENTS

Early Impressions

At one month the parents were asked whether they felt that they and the children were becoming attached. They also gave their views on whether they anticipated difficulties in establishing a bond between them. As might be expected the great majority of parents were taking an optimistic view at this point and expecting no problems in forming attachments with the children. However, 22% of both mothers and fathers were already anticipating a difficult time.

In practice, these early feelings proved to be highly predictive (Figure 9.1). When mothers foresaw a relatively easy time in developing attachments, in only 18% of cases was there no attachment between mother and child by the end of the year, compared with 83% of cases where mothers predicted difficulties. The prediction was similar for fathers.

The Relationship Between Placed Children and Parents at One Year

In summarising each parent's description of the parent–child relationship at a year a fourfold categorisation was used. The distributions are given in Figures 9.2a and 9.2b. Good attachments had developed for

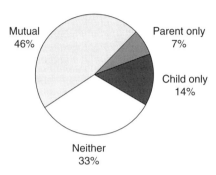

a   **Relationship with new mother
at a year (*n* = 57)**

Mutual 46%

Parent only 7%

Child only 14%

Neither 33%

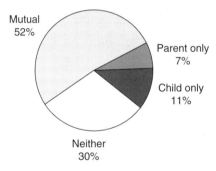

b   **Relationship with new father
at a year (*n* = 54)**

Mutual 52%

Parent only 7%

Child only 11%

Neither 30%

Figure 9.2: The level of attachment between parents and children at a year

about half of the mothers and fathers. In a minority of placements there was a one-sided attachment developing but for 16 fathers and 19 mothers there was no sign of a bond developing with their children. Whilst 8 children became attached to their new mothers despite the mothers not feeling attached to them, it was less common (*n* = 4) for the mothers to feel an unreciprocated attachment for the children. In the majority of cases, reciprocity of feelings was necessary for attachment to develop.

In general, attachment to one parent went along with attachment to the other and so, in order to explore the development of relationships further, we divided the sample into three groups. The first of these, a 'good attachments' group, included placements where good *mutual* attachments had developed between the placed children and both new parents. Twenty-five placements (43%) fell within this group. Seventeen placements (30%) formed an 'intermediate group', where, despite some level of difficulty, there were signs of attachments developing between the children and at least one of their new parents. The final group of 'poor attachments' included 16 placements (27%) where there were serious difficulties in the relationship with both parents, that is where the children were showing little sign of attachment to either parent and neither parent was bonding to the child.

These data lend support to the findings of Hodges and Tizard (1989b) and others that mutually rewarding relationships can and do form even in late placements of disturbed and disadvantaged children. Half of the sample adapted quickly and well to their new parents. But at one year into placement 27% of children had mutually poor relationships with their parents. This was higher than the 16% found by Hodges and Tizard. However, the children in their sample were followed through to their eighth year of placement and it is possible that the problematic relationships in our sample may improve in time, particularly with sensitive help from parents or practitioners.

Expression of Feelings and Interaction Patterns: Differences Between Sample Children and a Comparison Group

At one month into placement, 86% of the placed children scored 83 or above on the total amount of difficulty compared with only 2% of the comparison group.

The clear discrimination between the control and sample children, illustrated in Figure 9.3, suggests that the questionnaire was effective in targeting the appropriate expression of feelings.

Comparisons between the samples revealed substantial differences on many of the individual items. The placed children were described as significantly less open and more inappropriate in their expression of emotions; were more prone to bottle up feelings; were more likely to seek attention by misbehaviour or complaints of illness; were felt to be less genuine and more immature in their expressions of affection; and were much more likely to be over-friendly with strangers.

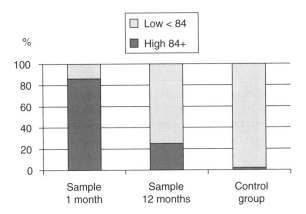

Figure 9.3: The proportion of high and low scores on the EFQ for sample at one and twelve months and controls

Differences at a Year Between Attached and Non-attached Children

Because the behaviours tapped by the questionnaire were so common for the placed children at one month, it was not possible to use the individual items or the pattern of ratings to explore the quality of the attachment to or relationship with the new parents. The differences between children who developed a good relationship with their parents and those who did not became much clearer by the one year point and the EFQ ratings became informative about the characteristics of the non-attached children.

The poorly attached children were far more likely than the rest of the sample to score highly on the EFQ at one year (means 94 v. 60, $F = 17.3$, d.f. $= 1,36$, $p < 0.005$). While the mean reduction in EFQ score over the year for most of the sample was 40 points, the mean reduction for the 'poorly attached' group was just 0.5 points ($F = 25$, d.f. $= 1,36$, $p < 0.001$).

The first area examined by the EFQ was the appropriateness and frequency with which positive and negative emotions were shown by the child. Responses were regarded as inappropriate if they were exaggerated, atypical or unexpected. Figure 9.4 shows the large differences between the appropriateness of expression of feelings between the attached and non-attached children.

In addition to the problems with inappropriateness of expression, there were also differences in the frequency with which the two groups

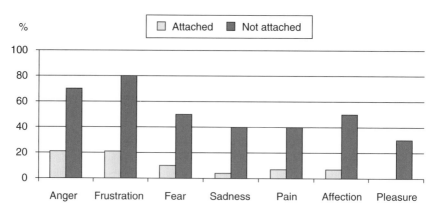

Figure 9.4: Proportions of attached and non-attached children showing inappropriate expression of emotions (EFQ). Group differences significant at $p < 0.05$ or better on all items

showed various feelings. Thus, those who were not making good relationships with parents tended to show 'negative' emotions, such as frustration, anger, sadness, pain and fear, more frequently but were more guarded in their expression of affection and pleasure. There was a tendency for significantly more of these 'poorly attached' children to reject the approaches of their new parents, and the parents more often felt that these children were bottling up their feelings.

The questionnaire also revealed differences in the patterns of approach to the parents (see Figure 9.5). For example, the non-attached children were much more likely to use inappropriate methods to gain parental attention, such as complaining of illness or misbehaving and more likely to be described as disliking cuddles.

There was a greater tendency for the non-attached children to display immature or sexualised affection. Parents were also far more likely to perceive the affection shown as non-genuine or 'phoney'. The parents found these children very difficult to feel close to and did not anticipate rapid improvements in their relationships.

THE DEVELOPMENT OF RELATIONSHIPS WITH NEW SIBLINGS

In the child care field, protecting and maintaining sibling relationships wherever possible is now seen as being of prime importance. In addition, where children have to be 'looked after' on their own, it is often

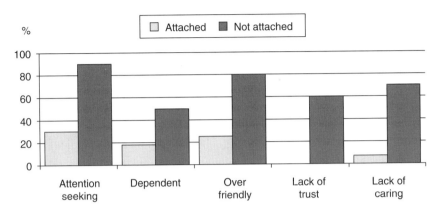

Figure 9.5: Proportions of attached and non-attached children showing interaction problems (EFQ). Group differences significant at $p < 0.05$ or better on all items except dependency (0.09)

seen as positive to choose a placement that lets them grow up with other children. Finding such a placement also allows practitioners to realise their often voiced desire to find experienced parents to care for children who have been exposed to considerable hardship and instability in their lives.

However, as Chapter 5 showed, children who joined established families tended to have poorer outcomes than those who did not. A major contributor to this appeared to be the formation of negative relationships with new siblings. As Part's study (1993) illustrated, the reaction of birth children towards foster children can range from altruism to intolerance.

We asked the new parents to describe the effect of the placement on each child in the family independently. The number of relationships where the impact was positive (52) far outweighed the negative (23), but it is important to register that 23 children were distressed at the arrival of the newly placed child and in six cases this distress was described as very marked. Several birth children were adversely affected by the placed child's misbehaviour and, in one case, a girl was frequently physically attacked by her new younger brother. Her mother explained:

> She sobbed her heart out – she just couldn't take him being nasty to her all the time.

On the other hand, some rivalry was often expected by the parents and was seen as normal:

We were told she would be sulky and get our kids into trouble, but we see this as just everyday kids' problems.

Reasons for Poor Sibling Relationships

Thirteen placed children had a poor relationship with 23 of their new siblings. At first glance, the reasons why these poor relationships developed did not seem obvious. There was a mixture of boys and girls among both the placed children and the birth children and a mixture of ages and age gaps. In 11 of the 13 cases, the birth child had been displaced as the only child or as the youngest in the family, but there were similar levels of 'displacement' where relationships with new siblings were generally good. Mothers felt that the placed child was at fault in 6 of 13 cases, their own birth child in 4 cases and that in the remainder blame was equally shared.

Despite the lack of clear reasons for difficulties, problems appeared to arise more frequently when the age gap between the placed children and the new siblings with whom they were having problems was relatively narrow or when the birth child was considerably older. Thus, 9 of the 13 children in these problematic cases were less than 38 months younger than the new sibling with whom they had difficulty and in the remaining four cases the birth children were considerably older. The issues that arose for these two groups are illustrated next.

Poor relationships when children are close in age

The nine children in this group were around 6 or 7 years old and their new siblings 9 or 10. These children were placed on their own into established families and showed significantly more behaviour problems than other singly placed children ($\chi^2 = 6.8$, d.f. = 2, $p < 0.05$). This often proved stressful to the new parents and was a source of considerable strife between the children. By the end of the year, three of these nine placements had disrupted and plans were being made to end a fourth. The effect the placement was having on the other children in the family was a factor in the decision to end these placements. EFQ data were available for four of the remaining children. Three of them had high scores, suggesting that the problems in relationships with new siblings were part of wider problems in relating that also affected attachments to the new parents. The following vignette gives an impression of the difficulties these families faced.

When Alison joined her new family she became the youngest (by just three years) in a family of three. She was a distractible child who could not concentrate, although she was described as reasonably bright. She would very often misbehave, mostly in an effort to gain attention, deliberately doing things she had been told not to do and failing to do things she had been asked to do. Her relationship with the eldest of her new siblings was fairly neutral because he was considerably older and often out of the home, but her relationship with her new sister was extremely volatile, and almost any minor incident would lead to friction. The two girls could not spend time together without arguing and fighting, but neither could they leave each other alone. Whenever the new sister wanted attention from her parents, Alison would be there verbally or physically 'muscling in' on the action, determined not to miss out. The new parents felt that each of the children was trying to eject the other from the family.

Poor 'new sibling' relationships when there is a larger age gap

The remaining four children tended to have poor relationships with much older new siblings, who were around 13 to 15 years at the time of placement. In contrast with the children described above, this group did not have more behaviour problems than other singly placed children who had developed good relationships with older siblings. There may be a number of reasons why there were difficulties in these four cases. Anecdotal evidence from three of them suggests that factors associated with early adolescence, such as embarrassment and general intolerance of others, may have had a bearing on the birth children's responses. In addition, these older children were of an age to understand to a greater degree the impact that the placement was having on their family.

However, these problems seemed less threatening to the placement perhaps because the parents concluded that their own children's 'adolescent problems', which would happen anyway, were part of the reason for the difficulties. A second parental conclusion may have been that their teenagers were preparing to 'fly the nest' and therefore difficulties arising from the placement were less serious. Some of these parents suggested that the placement had been positive because it reduced parental preoccupation with their teenagers. Some felt that parental interest and attention was less important for adolescents. Hannah's placement provides a typical example of this group.

Hannah was six when she joined her new family, who had a teenage son and daughter of their own. She did not have severe problems, although she had some very immature habits. Hannah had experienced a very difficult relationship with her birth mother and was reticent about accepting a new mother, although she was very happy with her new father. This not only caused difficulties for the new parents, but also divided their children. The younger son had many changes to get used to. Not only was he displaced as the youngest child, but he had always been close to his mother and could not bear to see her hurt. For this reason he, in turn, rejected the placed child. This scenario was complicated by his own teenage insecurities. He was embarrassed by the younger child's behaviour and at the same time was jealous of his sister who was favoured by the placed child.

The dynamics involved in such cases are complex and require skilled work from the practitioners involved.

THE DEVELOPMENT OF RELATIONSHIPS WITH PEERS

Research on peer relationships has identified a number of characteristics that are associated with a high risk of peer rejection (Asher & Coie, 1990). These include poor social skills, high levels of aggression, immaturity, antisocial behaviour and identification with other 'rejected' and aggressive children (Cairns et al., 1988). Ladd (1983) found that eight- and nine-year olds who were rejected by their peers spent less time in conversation and cooperative play and more time in arguing and fighting. Children with poor peer relationships have fewer social skills and lack strategies for joining the play of others. For example, Dodge and his colleagues (1983) found that popular five-year-olds watched and waited when they wanted to join the play of others, whereas peer-rejected children interrupted or disrupted the activity leading to their continued rejection.

We were not able to take direct measures of the children's peer relationships for reasons given earlier. Therefore our information on peer relationships comes from new parents and teachers only. We cannot be sure that these adult accounts reflect the views of the children's peers, but many of the problems outlined above were displayed by the sample children who were identified as having peer difficulties by both parents and teachers.

Reports from teachers (Rutter B2) highlighted peer relationship difficulties for a significant proportion of the sample children. Four items on the

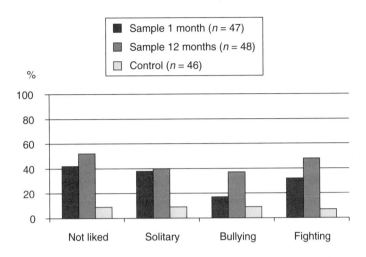

Figure 9.6: Level of peer relationship difficulties for sample at one and twelve months and control group

teacher's scale describe aspects of peer relationships. These are: 'not being liked by peers', 'tendency to be solitary', 'bullying' and 'fighting or quarrelling'. As Figure 9.6 demonstrates, the placed children were much more likely to show these problems, at both 1 and 12 months, than their classroom controls. In addition, those rated as having peer relationship difficulties were far more likely to show problems of conduct and overactivity than those who got on well with peers.

When we compared the teachers' responses (Rutter B2) with the corresponding items on the mothers' questionnaire (Rutter A2), we found a high level of correlation. However, there were eight instances where teachers' and mothers' reports did not match. In five cases, the teacher reported peer problems but the mother did not, whereas the reverse was true for the other three children. It is hard to say whether this was due to a difference in perception of the adults, or a situational difference in the interactions of the children.

There was a significant relationship between mothers' reports of peer relationship difficulties and poor relationships with the new parents but the same was not true of the teachers' reports of peer relationship difficulties. It could be the case that parents who had a mutually 'poor' relationship with their children were more likely to focus on negative aspects, or that these children behaved differently in the presence of their parents.

Reasons for Poor Peer Relationships

The interview data suggested six different kinds of problems in peer interactions. Four of these problems relate to an immaturity or ineptness in social interaction. These were: poor ability to attend when playing games; poor level of understanding the rules of games; over-enthusiasm in interaction; and an insensitivity towards the feelings of other children. These are very similar to those identified by Ladd (1983) and Dodge *et al.* (1983) as characteristic of peer-rejected children. Almost half the sample had marked difficulties in at least one of these areas and 13 children presented two or more of these problems.

The remaining two peer difficulties were quarrelling and aggression. These were prominent problems for only a minority of children (six), and all but one of these children also exhibited some immature or inappropriate social behaviours. The children who had difficulty with peers were more likely to show considerable behavioural problems and this was particularly true for aggressive children ($\chi^2 = 8.9$, d.f. $= 1$, $p < 0.01$). They were also more likely to have a high (poor) score on the Expression of Feelings Questionnaire ($\chi^2 = 6.6$, d.f. $= 2$, $p < 0.05$).

It remains to be seen whether these children will be able to overcome their difficulties with peer interaction as they grow older. Hodges and Tizard (1989b) found that peer relationships can continue to be problematic for children despite many years in permanent substitute families, even when relationships with the new parents remain good. Many of the parents we interviewed were very aware that their children were not forming good peer relationships. Competence in peer relationships has not been sufficiently studied in child care research, especially given the importance of friendships and partnerships in adolescence and adulthood (Quinton & Rutter, 1988). This is an area that deserves much more attention from both research and practice.

Children who Have Difficulties with all Relationships

From our sample of 61 children, we found that 29 had no major difficulties with relationships with other people. After one year in placement they were developing mutual attachments with their new parents, relationships with their siblings were on the whole positive and their new parents reported no problems concerning their peer interaction.

However, this leaves 32 children for whom at least one aspect of their social interactions was problematic. Sixteen children had problems in their relationships with other children: either siblings, peers or both. A further 16 children had difficulties in attaching to their new parents and for the majority of these children (14), their difficulties extended to include interaction with siblings or peers.

PRACTICE IMPLICATIONS

By the end of the year, 27% of children had not developed mutually rewarding relationships with their new parents and half the children had difficulties in at least one of their relationships with either new parents, new siblings or peers. This clearly needs to be anticipated in the pre-placement preparation and attended to in the post-placement support work. The child's social competence and relationship patterns need to be carefully assessed prior to permanent placement. Preparation of the child and new parents can then be geared far more accurately towards the impact that relationship difficulties may have on the entire family. Once the child is placed, the limited resources can be focused on those children for whom it is likely that forming significant new relationships will be a problem.

The analyses suggested that problems may arise between placed children and new siblings, regardless of their ages or the age gaps between them. Where there are other children in the family, assessment and preparation needs to focus on their needs and their understanding of the placement. Both the young people and their parents may need considerable help to think carefully about what they are expecting from the placement and how the inevitable adjustments may affect them both individually and in their relationships with one another.

It was striking that the new parents were able to predict enduring relationship difficulties very early on in placements and it may be too easy to dismiss early indicators as nothing more than initial adjustment difficulties.

SUMMARY

We found that of the placed children, just over a quarter had relationship difficulties with new parents throughout the year. In 13 of the 30 cases where children joined households with previously resident children there were difficulties in the 'new sibling' relationships and around half the sample were having problems with peer relationships.

Where there were problems in the relationships between the placed child and the new parents, there were also likely to be difficulties with relationships with other children. This fact is of particular importance, since it may be easy to assume that a child will be able to weather a placement despite not developing a fulfilling relationship with a parent. However, if one considers that all but two of those children with attachment problems also had difficulties with either siblings or peers, it becomes clear that the children who are not making attachments to their parents are in danger of failing to make *any* satisfying relationships. The relevance of these findings is important, not only for the children's current development, but for their transition into adolescence and adulthood.

Placements were more likely to be difficult for single children entering families where there were already birth children, especially where there were small age gaps. However, a small proportion of placements were in difficulty because of the impact on the new siblings despite large age gaps. Negotiating relationships with new siblings as well as new parents was bound to be complex. It is crucial to understand more about the added stresses caused by the increased number and complexity of relationships in placements which include the presence of birth children in the new home. For some new families there was considerable conflict and dissatisfaction and the impact on the new siblings could be severe.

10

THE CHILDREN IN SCHOOL

So far we have concentrated on the children's adjustment in their new families. However, all of them were between five and nine years old when they joined their new parents, which meant that attending school accounted for a significant part of their time. It was clearly important to learn how the children were getting on there and what difficulties, if any, they were experiencing.

As Maughan (1994) has pointed out, school is not just a place for academic learning, it is also a forum in which effective communication with others is practised and developed; in which socially acceptable behaviours are learned and where most opportunities for new friendships arise. It is possible that children who had had poor experiences at home might perceive school as a safe haven and flourish. However, it is also possible that the conduct, attentional and emotional difficulties that many of them were showing might impede their ability to fulfil their potential at school.

Many researchers have found that children within the care system consistently perform below national norms for their age groups. Indeed, Heath et al. (1994) reported that even when foster children had been in stable, long-term placements, their scores for reading, vocabulary and maths continued to be lower than the national average. The poorest achievement scores in Heath's sample were among those children who were taken into care because of abuse or neglect. Almost all of the children in our sample had histories of abuse or neglect and therefore might experience educational problems. In addition, children who are in the care of local authorities have been shown to score higher than general populations on indices of problems in classroom behaviour (Yule & Raynes, 1972).

This chapter focuses on difficulties at school, and addresses two main areas of concern: educational achievement and behaviour problems. The data are drawn from three sources: first, the new parents' impressions of the children's school experiences, at both 1 and 12 months after placement; secondly, the teachers' ratings on the Rutter B2 Scale of the children's behaviour in the classroom and that of the classroom controls; and finally, the direct assessments of the children's verbal and spatial abilities and their concentration. All these measures were described in Chapter 2.

THE NEW PARENTS' CONCERNS ABOUT EDUCATION

The Choice of School and Cooperation Between Home and School

At one month the majority of the children (90%) were attending their local state schools, appropriate to their ages. Four were at special schools for emotional and behavioural difficulties and two children were educated in the independent sector. It was clear from the interviews that almost all of the schools had been carefully selected by the new parents and, in the majority of cases, they had visited them prior to the children starting there, to discuss the children and their backgrounds with the head and form teachers. However, in most cases this discussion was limited to the information that the children had been looked after for some time and had recently had a change of carer. The new parents were very aware of the need for confidentiality and were anxious that other people should not know about the children's past. The teachers were fully aware of the children's history in only seven cases. There did not appear to be any particular sub-group whose histories were shared with teachers.

Overall, the new parents were very concerned about their children's education. Only three parents were rated by interviewers as placing little importance on education at this stage. Almost half (27) were rated as actively involved, discussing the school day with their children and showing distinct enthusiasm for their achievements. The majority of parents continued to liaise closely with the schools throughout the year, with 37% of parents making opportunities to speak with teachers at least once a month, and a further 25% at least once a week. Most of the parents felt that teachers were working with them to enhance the experience of school for the child. Half of the teachers were described as being actively involved in the children's progress and this view was supported by evidence of regular exchange of information. On the other hand, a minority of parents were less than happy throughout with the way the school was dealing with their concerns and by the end of the year nine parents were expressing some dissatisfaction. The reasons for complaint varied from a lack of response to concerns about bullying, to feelings that the schools were too concerned about emotional well-being and ignored significant under-achievement.

Homework

In about 70% of cases (44), new parents encouraged the children's interest in academic achievement by working with them at home. In most cases homework caused no more problems than it does for most children. However, 20 families found that work at home led to more serious difficulties. Some of these parents described a complete impasse developing, with the children simply refusing to continue. In two cases this became a source of severe difficulty. There was some improvement in the number of children who had difficulty working at home by the end of the year but there were still 11 children for whom homework could herald significant problems.

In the course of describing the children's academic problems, parents also described how they were trying to help overcome these. The majority of parents offered general encouragement, but about 12 parents showed considerable ingenuity in developing interesting and unusual learning methods. They used a variety of games and devices to encourage the children to learn to read, spell or tell the time. On the whole these ideas came from the parents themselves, although in one or two cases social workers had been involved.

Children's Abilities and Educational Needs According to Parents

Impediments to Learning

At the start of the placement the majority of new parents (80%) felt their child's level of ability was at least average. On the other hand, many parents (72%) thought their child was having some difficulty in turning their abilities into achievements. Some of these difficulties were to do with grasping particular concepts, for example the concept of time or money. Others were to do with a lack of age-appropriate basic skills, like

Table 10.1: The prevalence of learning difficulties at
1 and 12 months

Type of problem	1 month ($n = 57$)	12 months ($n = 58$)
Conceptual problems	16%	3%
Reading problems	32%	17%
Emotional problems	21%	22%
Behaviour problems	32%	29%

writing or reading. Sometimes, they involved the children's emotional approach to learning. Some parents felt their child was afraid of failing and would employ ways of avoiding a challenging task. Disruptive behaviour and lack of concentration in class were also mentioned.

Table 10.1 outlines the extent to which new parents felt their children suffered these impediments early in the placement and at the end of the year. For the sample as a whole parents saw some improvement in conceptual abilities and reading. However, the other difficulties appeared to persist for longer.

There were 53 children for whom information on schooling was available at both interview points. Of these, 16 (30%) were described as having no serious impediments to learning at the time of placement and continued to cope well in school throughout the first year. Five children (9%) had at least some significant difficulties with learning at one month and these continued to cause concern throughout the year, although they did not get worse. Sixteen children (30%) showed a reducing number of difficulties suggesting an improvement in their ability to learn, but 13 children (24%) showed a tendency to exhibit more of these barriers to learning as time went on.

Throughout this chapter there are areas where difficulties appear to rise over time for some children. At this stage it is not possible to be sure whether this is due to a true rise in problems, or whether, at one month, some respondents had not had sufficient time with the child to have acquired a complete picture of his or her abilities. In the current context it is quite likely that the latter explanation is correct. Some parents described the considerable skills their children had developed to conceal their academic deficits. For example, some children appeared to read quite well. It took time for their parents to realise that they had memorised the stories word for word from listening to them and, with the pictures as prompts, were able to recite them back. It was only as their story books became more complex that problems became apparent.

Table 10.2: The extent of remedial need, identified and provided for

	1 month (*n* = 61)	12 months (*n* = 58)
Remedial help suggested	20	30
Statement completed/in progress	5	11
Receiving any sort of help	13	24

Categories are not exclusive.

Remedial assistance

By the time of the first interview remedial help had been suggested either informally or formally for about one-third of the children. Statements of educational need under the 1981 Education Act are designed to ensure appropriate provision for pupils formally assessed as having special needs. These had been prepared for five children and assessment was proposed for a further six children. However, apart from those children who were attending special school, only 10% were receiving any extra help at school in the early weeks. Table 10.2 shows that there was a gradual recognition of the level of help the placed children required to enable them to achieve their potential in school.

By the end of the first year over half the children were thought to require some level of remedial help. Eleven of these either had been or were being assessed for statementing. Despite this, as Table 10.2 shows, the level of provision continued to be below the level of need identified. Overall, more than half of the parents (35) had reported some anxieties about the educational assistance being offered to their children at the start of the placement. By the end of the first year there was a small decrease in anxiety about educational provision and for 28 families this continued to be a source of concern.

Some of the new parents felt that they had not been fully informed of the extent of their children's educational needs prior to placement. They felt they had to press their case extremely hard to obtain the necessary help for their children and expressed concern that such obvious under-achievement had been accepted for so long, while the children had been in the care of local authorities.

Parental Distress Concerning Education

At the first interview it was clear that for some parents schooling was an issue that was causing them distress. This became more pronounced in some placements as it became clearer to the new parents that the children were not going to make immediate improvements. At one month, education was a significant source of distress for 12 mothers and 10 fathers. By 12 months this had increased to 18 mothers and 14 fathers. These parents discussed how shocked they had been by their children's limitations, even where learning difficulties had been mentioned prior to placement. They nevertheless felt unprepared for what that implied and for how long those difficulties might persist.

SOCIAL WORKER INVOLVEMENT WITH SCHOOLING

The children's social workers were not generally perceived by the parents to be involved with their new child's schooling. At one month, a total of 43 social workers were described as having no contact with the school at all. Only three were described as being actively involved in what was happening with the school. The remainder had some minor involvement only. The level of social worker activity regarding education remained the same throughout the year.

The impression given by many social workers during the interviews with them was that, in permanent placement, they felt schooling to be the responsibility of the new parents and, indeed, the majority of parents agreed. In the early months there was more involvement in education by practitioners in some of the fostering placements, although this was not always the case, and the active involvement did not necessarily persist. During the course of the year there were three adoptive placements in which the social worker became more actively involved with schooling. In all of these, schooling was the source of particular difficulties within the placement, because of either poor behaviour or previously unrecognised learning difficulties.

Despite the new parents' commitment to their obligations regarding education, there were a few new parents (four) who expressed some frustration that social workers seemed reluctant to become more involved. This usually occurred when parents were trying to argue for extra resources for their child and felt the intervention of another professional would lend extra weight to their case.

CLASSROOM BEHAVIOUR ACCORDING TO TEACHERS

Teachers were asked to fill in the Rutter B Scale for the placed child and for the child in the same class nearest in age and of the same sex. Some

Table 10.3: Rates of disorder on the teacher questionnaire at one month for boys, girls and controls

	Boys (%)	Controls (%)	Girls (%)	Controls (%)
Score of 9 or more	50	11	29	10
Emotional sub-score	11	0	10	5
Conduct sub-score	37	11	19	5

n: boys = 27–28 (controls = 27), girls = 21 (controls = 20).

teachers were unwilling to do this and some parents did not give permission for the teachers' ratings to be made. At one month, data were available on 49 of the placed children and 47 controls. Questionnaires were more likely to be refused for girls than for boys. Comparisons between placed children and their controls are given in Table 10.3.

The overall level of disturbance was significantly higher in the placed boys (χ^2 = 7.99, d.f. = 1, $p < 0.005$), but this was not the case for girls, even though the placed children were nearly three times as likely to be rated above the cut-off. As is clear from the sub-score ratings, the differences between the groups applied to both emotional and conduct disorders.

In general population studies, between 10 and 19% of children have been found to score above the cut-off, with boys showing approximately twice the level of problems as girls (Rutter *et al.*, 1975). The placed children were showing substantially more problems at school than their classroom controls and in comparison with general population data. The individual scale items showing the largest placed–control differences are given in Table 10.4.

The following items did not show sizeable or significant differences between the samples: truants, worried, miserable, has twitches, sucks thumb, bites nails, absent from school for trivial reasons, disobedient, fearful, steals, complains of aches and pains, has tears on arrival at school, stutters or bullies.

There are larger differences for boys and more of these are statistically significant. However, caution is necessary in drawing conclusions about gender differences because there were more missing data for girls, which may have been related to the level of difficulty in those for whom parents refused permission. Nevertheless, the differences on the items relating to activity and attention are striking for both sexes. In addition, the teachers' ratings reveal substantial problems in relationships with other children.

Table 10.4: Individual items on the Rutter B Scale at one month

	Boys (%)	Controls (%)	p	Girls (%)	Controls (%)	p
Restless	79	19	0.002	71	15	0.002
Squirmy	70	25	0.001	48	20	NS
Poor concentration	71	11	0.001	67	20	0.007
Destructive	29	7	0.07	0	0	NS
Fights	44	15	0.04	19	11	NS
Not liked	46	15	0.02	38	10	NS
Solitary	41	15	0.07	33	5	0.06
Irritable	36	11	0.07	19	10	NS
Disobedient	54	30	NS	19	10	NS
Lies	32	11	NS	14	5	NS
Apathetic	33	7	0.04	19	10	NS
Resentful	32	11	NS	24	10	NS

n: boys = 27–28 (controls = 27), girls = 21 (controls = 20). NS: not significant.

Teachers' questionnaires were available on 44 children at both points in time. Table 10.5 gives a parallel analysis to that in Chapter 8 for the parent questionnaire, examining the proportions of the sample whose questionnaire scores moved across the cut-off.

At one month just over one-third of children scored 9 or more on the teachers' questionnaire, but by 12 months the proportion had risen to 52%. This rise was not statistically significant but was nevertheless quite large and appeared to apply more to boys than to girls. An analysis of changes in average rather than categorical scores illustrates this gender difference more clearly (Table 10.6).

At both 1 and 12 months boys were showing significantly more problems at school than girls and boys also showed a larger, though not significant, rise in problems at school over the year (t = 1.96, d.f. = 23, p = 0.062).

For some of these difficulties the increases may be understood in terms of the children behaving differently in their early weeks at school. It would be understandable if children showed less confrontational behaviour in a new environment. For problems that are by their nature more deceptive, like lying or stealing, it is possible that after only a month at school teachers had not realised these behaviours were occurring. The most conservative conclusion is that there were no significant changes in school behaviour over the year. This finding underlines the need for longer-term prospective research to see whether these difficulties diminish after a longer period of stability.

Table 10.5: Changes in teacher questionnaire score. Moves into and out of disorder groupings between 1 and 12 months

Never scored above the cut-off	36%
Above cut-off at 1 month, below at 12 months	11%
Below cut-off at 1 month, above at 12 months	25%
Always above the cut-off	27%

The cut-off for the teacher questionnaire is a score of 9 or more.

Table 10.6: Changes in teacher questionnaire scores. Mean scores at 1 and 12 months for boys and girls

	1 month mean score (s.d.)	12 months mean score (s.d.)
Boys	9.00 (7.7)	11.75 (9.4)
Girls	6.95 (5.9)	7.84 (6.9)

Difference between 1 and 12 months not significant.

DIRECT ASSESSMENT OF THE CHILDREN

In the course of the study, direct assessments of the children's verbal and spatial abilities were undertaken 6 months into the placement and measures of impulsivity and concentration at 1 and 12 months (see Chapter 2 for a description of measures). A total of 26 children took part in all assessments, and a further 22 children took part in some assessments but not all. There was a non-significant tendency for children who did not complete all of the tests to be described by their new parents as either brighter or more overactive than those who did. The missing data have implications for comparisons with general population norms, since the distribution of scores may have been substantially different had these children been included. Despite these limitations, the measures of intellectual ability and attention are able to add to the descriptions given by parents and teachers and to contribute to a discussion of the educational potential of the group, although the findings should be treated as suggestive only.

Direct Test: Within Sample Differences

The children's performance on the spatial test was somewhat better than that on the verbal ability test, although there was a strong relationship between the two. Both verbal and spatial ability were also significantly associated with parental reports of the children's level of attainment at school at one year and with need for remedial help. Boys and girls performed similarly on all tests with the exception of verbal ability, where girls did somewhat better than boys. There were significant improvements in the children's performance over time on the tests of impulsivity and attention. However, the analysis suggested that this was probably due to increasing age.

Spatial ability was related to performance on the impulsivity and attention tests but verbal ability was not. Although the children's scores on the verbal and spatial ability measures, as a group, were somewhat lower than the general population norms, their performances on the other tests compared favourably to the control group scores reported by other studies using these instruments (Cairns & Cammock, 1978; Taylor *et al.*, 1986).

The Children's Behaviour During the Testing

Although the testing was carried out in the children's homes, it was administered on a 'one to one' basis and followed a standard format. The structured nature of the assessment task offered a valuable opportunity for examiners to rate the children's behaviour on the following: their approach to the testing situation; their emotional tone throughout the test; their cooperativeness with tasks; their attention and goal orientation; their activity level; their need for facilitation and encouragement and the overall difficulty for the examiner in helping the child complete the tasks.

These ratings were made at both one month and one year. The most important features of the children's behaviour that made it difficult or easy to engage them in the tests were their level of activity, the degree of attention and the amount of cooperation shown. A total of 9 children improved in their ability to attend over time, 2 deteriorated, 12 were free of attention difficulties throughout, while 12 continued to be difficult to engage because of an inability to be still and maintain their concentration. Of the 38 children who were seen by examiners at one year, 15 were rated as having difficulties in one or more of these areas.

OVERACTIVITY AND ATTENTION ACROSS SITUATIONS

So far poor attention and overactivity have come up again and again as problems for the children. Information from parents, teachers and research examiners has all led to the conclusion that these difficulties are very common. This finding confirmed those of the pilot study, which had highlighted the persistence of overactivity and restlessness in late placed children over eight years.

Since these particular difficulties have major implications for the children, we were interested to establish the extent to which reports of overactivity and poor concentration were in agreement and what impact these factors might have on the placement.

Overactivity at School and at Home

Both the Rutter A and B Scales contain three items on overactivity: 'squirmy/fidgety', 'restless', and 'unable to settle to things for more than a few moments'. A score of 3 or more (out of a possible total of 6) on either of these scales has been shown to indicate overactivity (Taylor *et al.*, 1986). A score on only one of the scales indicates *situational* hyperactivity whilst a score of 3 or more on each scale indicates *pervasive* hyperactivity. A and B Scales were available for 42 children at one month and 38 at a year. The excess of pervasive overactivity in the placed group is very striking, with over a third (35%) rated as having such difficulties at a month and 20% at a year. This compares with only 2.2% in Schachar's analysis of the Isle of Wight sample (Schachar *et al.*, 1981).

Overactivity in Three Situations

Next we compared our data on overactivity and inattention from new parents, teachers, the testers' ratings and objective tests. Data were complete for 33 cases at a year.

Table 10.7 gives the correlations between the activity scores from these four sources at one year. Although the relationships between the three adult reports were quite strong they were by no means consistently so and the association between the tester and teacher reports was only marginally significant.

We were interested to explore the extent to which overactive behaviour occurred across different situations; therefore we classified the children according to whether or not they were overactive on each of the measures used. For the activity sub-scales of (a) Isle of Wight interview for the parents and (b) Rutter (B2) for teachers, a score above the median

Table 10.7: Correlations between adult reports of overactivity
and relationships with test results (n = 33)

Source	Teacher report	Examiner report	Sensitivity CPT	Errors MFF20
Parent report	**	*	**	0.064
Teacher report		0.055	**	*
Examiner report			***	*
Sensitivity				*

$*p < 0.05$; $**p < 0.01$; $***p < 0.001$ (Kendall's *tau* statistic).
CPT: continuous performance test; MFF20: Matching Familiar Figures
V20. See Chapter 2 for a description of measures.

Table 10.8: Mean test and behaviour scores according to number of overactivity
reports

Score	None	1 source	2 sources	3 sources	F =	$p <$
Sensitivity (CPT)	0.95	0.92	0.86	0.7	4.8	0.01
Error score (MFF20)	16.4	23.8	31.7	30.0	4.2	0.02
Behaviour score	1.3	5.6	15.0	14.0	22.9	0.001
Overactivity parent	0.7	2.5	6.3	6.2	15.5	0.001
Overactivity teacher	0.8	2.0	4.0	5.2	15.1	0.001
n	13	7	8	5		

CPT: continuous performance test; MFF20: Matching Familiar Figures V20. See Chapter 2
for a description of measures.

for the sample was taken to be indicative of overactivity/poor attention.
When we grouped the children into *overactive* versus *not overactive* for
each adult report and according to test results, we found that only a
minority of children were classified as overactive by all of them. However, as Table 10.8 illustrates, being identified as overactive, particularly
by multiple sources, was significantly associated with a greater likelihood of poorer performance on the attention tests and poorer general
behaviour.

In addition, the pervasively overactive children were significantly less
likely than others to have formed good relationships with their new
parents (χ^2 = 10.9, d.f. = 3, $p < 0.02$), or to have shown any improvements in their behaviour over the year (χ^2 = 12.8, d.f. = 3, $p < 0.005$).

Given the high incidence of overactivity and inattention reported by
both new parents and teachers, we were somewhat surprised by the
children's performance on the direct tests of attention and impulsivity,
which appeared to compare favourably with those of general population
samples.

The implication of these findings is unclear because of the possible biases due to missing data. Our small eight year follow-up study showed the persistence of problems of attention and restlessness, so such difficulties should be viewed with concern. On the other hand, the children's ability to perform within the normal range in a structured setting may indicate a potential for educational improvements given the right conditions. Whether the origins of and prognosis for restless and inattentive behaviour are the same as or different from apparently similar behaviours found in general population samples is an important question for future research.

PRACTICE IMPLICATIONS

It is clear that the educational needs of children in care must be assessed and provision made for them to be met through a multidisciplinary approach. The needs of looked after children require a higher profile within schools. New parents should be informed of the new children's level of academic development before they are placed, and supported in helping these children to reach their potential. Teachers also need more training on the potential educational and behavioural problems of these children.

Unfortunately, it was clear from the parent interviews that information about the children's education had sometimes been misleading, for within months of placement it became apparent that their children's educational needs had not been adequately assessed and certainly were not being met. Some new parents were surprised not only by the level of educational difficulty but also by their response to it, speaking of the frustration they experienced in trying to help their children learn. This has implications for both the preparation of new parents and the support of placements once made.

SUMMARY

This chapter has explored aspects of the children's school experience and their learning. The first section drew attention to the relatively high level of barriers to learning that were evident, particularly at the start of the placement. The increase in the number of children requiring or undergoing *statementing* over the course of the year suggests that perhaps more attention should have been paid to education at an earlier point in time. Some parents revealed considerable distress in relation to their children's limitations and there were indications that information given to parents about the children's achievements may have been misleading or at least insufficient for the parents to be able to think about how living with the limitations might have an impact on them.

Comparison between the teacher reports for sample children and their classroom controls revealed high levels of problem behaviour in the classroom and school environment, which tended to increase over the course of the year. The increased level of difficulties was true for both sexes but was particularly marked for boys for most types of poor behaviour. The exception to this is overactivity and attentional problems, which occurred with similar frequency in both boys and girls.

The final part of this chapter explored the overactivity across different situations; 35% and 20% of children were identified as pervasively overactive at 1 and 12 months respectively using the Rutter A and B Scales. Analysis of overactivity as identified by all four available sources (teachers, parents, examiners and test results) revealed that only a small minority of children (15%) were identified as being inattentive or overactive by all sources. This is a potentially important finding because it suggests that many of these children may be able to respond to a flexible and structured educational environment.

11

NEW PARENTS' EXPERIENCES: STRESSES AND SUPPORTS, CRISES AND DISRUPTIONS

This chapter covers aspects of the new parents' experiences through to the end of the first year of placement. It is divided into three sections. In the first we look at the parents' impressions of the children before they joined the family and their views on how difficult they might prove to be. We then examine to what extent these views changed once the placement had happened. The second section deals with the stress the parents experienced before the placement and then during the year, the main causes of this and their sources of informal support. The majority of information concerning the provision of, and parental satisfaction with, social work support appears in Chapter 12, although the final section of this chapter, which explores the reasons for placement crises and disruptions, does include some accounts of social worker perspectives and responses.

FIRST IMPRESSIONS

New parents were asked to describe their impressions of the children when they first met them and then at one month into the placement. These descriptions were rated by the interviewers as either negative, neutral or positive. Mothers and fathers gave very similar descriptions of the children and, for this reason, we report the mothers' responses only in order to simplify the presentation.

As can be seen from Figures 11.1a and 11.1b, the new mothers' first impressions of the children's appearance, sociability and behaviour were mostly positive or neutral. Many said they were pleasantly surprised and impressed at the children's ability to interact and be open with

a

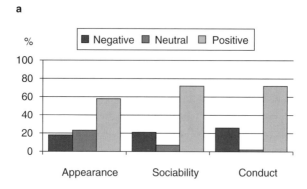

b

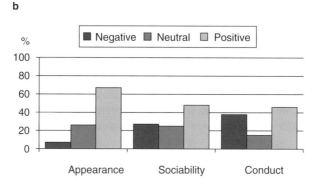

Figure 11.1: New parents' impressions of the child at first meeting (a) and after one month in placement (b) (n = 60)

them, although a few children were over-excited and over-friendly, accounting for the negative ratings.

After a month of living together very few parents had reservations about their child's physical appearance, but more parents felt negatively about the children's sociability and conduct. Some parents had come to realise that the cheerful, amenable child they had initially met could also show less pleasant behaviours, such as temper tantrums, sulking or stubbornness, or that the sociable behaviour concealed a need for constant parental attention.

At both the 1 and 12 month interviews, parents were asked to summarise the level of difficulties they had experienced in developing a relationship with the child and with his or her level of behavioural problems and whether they had expected difficulties (Figure 11.2). Expectations, prior to placement, of problems in conduct were relatively

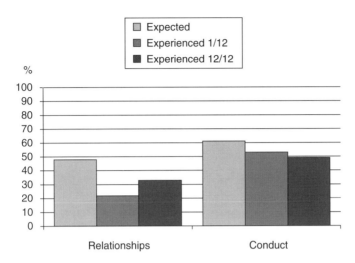

Figure 11.2: Relationship and conduct problems: pre-placement expectations and experiences at one and twelve months

accurate. Sixty per cent anticipated difficulties over behaviour and most reported that to have been the case over the course of the year. The development of relationships seemed less predictable. Prior to placement, nearly half the parents thought that it might be difficult to form a relationship with the child. However, at the first interview four-fifths felt that relationships were developing reasonably well, but a small proportion became more worried about this by the end of the year. Although in many cases the expectations about relationships prior to placement were more pessimistic than proved to be the case, the parents' views at a month were predictive of the status of relationships at a year (see Chapter 9). Of course the pre-placement predictions were based on very little information and may have been a general expectation about the problems these children would present, rather than a view based on the way they actually behaved.

NEW PARENTS' LEVEL OF SATISFACTION WITH THE CHILD AS A FAMILY MEMBER

A more specific question to the parents concerned the level of satisfaction they felt with the child as a member of the family. At the end of the first month, most parents were pleased with this. Only six mothers and three fathers had reservations but in four families this had led to serious concern about the viability of the placement. The problems generally concerned the effect of difficult behaviour on other children in the family. By the end of the year, however, the numbers of parents expressing reservations increased to 15 mothers and 10 fathers. Mothers' doubts had resolved in only one case and neither of the fathers who had initial doubts changed their opinion. But to look at it the other way round, 75% of mothers and 83% of fathers were at least reasonably happy with the child as a member of their family at the end of the year.

STRESSES AND SUPPORTS

Stresses Experienced by New Parents

Much has been written about the children's transition between homes, but the new families are undergoing major changes as well. The change involves a transition from preparation and anticipation to responsibility for the children and 24 hour engagement with the parenting task. Even those with their own birth children experience 'instant parenthood'. Are these changes and the accompanying stresses properly understood?

At each interview the parents were asked how much stress they felt and whether this was due to the child, to other factors related to the placement, such as contact arrangements, legal and financial concerns or other stresses unrelated to the placement itself. At the one month interview we also asked about the stresses they experienced prior to placement, again separating this out into the three categories. The proportions of mothers and fathers reporting significant stress in any of these categories are illustrated in Figures 11.3a and 11.3b.

Stress Levels Prior to Placement and in the Early Weeks

Figures 11.3a and 11.3b show that the pre-placement period could involve a significant amount of stress for both mothers and fathers. About one-third of parents experienced stresses to do with the child and two-thirds were under considerable 'placement-related stress' at this time. Only a small minority (6%) revealed other external unrelated stress such as a house move and loss of employment.

Maternal *child-related* stress rose a little when the children were placed but *placement-related stress* dropped significantly from two-thirds of

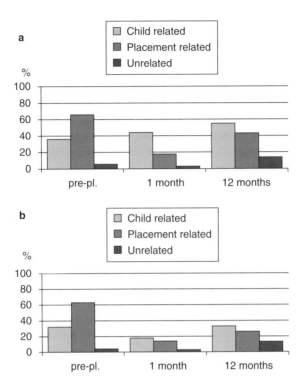

Figure 11.3: Reports of high stress: (a) by mothers, pre-placement (n = 60), and at one month (n = 60) and twelve months (n = 57); (b) by fathers, pre-placement (n = 58), and at one month (n = 58) and twelve months (n = 55)

mothers pre-placement to under a fifth afterwards (McNemar test, χ^2 = 22.1, p < 0.001). One mother said:

> I found the exhausting part was actually waiting for them to find a child. Then, when they first said they had one, it was even more exhausting. But once she came to live here the stresses and strains were nothing like as bad.

Once the children were placed, fathers' stress levels decreased for both sources of stress but more so for placement-related issues.

As is clear from Figures 11.3a and 11.3b, the period between the one month and one year interviews saw a fairly substantial rise in all types of stress for both mothers and fathers: to the extent that over half (54%) of all mothers were experiencing marked or extreme stress in relation to the placed child by the end of the year and nearly half (44%) in relation

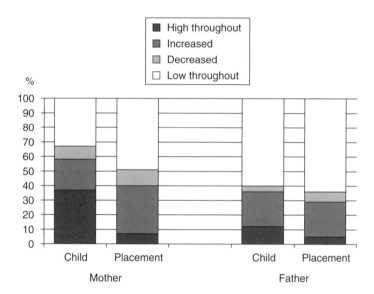

Figure 11.4: Changes in child-related and placement-related stress levels over the year ($n = 60$)

to the placement more generally. This compares with 36% and 29% respectively for fathers, who consistently reported less stress than mothers. The rise in maternal placement-related stress was significant ($p < 0.01$) as was the rise in paternal child-related stress ($p < 0.05$, two-tailed McNemar tests). Nineteen mothers (33%) were highly stressed throughout the year because of the child compared with seven fathers (13%). Figure 11.4 shows the direction of change in stress levels for both mothers and fathers.

In spite of the stress levels reported, only two mothers and two fathers reported health problems resulting from stress.

The Nature of the Stresses

Pre-placement stressors

What accounts for such high pre-placement stress levels and why did placement-related stress drop so significantly? A search of the interview records revealed a great deal about the content of the stress. The families told us how difficult it was to have their motives scrutinised by social workers and the unpredictable length of waiting, which generated apprehension, uncertainty and doubts about their own adequacy. Experienced parents were concerned beforehand about the effect of placement on their resident children and whether it would jeopardise their happiness. One mother's level of stress reduced immediately after placement following considerable apprehension during the introductions about compatibility with the other family members:

> She has slotted in so well! The relationship with our children is brilliant. It would have been an absolute nightmare if our two had hated her, but the youngest idolises her and it has brought out a lovely side of our son.

There were those who had doubts about this way of creating a family and worried whether the child would come to 'belong to them' or be compatible with other family members. Theorists about adoptive parenthood have been concerned with the psychological adjustments required of substitute parents (Katz, 1977, 1986) and possible intra-psychic conflicts (Brodzinsky, 1990) but the *external* stressors in later placements should not be under-emphasised. These often involved frequent meetings in foster homes (some involving cross-country travel taking two or three birth children) and the awkwardness of trying to relate to the new child on someone else's territory.

Because we interviewed families early in the placement we heard rich descriptions of these significant pre-placement stresses which can be so easily overshadowed by the day-to-day task of parenting once the children arrive.

In-placement stress – child-related

Reports of stress caused by the child were significantly related to the parents' accounts of difficult behaviour and failure to develop a mutual relationship. For fathers, the lack of a relationship showed a rather stronger association with stress ($\chi^2 = 16.6$, d.f. $= 1$, $p < 0.0001$) than behaviour problems ($\chi^2 = 9.11$, d.f. $= 1$, $p < 0.01$). This was reversed for mothers, with difficult behaviour seeming very important in determining stress levels ($\chi^2 = 27$, d.f. $= 1$, $p < 0.0001$), although relationship difficulties were also very influential ($\chi^2 = 8.14$, d.f. $= 1$, $p < 0.005$). Parents illustrated these points when discussing how stressful and tiring it was when they needed to be ever-vigilant because of the children's behaviour:

> You can never relax and leave them alone in case of an eruption from their constant squabbles.

Nobody tells you that a disturbed child is going to jump up and down on the work surfaces and swing from the doors.

Sometimes a continually argumentative child would succeed in making the mother angry, her bad mood would then affect the father and thereby family life generally. These problems brought out contrasting emotions in mothers. One said:

This has brought out the best in us and the worst in us. I don't think I've ever felt so happy about something, but at the same time I've never felt so angry.

Parents might have been better able to deal with these unexpected problems with more sophisticated preparation and more detailed information about the child. One mother said:

The 'Form Es' could be more explicit. What the social worker tells you she feels [about the child] gets in the way of really knowing what the child is like. After all, it's where you get your first information about the child. It needs much more detail.

In-placement stress – placement related

New parents often accepted that taking on these children was bound to be stressful and one family said if it did mean more pressure, it was pressure they had wanted. Many placement-related stresses were due to expected changes, such as the need for more washing and ironing, the restrictions on their social life, the logistics of managing the children's social activities and finding time for several lots of homework. These everyday and, in some ways 'wished for', pressures could, nevertheless, have an impact on the parents' sense of well-being. Other placement-related stressors included making sure everyone would be home when the social workers called and making arrangements for the children to keep in contact with important people from their past. Sometimes contact arrangements with birth families led to more specific stresses and, as moves were made toward adoption, the prospect of a contested hearing could lead to a good deal of worry.

In-placement stress – other stressors

Placements do not occur in a vacuum. Life continues and changes for all family members, regardless of the fact of placement. Individuals develop ailments, become pregnant, find themselves bereaved, out of work or needing to work longer hours. Over the course of the year nearly half the families experienced a change in life circumstances, some positive and others not. While there was no evidence that the changes had any significant impact on the success or otherwise of the placement, a few families (eight mothers and seven fathers) were reporting considerable additional stress from these experiences.

Some placements were relatively stress-free and brought great reward, but for others it was a very taxing first year and it was not surprising if some wavered:

> Well, every day we say that they're going back tomorrow, but we know that is a no-no and we'll never send them back.

When asked if they had any advice to give after their first year as new parents, one father said:

> Yes. Buy a pair of earplugs!

Sources of Support for New Parents

Where did the parents find support in coping with these stresses? For the most part the support that parents wanted was simply the opportunity to talk to others, for confirmation that their experiences were within or outside of the 'normal range', for reassurance that they were handling things in the best way or for ideas about alternative strategies to tackle problems. New parents rarely called on others to help with the practicalities of child care. There was, for example, surprisingly little use of the services of babysitters or childminders. Even at the end of the first year only half the parents reported having left the children with other carers to go out for an evening.

Figure 11.5 shows the frequency with which new parents used different sources of support. Couples most commonly turned to each other. This confirms the findings of our earlier study (Rushton et al., 1988) that new parents turn most frequently for support to those who have an intimate knowledge of the situation. Close friends were important in 30–40% of cases, although issues of confidentiality meant that there was often much that could not be fully shared. Extended families were important for some parents, although their reactions could occasionally add even more strain.

Formal support came mostly from family social workers (FSWs), then child social workers (CSWs) and then other professionals. In fact, it was

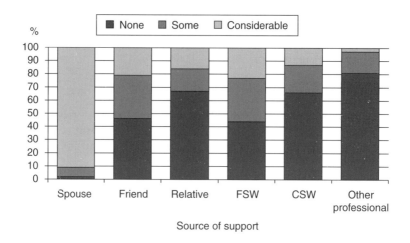

Figure 11.5: Parents' sources of support at a year ($n = 58$)

notable how rarely other professionals were used. Parents seemed to have to rely almost entirely on the strengths and weaknesses of the social work service but links with other organisations, originally formed with the help of social workers, could remain important. For example, a small number of parents gained support from members of their adoption and fostering preparation group who had kept in touch and become friends. Sometimes social workers had arranged a 'link family' which was very much appreciated. Such support from others with similar experiences was often more helpful and more comfortable than a professional service where the sense of being investigated seemed to linger.

CRISES AND DISRUPTIONS

The Incidence of and Reasons for Crises in Placements

Just over one-third of parents (20 of the 58 placements intact at 12 months) reported periods during the year when they had seriously questioned whether continuing with the placement was the right thing to do. For seven of these families, the period of doubt had been quite short-lived. Nine families reported more significant periods of questioning, although they felt these had resolved in time. There were four families who remained sufficiently unsure to be still considering the possibility of ending the placement.

The children's behaviour was a very significant factor in all of the incidents of doubt, but was the sole cause in just two cases. Serious anxieties about the parent/child relationship were present in 14 cases. Sixteen of the 20 families had birth children at home and worries about the effect of the placement on these children were important in all but two of them. The crises occurred in both singleton and sibling placements and affected both child-free and established families. Age at placement, gender, in-care experiences and abuse history were all unrelated to the occurrence of crises.

Generally, social workers seemed to be aware of these periods of crisis and had been able to respond in an appropriate manner. Five of the 13 families who had experienced significant doubts reported that they had received good support from both social workers, a further four felt that at least one had offered adequate support, but two felt totally unsupported throughout their ordeal. One family found themselves in a crisis during a bank holiday and turned to the duty social worker for help, only to be told, 'a child is for life not just for Christmas'. Despite their difficulties, these placements were still intact after a year in placement, although it remains to be seen whether all of those in crisis at the one year point succeeded in weathering the storm.

For three cases in our study the outcome was rather different and the placement was ended within the year. Many of the difficulties which beset these disrupted placements were the same as those in the placements that remained intact after crises. The remainder of this chapter presents the themes that emerged from the post-disruption interviews with new parents and social workers.

Placement Disruption

There were three disrupted placements in this interviewed sample, making a rate of only 5%, a figure that is low when compared to the findings of other studies of children of this age (Kadushin & Seidl, 1971; Boyne et al., 1984; Tremitiere, 1984; Barth & Berry, 1988; Fratter et al., 1991; Rushton et al., 1995). If the information we obtained on the eligible families who did not take part in the study is added in, the resulting rate of 11% is comparable with other studies.

The disruptions have some common features, although these frequently occurred in the cases that remained intact as well. All three children had suffered physical abuse, sexual abuse and neglect separately or in combination and two had shown previous difficulties in forming an attachment to a foster mother. All three showed conduct difficulties early in the placement that did not improve or worsened during the year. This, coupled with difficulties in achieving a close relationship with the child and the reactions of their own birth children, ultimately proved too much for the parents. All of the social workers discussed the difficulties the families faced in trying to hit the right balance between protecting their own children and not rejecting the new child.

In two cases the risks were known from the start and it was acknowledged that the placement could be unstable. One mother said:

> We thought he would be a quiet, shy child who would need to be brought out of himself, but during the introductions we realised the more attention you gave him, the more he demanded, and if he didn't get it, the more problems we had.

The other child's problems were completely unexpected and it seems unlikely that anyone could have anticipated them, since the difficulties did not come to light until the child was in the new home.

All three of these families felt that the information they received about the child prior to placement was inadequate. One family went so far as to say that if they had been given fuller information, they would not have proceeded with the placement. Two of the three families were dissatisfied with their preparation to become adopters. One of them would have welcomed more opportunity to discuss whether the child was the right one for them before he moved in,

> It was all cut and dried – yes, we were going to have him. There didn't seem to be a point where everybody took stock of what was going on and asked 'OK do you think this child suits your family?'.

Social Workers' Perspective on the Disruptions

The social workers preparing and supporting these placements varied in their level of experience and confidence. Two of the CSWs felt inadequately trained and ill-prepared. They were both working in generic or child care teams and were receiving little support from their supervisors. In contrast, two of the three family workers were experienced in placing older children and both felt adequately trained and prepared for this work. However, there were problems with liaison and agreement about the management of the placement between the FSWs and CSWs in all three cases. The problems varied but included unspoken conflict over the level of involvement of one of the workers with the placed child, lack of agreement regarding the timing of the placement, arrangements for introductions, handling of the child, and the financing of the placements.

Social Work Predictions

When asked at the one month interview what, if anything, might cause the placement to disrupt, five of the six social workers accurately predicted the eventual cause of the disruption. In one case, the social worker outlined a course of action that might help to prevent such an outcome, but added that this would not be possible due to lack of flexibility in working hours.

In two of the three cases, the placement differed substantially from what had been sought for the child. The social workers acknowledged that the situation was not ideal. One children's worker remarked:

> You don't wait for the perfect family, you make compromises and hope the family will be good enough.

The Families' Perspective

The families were all very badly affected by the disruptions and were all angry with the social services departments for the way in which they were treated. All of the birth children were thought to have suffered, some more severely than others. One child asked wistfully if his family could go back to the way they used to be before the placed child arrived. A lot of the parents' anger came from the knowledge that this was not possible and that their children had been hurt by the experience:

> We felt on our own to be quite honest, like nobody cared. It was just the placed child that they bothered about and we didn't matter. I was really angry afterwards at the damage done to our children.

All three families felt inadequately supported in the aftermath of the disruption. This may always be a difficult time for social workers to offer help and for families to accept it.

PRACTICE IMPLICATIONS

No one working in family placement or children and families teams will be surprised to find that placement can lead to significant stress for many parents and that much of this is due to behavioural and relationship difficulties. However, there are aspects of the findings presented in this chapter that deserve particular mention. The *first* is the high level of stress reported in the pre-placement period. Assessment and preparation is bound to be challenging to prospective adopters and foster carers; indeed, without challenge it might be less effective. However, there are features of the pre-placement process that can and should be addressed by practitioners. Regular contact with those waiting and explanation of what is happening, at whatever stage of the process, would be well received. There should be much greater consideration of the needs of the new family, including those of their birth children, when planning introductions. This was seen as important also for those who stood to lose money for time taken off work.

The *second* point concerns the handling of placements in crisis. Only 5 of 13 families who reported significant crises during the year felt that they had been fully supported by both social workers and 2 felt totally unsupported. There is a clear need to ensure that adequate post-placement support systems are established and support plans drawn up that are shared with and agreed to by the family.

Thirdly, liaison between the social workers was emphasised as a problem in disrupted placements, as was the level of agreement between them. It is crucial that those involved in this work are able to allocate sufficient time to ensure that information is exchanged effectively and efficiently. Disagreement between individual professionals is bound to occur but can be very unhelpful to the families if not resolved. Access to a supervisor who has experience of permanent placement work is essential and there may be a case for considering joint supervision of workers in these cases.

Finally, the experiences described by families suggest that improvement in post-disruption services is necessary and thought should be given to the possibility of involving another agency or worker capable of providing an independent viewpoint and appropriate support.

SUMMARY

This chapter has detailed the new parents' first impressions of the children and how their reactions changed as the new families became used to living together. The research should alert us to the high anticipatory stress experienced by new parents prior to placements and the continuing stress for many parents over the first year. This applied to one-third of mothers, with difficulty being particularly related to difficult behaviour and the failure of a rewarding relationship to develop.

Consideration of the disrupted placements within the sample high-lighted a number of practice issues which are discussed above.

12

POST-PLACEMENT SOCIAL WORK SUPPORT

Social work support has come to be regarded as essential to the establishment of secure placements for older children. In the current climate of 'service efficiency', we felt it was important to learn whether parents were satisfied with the service, whether it was effective and where the shortfalls were to be found. While the agencies' responsibilities towards children placed for permanence are very clear, the published statements about the services they will offer are usually couched in very general terms, for example 'to give support and advice to the new parents'. There is no legal requirement about the volume of service or guarantees about its duration, its quality or the rights of new parents to challenge what is on offer. This poses something of a problem for the families, who frequently lack specific information about what level of service might be expected and how it may best be accessed. It poses a problem of similar magnitude for the researcher, who cannot easily evaluate a service if there is nothing approaching a standard description of the task.

This chapter explores firstly the extent to which there was social work involvement with the placements and the new parents' satisfaction with the help that was on offer. Acknowledging that there are many factors that may influence the way in which parents perceive support, we go on to present our research judgements of the quality of support available to the new families. Finally we explore whether there were specific factors, in either the child or the new family, that determined the level of support offered. The majority of these data are drawn from the one year interviews with the children's social workers (CSWs), the family social workers (FSWs) and the new parents.

OVERVIEW OF SOCIAL WORK INVOLVEMENT THROUGHOUT THE YEAR

At the start of placement, almost all of the CSWs and FSWs considered themselves to be offering a supporting and sustaining presence to the placement, a role seen as shared between them. The common perception among parents was that CSWs were there to monitor and assist in the children's settling in, and that the role of the FSW was to support them as parents. In practice, these roles frequently overlapped and either or both workers could be involved in almost any aspect of support work. By the end of the year, CSW support was continuing in 37 cases and FSW support in 43 cases. Families were three times more likely to have a change of CSW than a change of FSW. The direct support received from the FSWs provided the continuity that is highly desirable through the critical first year. The families who had a change of FSW were usually sorry that this happened, but a change of CSW was welcomed in over half the cases (8/13). This was partly because relationships with the CSWs had more potential for conflict than those with FSWs.

Social work involvement had ceased entirely in only 9 of the 58 intact placements. Six CSWs and 12 FSWs were holding the support role on their own and in 31 placements both workers continued to do so. Visiting was continuing, on average, once every five to six weeks by both types of worker (range 1–12 weeks, s.d. = 2.8–3.1). Complete cessation of social work activity usually occurred where adoption proceedings had been completed and there was no reason for further involvement. All of these nine placements appeared stable at the 12 month interview. Parent views concerning social work support varied considerably; some parents had very complimentary opinions of social workers:

> She couldn't have done more than she has. She has shown a lot of compassion and understanding

> The social worker was more like a friend than an official – she's been ever so helpful.

Others felt that social workers needed less theory and more hands-on child care experience. One father was strongly critical:

> So many social workers live in cloud cuckoo land – they've no experience of life.

While most of the families looked forward to the visits stopping, permitting a return to 'normal life', some felt abruptly abandoned by the child's social worker after the adoption:

> It annoys me that her own social worker hasn't even phoned to see how she is. It is like she is adopted and that's it.

Looking back over the year, many parents (41%) reported that they had found both their CSW and FSW responsive and supportive. Sixteen families (28%) felt supported by their FSW only and nine (15%) by the CSW only. A further nine families (15%) reported either inadequate, or in two cases intrusive social work. Parents who had taken children for long-term fostering were more likely to be dissatisfied with the support from both CSWs and FSWs, but particularly the latter ($\chi^2 = 9.64$, d.f. = 3, $p < 0.05$). A permanent fostering placement sometimes received a routine monitoring service if the family had fostered before, rather than the higher level of service to the placements planned as adoptions.

In cases where one worker was carrying the role alone this was often because the other worker had left and the case had not been reallocated, or because the family had moved away from the area.

ASSESSING THE QUALITY OF SOCIAL WORK SUPPORT

The families did not normally welcome the involvement of a new worker. While the continuity of the service is interesting from some perspectives, information about the work undertaken with the families and the way in which it was received seemed far more important. At the time the study was conducted, there was no published research that had attempted to categorise the volume, content and quality of social work support. Therefore, it was necessary to obtain a comprehensive description of its role, acknowledging that social work commonly embraces both relatively routine tasks and complex activities. As discussed previously, there is no recognised standard in relation to the provision of post-placement support. Therefore, we compiled a list of areas in which parents might need social work assistance which we used in the interviews with both the social workers and the new parents. This format allowed us to assess the level of need, parent satisfaction with each worker's response and the social worker's views on their own ability to meet each of these needs.

Parents' Need for and Satisfaction with Social Work Support

Table 12.1 gives the percentage of families who acknowledged that they had felt a need in any of these areas, the social worker from whom they expected a response and the percentage who reported satisfaction with

Table 12.1: Parents' need of and satisfaction with supportive social work activities

Type of need	Number needing response (n = 58)		Number satisfied with response (n = 58)	
	From CSW	From FSW	From CSW	From FSW
Material needs	13	13	5	5
Understanding behaviour	17	17	10	10
Practical advice	33	37	21	24
Administrative tasks	36	33	22	25
Information	37	28	22	19
Reassurance	46	53	40	40
Direct work with child	22	4	11	4
Negotiate with birth parents	28	3	19	2

it. Parents were likely to approach either the CSW or the FSW for most of their needs, and were likely to record similar levels of satisfaction with the responses of both types of worker. The differences were, not surprisingly, that parents were more likely to expect the CSW to continue with direct work with the child and undertake negotiations with birth parents. Where parents needed further information about the child they were also more likely to look to the CSWs.

The most frequently acknowledged need was for reassurance, with 80–90% of families wanting confirmation that they were approaching the task of caring for the child in a reasonable way and dealing appropriately with issues that arose. On the whole this need was satisfied by both types of worker for the majority of families. There were a cluster of other needs that were present for half to two-thirds of families. These included a need for practical advice concerning the management of difficult behaviour, completion of administrative tasks, such as the Schedule 2 report and providing further information about the child. Parents reported less satisfaction in these areas, particularly with the CSW's response. About one-third felt they wanted help in understanding what lay behind some of their child's behaviour and how to respond to it. In only about a half of cases were the parents happy with the answers they got.

Material need was a less frequent requirement but was satisfied in only 40% of cases. This probably reflects the financial constraints on local authorities but, nevertheless, there were families who felt that they had been promised financial support which failed to materialise.

When we looked at the social work perception of need in the listed areas, we found that both CSWs and FSWs tended to over-estimate the extent of need in relation to understanding the children's behaviour and under-estimate the importance of practical advice. Parents frequently told us that they were looking for ideas or strategies on how to deal with the day-to-day problems they encountered. A frequent reservation was that the social workers were simply passive listeners who did not have sufficient understanding of parenting to suggest problem-solving strategies. Tardiness in the completion of administrative tasks could also be a source of frustration for parents, who often felt that processes, like the adoption hearing, were being held up unnecessarily. CSWs tended to see direct work with the child as a greater need than the parents did and FSWs were less likely to view information-giving as of prime importance.

Supportiveness as perceived by parents was not related to the length of social workers' service or training. Rather, it was strongly related to the parents' perceptions of the availability of the social worker, the relationship that developed between them and the extent to which they made space for discussion. The parents' perception of the supportiveness of the FSW was also coloured by their view of the FSW's allegiance to the family and reliability in keeping to arrangements. This was not the case for the CSWs and this may have been due to the parents' awareness of the pressures on CSWs as a result of the other aspects of their work. Nevertheless, perceptions of divided loyalties and unreliability were a feature for some CSWs and could lead to tensions. Some parents reported that failure to visit when expected could cause significant upset for their children. Seven parents said that the children showed a marked rise in problems at the time of the CSW visits, which was never true for the FSWs. One father said:

> If he comes home and sees her [CSW] sitting there he thinks – Oh God what has happened now?

Parents also disliked the tendency for the child to be singled out from the birth children by CSW visits when they were doing all they could to integrate the child into the family.

The importance of the relationship that develops between parent and support worker is underlined by the reports of the social workers as well. While most felt they had good working relationships with the new parents, 4 FSWs and 10 CSWs thought that the relationship was not ideal and this had made it difficult for them to offer the support they would have liked to give.

A further difficulty arose when conflicting messages were given by each worker. This happened rarely but could be confusing and distressing. The social workers were asked about the liaison between themselves: 5 CSWs and 17 FSWs reported significant difficulties with establishing efficient channels of communication and 4 CSWs and 5 FSWs felt that there was considerable disagreement on the best way to support the placement.

Research Assessment of the Level of Social Work Support

There are clearly a number of factors that may influence parents' satisfaction with their social workers and, while satisfaction is clearly important, it may not be entirely synonymous with the quality of work. For this reason we constructed a systematic and independent assessment of the level of service comparable to that of the CSW's preparatory work reported in Chapter 6. The records of the interviews with the FSWs were examined and three categories of support were defined, representing recognisably different levels of work.

Low level service

This group included workers who were not very available to the families and visited infrequently. They provided minimal support and only did so when parents requested it. They did not appear fully aware of the level and range of problems faced by the families and they used no specific techniques of intervention but relied almost entirely on general reassurance. Promises of action would frequently not be fulfilled.

Moderate level service

Social workers providing a 'moderate level' service tended to visit frequently (averaging more than once per month during the year) and were readily available at other times. They were able to be flexible in the level of service offered and increased the frequency of visiting in times of greater difficulty or crisis. They offered the parents the opportunity to ventilate their strong feelings, including anger, self-doubt and a sense of panic. They acknowledged the stresses and anxieties experienced by the parents, provided encouragement and offered interpretations of the children's difficult or strange behaviour. They carried out activities discussed with the parents, within the agreed time-frame. However, they seldom translated their diagnosis of the difficulties into a purposeful plan of intervention, like advising on well founded parenting strategies for dealing with problem behaviour or on conflict between siblings.

High level service

This group provided a more comprehensive and skilled service. They were confident practitioners, having thought through their responsibilities and the challenges inherent in the role. They made an assessment of the level of difficulty presented by the child and related this to the capacities and experiences of the new parents. They were involved in detailed discussion of problems and considered possible tactics and approaches to them jointly with the parents. They employed specific methods for helping the parents to deal with attachment problems, overactivity and other psychosocial difficulties. They helped the new family to think about concerns for the future: fears of later delinquency or unwanted pregnancy or anxieties about contact with birth parents. They took account of the formation of new relationships in the new family, including sibling interactions within the placed group, as well as relationships with birth siblings.

As illustrated by Figures 12.1 and 12.2, the distribution of 'service levels' across CSWs and FSWs is somewhat different. A higher proportion of FSWs were considered to have been working at a high level and fewer to be offering a low level of service.

When the FSW and CSW ratings were combined, 5 families were without adequate support from either worker, 7 were receiving at least a reasonable degree of support but only from a CSW, 22 families were receiving support from their FSW but little or nothing from the CSW and 27 families were in receipt of fair support from both. It was somewhat reassuring to find that none of the placements in difficulty at a year were without at least some support (Table 12.2), although over half of these placements only had access to one effective worker.

THE ROLE OF THE FAMILY SOCIAL WORKER

Unlike CSWs, who may have a number of very different clients to deal with, supporting permanent placements constitutes a good proportion

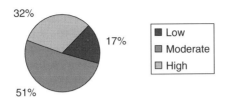

Figure 12.1: Distribution of FSW service levels ($n = 59$)

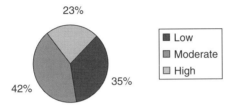

Figure 12.2: Distribution of CSW service levels ($n = 52$)

Table 12.2: Availability of social work support according to stability of placements at one year

Placement stability	Neither	CSW only	FSW only	CSW and FSW	Total
Less stable	–	1	8	8	17
More stable	5	6	14	19	44
Total	5	7	22	27	61

of the work of family placement workers. But despite their more focused role, none of the FSWs claimed that they had received anything amounting to specific, in-depth training in post-placement support work. Most of the FSWs (65%) said the only related training they had received had been on their basic social work courses and only 35% had subsequently attended short courses and study days. Although much of their knowledge had been absorbed informally in the work setting and through attending team discussions, in general the FSWs felt confident in the role. Therefore, it was reasonable to expect the FSW to have an informed view on the way a placement was working out and the type and extent of support that may have been needed.

FSWs' Views of Levels of Demand by the New Parents

The FSWs were asked to give their views on how the families were coping with the child and to rate how demanding the case was for them during the first year. These ratings produced three broad groupings. In the first group, FSWs thought that no more than average demands were being made, while in the second and third groups they described high or very high demands.

Average demand cases (76%, n = 42)

This was the largest group and contained the families who took on the task of parenting a new child without expressing strong needs for support. In these cases the FSWs said parents were rising to the challenge, demonstrating their capacity to cope with difficulties. The FSWs had confidence in the parents' handling style because they took on the new responsibilities without exhibiting too much anxiety or requiring excessive reassurance and they were often impressed with their inventive, insightful and resourceful approach. Close supervision of these placements beyond the initial stage was not deemed necessary when the social worker judged the child to be well cared for, the new parents were keen to adopt and there was ease of communication between worker and family.

High demand cases (15%, n = 8)

These placements ran less smoothly and problems arose that were more demanding of the FSW's decision-making and intervention skills. 'High demand' was identified when the expectations or handling style of the new parents gave the FSW cause for concern. When the FSWs identified unrealistic parental expectations about the child's pace of recovery, they had to persuade the parents to adjust these to a more reasonable level. FSWs had to assess whether the parental reactions they encountered (sometimes including exasperation, loss of temper and frequent interparental disagreement) were passing concerns or more serious warning signs. In one case, the FSW had to decide whether a parent's apparent lack of feeling for the child was likely to improve over time and with social work help and whether it would be contrary to the child's interests if the lack of feeling persisted.

The delivery of a support service did not automatically involve a positive response from the parents. The FSWs found this group harder to communicate with as they were not always cooperative or ready to consider the FSW's suggestions or eager to reflect on their own parenting style. Three mothers and one father were rated as not at all receptive and were seen as defensive, over-confident or unused to a 'helping relationship'. One family resisted social work attention. The FSW did not feel comfortable visiting them and began to do so less frequently. Clearly she was not then able to supervise the placement and safeguard the child's welfare adequately under these circumstances.

Some of the difficulties in this group arose in the context of families whom the FSW would not personally have approved as prospective adopters. This was more likely to be the case when there was an urgent need to find a placement but no satisfactory match had been found.

Very high demand cases (9%, n = 5)

Cases were rated as 'very high demand' if the level of difficulties meant that the advisability of the placement was being called into question. In cases where the child was slow to develop a warm relationship with the new parents, or was actively rejecting them, families became disheartened and FSWs needed to spend time encouraging them to continue with the placement. This was difficult to achieve if they had developed ambivalent or negative feelings towards the child. In other cases, when the FSWs detected inflexible or consistently inappropriate parenting, a lack of willingness to adapt or to make use of the social work help on offer, they wrestled with whether the placement should be terminated.

Parents' Account of the FSW Service

Parents reported that, in the first months of the placement, the FSW had visited every fortnight, on average. Of those continuing to receive a FSW service at a year (n = 43), 84% were visited every five to six weeks. The frequency of the service inevitably declined after the initial phase but the support service was still considerably in evidence at a year. In a third of cases the FSW always saw the mother alone and in two-thirds of cases both parents were seen together. The quality of relationship between the FSW and new parents was rated as adequate (19%), good (35%) or very good (35%), but a small minority (11%) of parents described a poor relationship.

As for the parents' opinion of the volume of service, the majority (74%) were satisfied with the frequency of visits, but 12% thought they had seen too much of them and 12% complained that they had received a negligible service and were dismayed to discover how little face-to-face support was provided.

In those cases where there was dissatisfaction, the new parents' most frequent complaint was that, although the FSWs were good listeners, they did not have sufficient experience of parenting to suggest ways of tackling problems. New parents who had taken children for permanent fostering rather than for adoption were more likely to be dissatisfied with the FSW service (χ^2 = 9.64, d.f. = 3, p < 0.05). Permanent fostering arrangements were more likely to be offered routine monitoring compared with the greater attention devoted to planned adoptive placements.

The families were especially concerned about the impact of the incoming child or children on the whole family, including their own children. Forty per cent of the established families with children (n = 30) did not feel their own children's needs had been properly taken into account, although 37% said they had been to some extent and 23% to a considerable extent. It was very unusual for the FSWs to become involved directly with the whole family group. They rarely saw the placed child separately, or the siblings together, and most of their work was conducted with the parents alone.

Determinants of FSW Service Levels

We then examined which factors explained these variations in service levels by looking for associations with characteristics of the child, the new family and the family social workers. As cell frequencies were too small for statistical testing when using the three-way classification, the level of FSW service was collapsed to a high level of service compared with combined low and moderate levels.

Children's characteristics

Table 12.3 shows the relationship between child factors and FSW support. The level of FSW service was not associated with differences in the child's difficulty initially, presumably because most families were receiving a more uniform service at the very start of the placement. However, by a year, the high level service was associated with placements in which the child was showing many psychosocial problems and was not attached to either parent. Other characteristics of the children, such as age, sex and previous experiences, were not associated with

Table 12.3: Determinants of level of FSW service (child factors)

Child's characteristics	Level of FSW service		Statistical significance
	Low/Moderate	High	
Sex			
Boys	21 (70%)	19 (30%)	NS
Girls	19 (66%)	10 (34%)	
Age at placement			
5–6	18 (78%)	5 (22%)	NS
7–9	22 (61%)	14 (39%)	
Singled out and rejected			
No	29 (82%)	6 (18%)	$\chi^2 = 8.9$, d.f. = 1,
Yes	11 (46%)	13 (54%)	$p < 0.003$
Child's attachment (1 year)			
Not either parent	11 (46%)	13 (54%)	$\chi^2 = 8.9$, d.f. = 1,
Attached to one or both	29 (83%)	6 (17%)	$p < 0.003$
Problems (1 month)			
Low	16 (80%)	4 (20%)	NS
High	24 (62%)	15 (38%)	
Problems (1 year)			
Low	22 (92%)	2 (8%)	$\chi^2 = 9.6$, d.f. = 1,
High	17 (53%)	15 (47%)	$p < 0.002$
Aggressive (1 year)			
No	21 (70%)	9 (30%)	NS
Yes	19 (66%)	10 (34%)	
Background history			
Relatively good	4 (67%)	2 (33%)	NS
Adverse	36 (68%)	17 (32%)	

NS: not significant.

levels of service, with one notable exception: families with children who had been singled out for rejection by their birth parents were more likely to receive a high level service. The experience of being singled out and rejected by birth parents was strongly associated with poor attachment to new parents and a multiplicity of behaviour difficulties. It is likely that the combination of these two factors attracted the attention of the FSWs, leading to a high level of service.

New family characteristics

The other set of factors that may have influenced the FSW service concerned the new families (Table 12.4). Mothers who expressed reservations

Table 12.4: Determinants of level of FSW service (new family factors)

Family factors	Level of FSW service		Statistical significance
	Low/Moderate	High	
Mother's satisfaction			
Reservations	4 (24%)	13 (76%)	$\chi^2 = 21.4$, d.f. = 1,
Happy	36 (86%)	6 (14%)	$p < 0.001$
Mother's stress			
Low, reducing	19 (79%)	5 (21%)	NS
High, increasing	19 (61%)	12 (39%)	
Parental responsiveness			
0/1 problems	28 (78%)	8 (22%)	$\chi^2 = 3.6$, d.f. = 1,
2/3 problems	10 (53%)	9 (47%)	$p < 0.05$
Mother's age			
< 40	23 (59%)	16 (41%)	$\chi^2 = 4.1$, d.f. = 1,
40+	17 (85%)	3 (15%)	$p < 0.04$
Previous parenting			
Neither	9 (90%)	1 (10%)	NS
One or both	31 (63%)	18 (37%)	
Status			
Fostering	5 (62%)	3 (38%)	NS
Adoption	35 (69%)	16 (31%)	
Placed with established family			
Child free	21 (84%)	4 (16%)	$\chi^2 = 5.8$, d.f. = 1,
Established family	19 (56%)	15 (44%)	$p < 0.02$
Sibling relationships			
No poor relationship/s	29 (85%)	5 (15%)	$\chi^2 = 18.9$, d.f. = 1,
1+ poor relationship/s	4 (24%)	13 (76%)	$p < 0.001$
Crisis			
No crisis	35 (80%)	9 (20%)	$\chi^2 = 10.9$, d.f. = 1,
Crisis	5 (33%)	10 (67%)	$p < 0.001$
Level of demand			
Average	34 (77%)	10 (23%)	$\chi^2 = 5.8$, d.f. = 1,
Demanding	6 (43%)	8 (57%)	$p < 0.01$

NS: not significant.

about the placed child received the high level of support, but this was not so for mothers with rising stress levels during the year.

Where the parents were seen to have problems in demonstrating sensitivity and expressing warmth, the high level service was provided. The adoptive placements did not receive a higher level service but there were only eight fostering placements with which to make the comparison. The extent of previous parenting experience was not in itself related to service level but the placement pattern was. A placement in which a child joins an established family has the potential for more relationship difficulties and may be in need of more service. The high level of service was, indeed, provided for established families and for families where there were negative relationships amongst siblings. The age of the mother was also an influence. Thus, 61% (14/23) of the younger mothers (under 40) with an established family were receiving a high level service compared with only 9% (1/11) for older mothers with established families (Fisher's exact test, $p = 0.003$). This may be because the children of the older mothers had reached later childhood and conflict between children was less worrying (see Chapter 9).

An important task of the FSW in sustaining placements was likely to be their capacity to respond appropriately in the event of a family crisis. Fifteen families said they had experienced at least one crisis during the year and it was encouraging to find that they were significantly more likely to receive a high level service.

A further possible influence on the FSW service was their own experience and training. However, those FSWs who had been longer in this post were no more likely to be providing a high level service and nor were those who had attended short post-qualifying courses about placement practice, but then specific training for this work was found to be noticeably absent. The provision of high level work was significantly associated with the FSW's assessment that the placement was progressing poorly ($\chi^2 = 18.4$, d.f. $= 1$, $p < 0.001$). This suggests, at least, that the level of response was consistent with their own judgements.

The Parents' Level of Demand in Relation to the Level of Service

Another possible influence on the level of service by the FSW was the extent of demand placed on them by the new parents. The association between 'parental demand' and the level of FSW service, each measured at one year, was significant and in the expected direction ($\chi^2 = 5.8$, d.f. $= 1$, $p < 0.01$). It is reasonable to conclude that higher levels of service were in response to higher demands by the families. However, there were 10 families who were regarded as 'average demand' but who were receiving the high level of service. The interview records revealed that this occurred in two types of circumstance. In some cases tasks such as negotiating with birth parents placed a demand for more intense activity on the FSW. In other cases the FSW identified a need for work to help families with difficulties they were not acknowledging, like understanding the strength of their own feelings and reactions to the child.

The Parents' Response to FSW Support

In general, a high level service was available to families where there were serious threats to the stability of the placement. However, it should not be assumed that having a high level response necessarily meant that these families experienced the service as supportive. In fact, the level of the FSW service was not related to the new parents' ratings of FSW support at a year. Whereas in the low/moderate level group 80% (29/36) of the FSWs were regarded as supportive, 41% (7/17) of the high level FSW help was not regarded as supportive by the families. In these cases there was more conflict in the relationship between the FSWs and the parents. Where the parents appeared to be showing less warmth and sensitivity, or had very high expectations, the FSWs were having to encourage different responses. In one example, the FSW thought the mother's parenting was inappropriate and might ultimately destabilise the placement. The FSW thought the preparation for taking this child had been poor and decided to address aspects of the parenting that had not been discussed openly before. When she did so this was not well received by the mother and this may have accounted for the low support rating.

THE RELATIONSHIP BETWEEN LEVEL OF FSW SERVICE AND PLACEMENT PROGRESS

The key question to tackle next was whether variations in levels of post-placement family support were related to progress in the placements. It should be remembered that none of the pre-placement preparatory work had been found to be related to placement progress. In order to explore ways in which the social work help may have influenced the children's progress and the stability of the placement, three outcome measures were used: children's problems at a year (categorised as many or few); placement stability; and maternal stress.

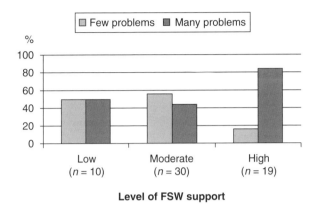

Figure 12.3: FSW service levels and child's problems at one year

Children's Problems After a Year in Placement

The sample was divided at the 25th percentile on the total symptom score (as described in Chapter 6). Those at or above this level comprised the many symptoms group and those below the few symptoms group. The three disruptions were added to the many problems group. This was justified because these children had shown many problems when they were with the families. There was a strong association between level of FSW service and the problem group categories (χ^2 = 8.24, d.f. = 2, $p < 0.01$). A high proportion of families receiving high level work (84%) had children with many problems (Figure 12.3), whereas the low and moderate levels showed comparably low problem levels. Indeed, a moderate level of service was slightly more likely to be provided to families with children with few problems. In these cases the level of service may be related to the demands of the parents, the preferences of the practitioner or ease of visiting; or perhaps the FSW chose to work on anticipated rather than current difficulties. Of course, this raises the question of whether a moderate level service was necessary for some of these families.

Five (15%) of the 34 children in the high problem group at a year were nevertheless receiving a low level FSW service. This may indicate a worrying failure to respond to the difficulties the parents were experiencing. On the other hand, it is possible that these might have been overly independent parents who were having considerable problems but who made few demands. In order to test this possibility, the relationship between the child's problems at a year and the level of FSW service was examined while controlling for the level of parents' demands. There was some evidence that the demandingness of the family made a difference. A minority (38%, 8/23) of low demand families with high problem children had a high FSW service, whereas the majority (70%, 7/10) of demanding families with high problem children had a high FSW service, a prediction that just fell short of statistical significance at the 5% level (Fisher's exact test, $p = 0.068$).

FSW Service and Placement Stability

The association between the FSW service and placement stability was then examined (see Chapter 3 for definition of this measure). As might be expected, a higher level of FSW service was associated with less secure placements ($\chi^2 = 16.11$, d.f. = 1, $p < 0.001$). Twelve out of 19 insecure placements had high level service (63%). This association was likely to have arisen because the more problematic cases received more intensive work and this would work against detecting a positive effect from intensive input. In order to examine this further we examined the effects of the service *within* the group of children with many problems at the start of placement and looked to see whether the level of FSW service affected placement security. In fact, even within this group the level of work was found to be inversely related to outcome, that is, the low/moderate service level was associated with more stable placements and a high level with placement insecurity ($\chi^2 = 12.1$, d.f. = 1, $p < 0.001$). Nearly all the low/moderate service cases had stable placements by a year (21/24, 88%) but the high service cases had mostly insecure placements (10/15, 66%). This suggests that high level service to the parents was not able to achieve stable placements over the first year, perhaps due to other more powerful factors at work. However, we are not in a position to know whether these placements would have survived to the first anniversary without the efforts of these FSWs nor whether the level of service was in response to other kinds of problem nor whether a high service level developed only when placements began to run into difficulty.

Maternal Stress and FSW Support

One reasonable expectation of the high level FSW service was that it might lead to a reduction in maternal stress. We have shown earlier that the mother's stress was significantly related to the child's problems. An increase in a child's problems led to more maternal stress and when they diminished stress levels did as well. In order to explore the effects of FSW input on stress we divided the sample into two groups depending on whether stress was *always low or reducing* or *always high or increasing*. It was striking that the level of FSW service made no difference to the levels of stress the parents were feeling at one year. This may mean that the daily stress generated by the child was too great to be counteracted by the FSW's visits, that the interventions were not sufficiently intensive or well directed to achieve reductions in stress levels, or that effects will only become apparent after the one year point.

THE SOCIAL WORKERS' PREDICTIONS OF PLACEMENT PROGRESS

Finally, we asked how accurately the FSWs had predicted the progress of the placements. They gave us their predictions at the one month interview when they would already have had evidence on which to base their judgements. At this point the majority were confident or very confident that the placement would be stable (53/61, 81%). The FSWs' predictions were significantly associated with placement stability (χ^2 = 10.1, d.f. = 1, p < 0.001). Six of the eight (75%) more pessimistic predictions were, indeed, unstable or had disrupted whereas 42 of the 53 confident predictions (79%) were secure. All but one of the eight placements that were expected to be problematic were in receipt of high FSW service at a year.

CSWs tended to be more pessimistic in their predictions, anticipating difficulties for 11 placements, which materialised in 7 (64%) of cases. Conversely, 39 of the 49 they anticipated would go well (80%) fulfilled their prediction. The relationship between these predictions and the level of CSW service was less clear-cut than that of the FSWs although the majority of placements thought to be doubtful were receiving at least some ongoing work from CSWs at 12 months.

CONTINUING WORK WITH THE CHILD

At the one month interview, CSWs for all but 11 index children had indicated an intention that Life Story Work, or some aspect of direct work with the child, should be continued into the new placement. But at the one year interview the social workers reported that further work had been carried out in only 22 cases. In three cases the work focused on the

Life Story Book only, in eight cases specific work was done with the child and in 11 cases direct work was combined with Life Story Work.

The objectives of the direct work varied. For example, one social worker tackled a very complex topic with a young child who made a false allegation about a previous carer, another social worker spent a considerable amount of time working with a bereaved child who had not had the opportunity to talk about the death of the parent. However, in most cases the main emphasis of the work was on 'permanence' and 'identity'. The majority of the work was conducted by the CSWs, although there were one or two examples of FSWs or other workers taking over. In 18 of the 22 cases, the CSWs thought that their objectives had been achieved while the other four were uncertain. This work was more likely to occur in more difficult placements. The average behaviour problem score was higher at both 1 and 12 months for children who received further work than those who did not, although the difference was only significant at one month ($t = -2.051$, d.f. = 56, $p < 0.05$). This suggests that at least some of the impetus for completing the work was that the children appeared unsettled in the placement, although the work did not have an immediate effect on the way the children behaved. It was also more likely that placements in receipt of this work were classified as unstable at the end of the year (Fisher's exact test, $p = 0.028$).

Like the work of the FSWs, the association indicates that increased social work effort is related to poorer one year outcome, but as with the FSWs' post-placement work, we do not know if the placements would have progressed this far without the support, nor whether the children and families will benefit in the longer term.

PRACTICE IMPLICATIONS

A number of practice questions have been highlighted. *Firstly*, it is important to recognise how new parents differ in their attitudes to and needs for a support service. Thought is required on how best to decide on the appropriate frequency of visits and focus of the task. There can also be confusion in the parents' minds on the roles of the two social workers and what they might expect as a service from each. Much more clarity is needed at the stage of making the match and planning the placement in relation to roles, responsibilities and expectations.

A *second* issue concerns preparation, training, support and supervision of social workers in this specialist area. The processes mediating the effects of a service are complex. Many factors are involved in this, including the way the parents choose to present their difficulties and to seek help, their receptivity to reassurance, to information-giving and to parenting advice. Nevertheless conflicts between parents and social workers do arise and it is necessary to ask whether there is room for parents to have more choice of social worker in these cases. This could be resolved without apportioning blame but with the simple recognition that not every combination works equally well.

Thirdly, parents' views on the support they received were very much coloured by their perceptions of the availability, reliability and allegiances of their workers. It is clearly important that social workers are able to 'ring-fence' the time to visit or telephone when they have arranged to do so, or at least to advise families in advance if they have to alter arrangements. The difficulties of working with a substitute family and a birth family simultaneously can be immense, especially if the birth family are antagonistic to the permanence plan. That such dilemmas were perceived by parents as detracting from the support they received suggests that such cases require, at the least, very close supervision, and the possibility of a separate worker for child and birth family might be a useful strategy in some cases.

Finally, the study found examples of cases where families with highly problematic children were receiving very low levels of support. Although the reasons for this may be complex, it is important to monitor cases so that the best match between placements and resources is made.

SUMMARY

The first part of this chapter presented data concerning the level of ongoing support work from both CSWs and FSWs. The support task was seen, for the most part, as a role to be shared between the two workers and in many cases both continued to be involved with the placement throughout the first year. Around 42% of parents described both their CSW and FSW as supportive, a further 43% felt supported by only one or other of the workers and a worrying 15% felt that they had not received adequate or appropriate help from either.

Social workers tended to under-estimate the need for practical advice and guidance and the importance to the families of promptness in dealing with administrative tasks. Parents were less likely than social workers to feel that they needed help in interpreting their child's behaviour or that the child was in need of some form of direct work.

There was considerable variation in the amount and quality of support work offered by both social workers.

The second section explored the activities of FSWs in more detail. Their work appeared to be logically determined by the changing needs of the placements, especially the problems in the children, the demands of the families and by immediate responses to crises. FSWs were able to predict fairly well which placements were likely to prove unstable and to direct more work towards them. Nevertheless, it must be concluded that high level FSW support work with families with multiple problem children still resulted in the majority of these placements being rated unstable at a year. This raises the question as to whether a different model of intervention may be necessary.

The focus of the social work service was largely on the new parents themselves rather than seeing their responsibility as being for the whole family. There were, however, some notable exceptions in which a more comprehensive assessment of the families' difficulties was made, resulting in an overview of family problems instead of attention being given exclusively to the parents.

Clearly our assessment of the impact of the support work depended on the classifications of social work intervention and of outcome. In both cases we were looking for sensible ways of testing key questions in the absence of any generally agreed definitions of social work activity. The design of the study also restricted us to within-sample comparisons and this, along with the sample size, restricted the statistical controls we could apply.

Nevertheless some conclusions are in order. Social work activity was quite well targeted on the families with problems although there was considerable variation in the quality of the service provided. Social workers were good at predicting which placements were likely to prove unstable but there was little evidence that their efforts to support these families made much difference either to placement stability or to parental stress or to children's problems at least during the first year. Even so, the great majority of placements were surviving at one year and there did seem to be evidence that social work intervention may have helped parents deal with crises that might otherwise have threatened the placement.

13

PARENTING APPROACHES AND RESPONSES

Most of the literature on the correlates of success in permanent placements has focused on factors in the children's backgrounds, the structure of the new family and the motivations of carers. Very few studies have attempted to measure the parenting responses to the challenge of the newly placed children directly. One purpose of our research was to take forward the study of the processes leading to successful placements through detailed assessments of parenting.

We employed a method of assessment that followed well-established techniques developed in other studies of parenting (Quinton & Rutter, 1984, 1988; Taylor et al., 1991). In the course of the interviews the parents provided detailed descriptions of their responses to the children's anxieties or worries, to episodes of management and control and their ways of encouraging the children's social development. Separate ratings were also made for each parent, on the content, context and the tone of their descriptions, according to established and reliable rating rules developed in studies of expressed emotion in parents with mental health problems and more recently applied to parents of children with behaviour disorders (Vostanis et al., 1994).

These descriptions and codings were used to make eight summary ratings for each parent on key dimensions of parenting, together with a rating of the degree of consistency between them in their handling of the children. In practice, mothers and fathers gave very similar accounts of their own behaviour, possibly because these were given in a joint interview. The only difference was a non-significant tendency for more fathers to use a degree of verbal aggression in their methods of discipline. Because the ratings were similar this chapter uses the ratings for the primary carer (usually the mother). The eight summary ratings were grouped into three broad categories: *responsiveness*, *management* and *aggression*. We used reliability analysis to check that the items formed a reliable scale. This produces the statistics' alpha, which can have a value between 0 and 1. The alpha values for responsiveness and management were 0.078 and 0.070 respectively.

Responsiveness included three ratings: 'emotional involvement', 'expressed warmth' and 'sensitive responding'. *Emotional involvement* describes the extent to which the parents showed empathy with and feelings for the children. *Expressed warmth* is an indicator of the positive feelings expressed by parents when discussing them. The evidence used for this rating included: the parents' account of the warmth they felt towards the child, the quality of interactions at bedtime, their ways of comforting the child and the style of reconciliation after confrontations. *Sensitive responding* refers to the degree of understanding and sympathy with which parents handled both anxiety and distress and defiance and misbehaviour. This rating reflected the extent to which parents tried to interpret their child's cues accurately and to respond with flexibility and imagination. Sensitive responding is not the same as warmth. Parents may be quite reserved in their expressions of warmth but nevertheless be very sensitive in their responses to their children.

The rating of *management style* took into account the levels of strictness or indulgence in discipline, the style of control, the effectiveness of supervision and the extent to which parents facilitated the children's interests. Ratings on this dimension indicated problems if parents were at either extreme, that is, either over-controlling, allowing the child very little autonomy, or extremely lax and failing to provide boundaries for the child.

The final area, *aggression in parenting style*, indicated the use of smacking or shouting. In practice, disciplinary aggression among these parents usually involved a loss of control leading to shouting at the child. Incidents of smacking or other physical punishments were extremely rare although there were a few examples of harsh or humiliating punishments.

Before we discuss these problems in more detail it is important to emphasise that the difficulties the parents were showing were not of an order that would imply that a placement should be ended or, indeed, that intervention was clearly necessary. Rather, they reflect departures from an optimum parenting style that might hinder the establishing of the placement or the developmental recovery of the children. In many cases the parenting difficulties were understandable responses to the persistent problems presented by the children.

FREQUENCY OF PARENTING PROBLEMS AND CHANGE IN PARENTING STYLE OVER TIME

Table 13.1 shows the proportion of parents experiencing difficulties in each area at 1 and 12 months and Table 13.2 shows moves into and out of problem categories. While there is some consistency across time, some parents manage to resolve their problems and others develop difficulties. The positive and negative cycles of interaction between the children's behaviour and the parents' responses are considered in Chapter 14.

Problems with Responsiveness

For all three of the responsiveness items, a larger proportion of parents than expected were rated as showing difficulties. Of course, a lack of emotional involvement with the child or a guardedness in expressing warmth at one month into the placement is not that surprising. However, this has to be balanced against the fact that two-thirds of parents were rated as positive in these areas.

As is clear from Tables 13.1 and 13.2, when all items related to responsiveness and warmth were taken into account, a large proportion of parents were having some problems at one or both points in time. Only one-third of parents never showed a difficulty on any of these items. By the end of the year just over half the sample were showing either continuing or recently developed problems in this area.

Problems with Management

There were fewer management problems than problems in sensitivity and responsiveness. The majority of parents used reasonably imaginative and flexible strategies to promote desirable behaviour, gave the child responsibilities and freedom appropriate to their age and struck a balance between allowing 'treats' and being clear about boundaries. As is clear from Table 13.1, difficulties with individual aspects of management occurred relatively rarely and, even when they were combined, there were never more than about one-third of parents with problems of this sort. On the other hand, 20 parents had continuing or worsening problems with some aspect of management. Ten of them tended to be over-controlling and ten were excessively lenient. With the exception of four parents who had difficulty in this area alone, all instances of management difficulty occurred in conjunction with problems in responsiveness.

Table 13.1: Parenting characteristics at 1 and 12 months (primary carers n = 61 at 1 month, 57 at 12 months)

Parenting characteristic	Very little of characteristic		Rather too much of characteristic		Appropriate	
	1 month (%)	12 months (%)	1 month (%)	12 months (%)	1 month (%)	12 months (%)
Emotional involvement	36	28	2	7	62	65
Expressed warmth	34	49	–	–	66	51
Sensitive responding	23	23	–	–	77	77
Any responsiveness problem	*47*	*46*	*–*	*–*	*53*	*54*
Disciplinary aggression	5	5	2	16	93	79
Facilitation of interests	10	11	2	2	88	87
Control	5	7	5	4	90	89
Supervision	5	12	2	4	93	84
Disciplinary indulgence	18	16	5	4	77	80
Any management problem	*21*	*18*	*15*	*18*	*63*	*64*

Table 13.2: Changes in parenting style over the year (n = 57)

Type of problem	Never a problem (%)	Problem resolved (%)	Problem developed (%)	Continuing problem (%)
Emotional involvement	50	14	11	25
Expressed warmth	46	5	21	28
Sensitive responding	66	11	11	12
Any responsiveness problem	32	14	16	39
Aggression	74	4	18	4
Facilitation	81	7	7	5
Supervision	84	0	9	7
Control	79	11	11	0
Indulgence	70	11	7	12
Any management problem	53	12	10	25

Parental Aggression

Parental aggression featured in only a minority of placements across the year but there was a substantial rise in aggressive behaviour.

Three major questions arise from this initial analysis. *First*, to what extent can these differences in parenting style be accounted for by differences in the children or the placement configurations? *Secondly*, which factors are associated with *changes* in parenting behaviour? *Thirdly*, are there any differences in placement outcome according to the parenting style?

CHILDREN'S CHARACTERISTICS, PRE-PLACEMENT FACTORS AND PARENTING PROBLEMS

For each type of parenting difficulty we checked to see if there were any differences according to the sex, age or race of the child, whether the child had previously experienced abuse or rejection and the number of times the child had moved or returned home. Parenting behaviour was related to only two of these factors. There was a tendency for mothers of older children to show more aggression, although this difference was not significant. There was also a significant tendency for maternal aggression to be more of a problem when parenting girls (χ^2 = 7.12, d.f. = 1, $p < 0.01$). However, one factor stood out in relation to parenting diffi-culties more strongly than any other and that was the child's experience of rejection from the family of origin. The new parents of these children were more likely to have difficulties in all three parenting areas, although this was significant for responsiveness difficulties at a year only. Of the 21 rejected children, 16 parents (76%) were rated as having continuing or worsening difficulties with responsiveness compared with 15 of 36 (42%) parents of non-rejected children ($\chi^2 = 6.4$, d.f. = 1, $p < 0.02$). This link between rejection and parental responsiveness was almost certainly influenced by the much higher levels of persistent conduct problems in the rejected children ($\chi^2 = 7.6$, d.f. = 1, $p < 0.01$) and many more difficulties on the Expression of Feelings Questionnaire (EFQ) ($\chi^2 = 5.8$, d.f. = 1, $p < 0.02$). Both of these factors were significantly associated with lower maternal responsiveness.

PARENTING DIFFICULTIES IN RELATION TO PLACEMENT CONFIGURATIONS

There were differences in the level of all types of parenting difficulty according to whether children were placed with or without siblings, whether they were placed with established families and whether they were placed for adoption or long-term fostering. These factors tended to overlap in different ways and, for this reason, it is difficult to draw conclusions from these bivariate associations. For example, a high proportion of foster mothers had problems with aggression, a finding that runs contrary to the recent report of Gibbons and her colleagues (1995) who found that adoptive parents tended to be more aggressive than foster carers. However, there were very few foster placements in our sample, most foster families had other children at home and most had single children placed with them. Both placements into established families and singleton placements were associated with more parenting difficulties in our study. Thus the differences between fostering and adoption may have arisen because of other features of the placement patterns. In the analyses below we focus on the parenting difficulties shown in these singleton placements into established families.

Table 13.3 illustrates the extent of difficulties with responsiveness items at a month according to placement type. Parents of children placed alone with established families were more likely to be having difficulties with warmth, involvement and responsiveness. This was true both at the start of placement and at the end of the year. Differences also emerged for management and aggression by the end of the year. The differences in responsiveness were greater on emotional involvement with the child and expression of warmth. There was less of a contrast between the two groups with regard to sensitive responding. Perhaps it is not surprising

Table 13.3: Responsiveness problems at one month according to placement type

Problem with	Single with established family (%)	Other placement configuration (%)	Fisher's exact test ($p = $)
Emotional involvement	60	19	0.002
Expressed warmth	47	23	0.062
Sensitive responding	30	16	NS

NS: not significant.

that sensitive responding should present a profile different from the other two characteristics, since the descriptions of the items given above suggest that this may be more a characteristic of the parent, while emotional involvement and expressed warmth may take time to develop and be more influenced by interaction with and experience of the child.

Before concluding that these associations reflect some kind of necessary connection between placement type and parenting difficulties it is necessary to ask whether the associations can be explained by antecedent factors, especially those in the children's backgrounds and experiences. Maybe the links with placement type arise because children with different experiences and problems have gone into different types of placement, for whatever reason. This seems part of the explanation in this case. In particular, the majority of rejected children were placed singly with established families and this factor accounts for much of the difference in parenting by placement type, especially in relation to responsiveness difficulties (Table 13.4). Despite the low numbers in some cells, it seems clear that the experience of rejection was associated with lower parental responsiveness. However, this was not true for other parenting problems. Management problems were raised in the singleton/established family placements generally, not just in relation to the placement of rejected children. The same pattern was true for aggression where, if anything, the difference was more marked for the non-rejected group.

THE INTERACTION BETWEEN THE BEHAVIOUR OF PARENTS AND CHILDREN

Of course, rejection itself must operate through some features of behaviour and interactions, so it is next necessary to look more directly at the associations between placement type and behavioural problems. At one month the children's behaviour was only – but already – associated

Table 13.4: Differences in parenting difficulties according to placement configuration and the child's experience of rejection

	Proportion of parents with continuing or developing difficulties at a year		Significance
	Other placement type (%)	Alone, established family (%)	
Responsiveness			
Non-rejected children	43	38	NS
Rejected children	43	93	$\chi^2 = 6.4$, d.f. $= 1$, $p < 0.05$
Management			
Non-rejected children	26	39	NS
Rejected children	29	50	NS
Aggression			
Non-rejected children	4	31	$\chi^2 = 4.9$, d.f. $= 1$, $p < 0.05$
Rejected children	14	43	NS

NS: not significant.

with parents' responsiveness. By the end of the year overall behaviour scores and the total overactivity score were significantly associated with *all* types of parenting difficulties (Figure 13.1a). There appeared to be an association between parenting problems and changes in the children's behaviour. Where parents were without parenting difficulties by the end of the year, the children were significantly more likely to show an improvement in their behaviour but the children of parents who had continuing or increasing difficulties tended to develop more problems.

A similar pattern emerged on the EFQ (Figure 13.1b). Where parents were having difficulties, children failed to show the same level of improvement in the extent to which they expressed their feelings as those whose parents were coping better.

At first glance this might suggest that responsive parenting and appropriate management had led to an improvement in the children's behaviour. But we cannot conclude from these data that the direction of effects was from parent to child. Examining the *changes* in parenting behaviour over time we found that, although the groups were small, parents whose difficulties eased had children whose mean behaviour scores at a month were very similar to those of the parents whose children had never had any problems. In contrast, parents who developed problems had children whose mean scores were high at both 1 and 12 months. Table 13.5 shows

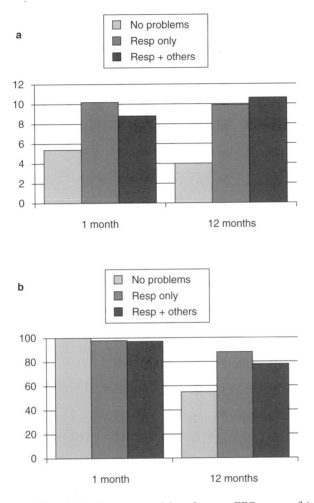

Figure 13.1: Mean behaviour scores (a) and mean EFQ scores (b) at 1 and 12 months according to parenting problems at 1 year. Group differences: Behaviour 1/12 $F = 5.2$ (2,54) $p < 0.01$; 12/12 $F = 8.4$ (2,54) $p < 0.001$; EFQ 1/12 NS; 12/12 $F = 6.7$ (2,54) $p < 0.005$. Resp: responsiveness

this with respect to responsiveness, but the pattern is similar for other types of parenting difficulty although the differences do not always reach significance.

These findings were reflected in the families' descriptions of the process of mutual adjustment. There were examples from the case records of families who were faced with only one or two major problems who managed to overcome these in time. Even there, a deliberate and

Table 13.5: Mean behaviour and overactivity scores according to change in parental responsiveness over the year

	Responsiveness problems over year				$F = ; p <$
	None ($n = 18$)	Improved ($n = 8$)	Developed ($n = 9$)	Continual ($n = 22$)	d.f. = 3,53
Behaviour score 1/12	5.8	4.0	8.9	9.9	4.4, 0.010
Overactivity sub-score 1/12	2.5	0.8	5.2	4.5	6.7, 0.001
Behaviour score 12/12	4.4	2.6	11.6	10.3	7.1, 0.001
Overactivity sub-score 12/12	2.1	1.1	4.7	4.4	5.2, 0.005

structured change of approach was sometimes needed. For example, one mother, who confessed to a stubborn streak herself, spent the first few months of placement embroiled in frequent and intense confrontations with her equally obstinate new son. However, these battles were always followed by reconciliation, hugs, apologies and explanations. Eventually, with the help of her husband, this mother was able to examine her own responses to her child's provocation and to make a deliberate effort to alter her own behaviour. It took her some time to settle into a habit of using non-confrontational strategies to control attention-seeking behaviours, but in time the effort paid off and, by the one year interview confrontations between mother and child were rare.

In other cases the behavioural difficulties that were evident at the start of the placement worsened through the course of the year. At first some parents were able to use their skills but, in time, their patience in doing so seems to have waned. For example, one family described in detail how they preferred to parent by negotiation: offering options, allowing choice and withdrawing privileges if sanctions were necessary. However, their new child was unused to such freedom and often abused it. His behaviour included determined opposition to his new parents, frequent and severe tantrums, overactivity and extreme rivalry with his new siblings. His new parents tried reasoning, ignoring, negotiating and offering rewards for good behaviour – all to no avail. Control episodes gradually became a shouting match. When asked to sum up the first year of placement, the new mother said it was 'like a whirlwind, a hurricane, . . . everybody's life has been taken by complete storm. I am amazed I am still standing'. These parents found their child unable to respond to attempts at reconciliation after confrontations and found it very difficult to establish boundaries or find effective sanctions and had not managed to do so even after a year.

REASONS FOR CONTINUING OR DEVELOPING DIFFICULTIES

There are two possible explanations for the association between increasing difficulties in the behaviour of children and parents: the first is that some of the parents were ill-prepared to take the child and failed to make the necessary adjustments to their approaches to parenting in order to accommodate the child's needs. A second interpretation is that the children themselves were unready for permanent family placement and failed to modify their behaviour, leading to a dissipation of the parents' energy to pursue strategies that would encourage positive change. We suggested earlier that the children's problems seemed to explain this association more than the parents'. However, the conclusion that the children's behaviour is a powerful factor does not mean that parental skills and capacities were not also implicated in the downward spirals. Nor does it mean that the associations between the type of placement and spiralling problems are unimportant. Parenting behaviour, as we discussed in Chapter 1, has to be seen within its context, not as a reflection of a quality that some people have and others do not.

At this point, therefore, we return to the relationship between behavioural problems and the type of placement. If this association were merely a reflection of the differential placement of more problematic children we would expect those placed singly into established families to show more difficulties. But, at one month into the placement this appeared not to be the case. Even the rejected children – who were differentially placed – were not showing more problems at this time. It seems that, while parenting difficulties were more likely in the presence of behavioural problems, the tendency for parents of children who joined established families on their own to have more difficulty than other placement types remained, even when the level of behavioural difficulties was taken into account (Table 13.6). This was particularly the case for expression of warmth and emotional involvement and was a pattern that was sustained throughout the year.

It is not difficult to suggest reasons why parenting difficulties should have been more common for parents who already had children at home. For example, parents who were previously without children might be expected to find special rewards in having children to care for and be more able to maintain warmth and responsiveness in the face of children's difficulties. Conversely, those who had parented before might expect techniques they had previously employed successfully to work with these children and might more easily become frustrated when they did not. It is also possible that the relationship between the placed children and other

Table 13.6: Parenting difficulties at one month according to placement type with regard to level of behavioural difficulties

Problem with	Behaviour problems at 1 month	Single with established family	Other placement types	Significance
Emotional	Few	57% (8/14)	27% (4/15)	NS
involvement	Many	63% (10/16)	13% (2/16)	$p < 0.01$
Expressed	Few	29% (4/14)	7% (1/15)	NS
warmth	Many	63% (10/16)	37% (6/16)	NS
Sensitive	Few	28% (4/14)	27% (4/15)	NS
responding	Many	31% (5/16)	6% (1/16)	NS

NS: not significant.

children in the family caused the parents difficulty and affected their tolerance, a factor discussed in Chapter 9.

THE IMPORTANCE OF PARENTING TO RELATIONSHIP DEVELOPMENT

It seems clear that parenting problems were associated with difficulties in the parents and children developing a mutually satisfying relationship. Responsiveness problems were associated with poorer expression of feelings by the child ($\chi^2 = 8.2$, d.f. $= 1$, $p < 0.01$) and poor attachment between the child and the new parents at a year ($\chi^2 = 18.7$, d.f. $= 1$, $p < 0.001$). The same was true for the other areas of parenting. Sixty-three per cent of placements where parents had continuing management problems showed little sign of the development of a mutually satisfying relationship, compared with 24% of placements where management did not appear to be an issue ($\chi^2 = 7.3$, d.f. $= 1$, $p < 0.02$). Problems with aggressive parenting were more likely in placements where relationships were slow in developing, although the difference did not reach statistical significance ($\chi^2 = 3.6$, d.f. $= 1$, $p = 0.076$).

PARENTING SKILLS AND OUTCOME MEASURES

As is clear from Figure 13.2, there was a tendency for the placement to be rated as less secure (see Chapter 3) and for behaviour to get worse when responsiveness was low. This association between outcome and parenting was even stronger when low responsiveness was associated with problems in the other areas of parenting. Possible models for the direction of these effects are explored further in Chapter 14.

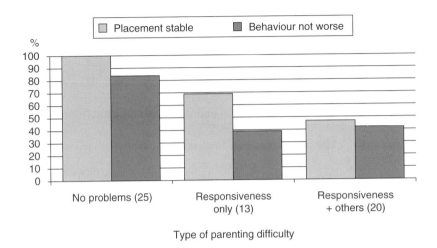

Figure 13.2: The association between parenting difficulties and outcome measures

PRACTICE IMPLICATIONS

The association between parenting difficulty and poorer outcomes should alert support workers to the importance of discussing and understanding the placement experiences of new families and to the need to explore alternative strategies both for managing challenging behaviour and for containing responses to that behaviour effectively.

There was a strong tendency for parents of children who had been actively rejected by their birth parents to be experiencing difficulties, particularly with showing warmth and sensitivity. It is possible that the experience of being rejected leads some children to act and react in a manner that reduces the likelihood of a warm parental response. It is important, therefore, for better assessments to be made prior to placement of the children's perception of their circumstances and ability to understand and live with their history. Parents may be better able to respond effectively to the children's behaviour if they are adequately informed and prepared. On the other hand, it must be admitted that research and specialist practice have not yet provided detailed guidance on handling these difficulties.

In this study we found differences in the level of parenting difficulties according to the type of placement, with the placement of single children into established families seeming particularly problematic. Rejected children were over-represented in these families but this did not seem to be the whole explanation. Explanations that are based on possible differences between experienced and inexperienced parents or on relationships with birth children seem plausible answers, but these findings would need to be replicated before strong conclusions are drawn. Nevertheless, in line with earlier research, it seems clear that an awareness of relationships with new siblings is essential. It is also possible that, when faced with unusually challenging behaviour, experienced parents may feel deskilled but find it hard to ask for help.

Outcomes were poorer when difficulties with parental responsiveness – which were relatively common among parents – were compounded by problems in management or aggression. Practitioners need to be aware of the difficulties new parents face in managing their child's behaviour effectively. Very often new parents bemoaned the fact that they knew they were not handling things in the best way, but they had run out of ideas. While their social workers were good at congratulating them for 'containing' difficult behaviour, they were of little help in suggesting other approaches when parents were having problems. For example, one mother mentioned having tried 'everything' to discourage bed-wetting. When asked to elaborate she mentioned no method that employed standard behaviour modification techniques.

It may be best to help parents focus on one or two aspects of behaviour that may be amenable to change in the short term and to provide ideas on strategies that may lead to that change. Once one aspect of behaviour shows signs of positive change, this may lead to wider improvements in the family's interaction.

Within this sample problems in parenting behaviour were generally apparent very early on in the placement and tended to persist or get worse. Our findings suggest that these issues should be addressed as soon as problems are noticed.

SUMMARY

In this chapter we have examined the parenting approaches of the new parents and found that, despite the aim of careful selection, training and matching of parents and children, around 60% of new parents were experiencing at least some difficulty with aspects of the parenting role. These problems were generally evident in the first month of the placement and tended to be persistent. The most common difficulties were in responsiveness, especially in emotional involvement and expressed warmth, but where there were problems with management or aggression as well, the likelihood of a poorer outcome increased substantially.

Poorer parenting was strongly associated with problems in the development of mutually satisfying relationships and also with the child's behaviour. It seems probable that the quality of the relationship is critical. Where this is satisfactory parents are better able to tolerate behavioural difficulties and handle them better.

Although the parenting characteristics of the majority of the sample were fairly stable, a minority of parents (around 13%) improved their techniques in the course of the year. The children placed with these parents tended to have a moderate level of behaviour difficulties at the start of the placement, which reduced further over the course of the year. A similar number of parents appeared to be overwhelmed and showed a decline in the quality of their parenting. Their children showed substantial problems at the start of the placement and these tended to get worse over the year. The implication is that where parents are rewarded by positive changes in their children's behaviour, parenting quality is maintained or improved and the children continue to recover. But where the behaviours are unaffected by the parents' efforts, the ability to feel warmly towards the child and continue with strategic approaches to manage behaviour seems to dissipate.

14

PREDICTING PLACEMENT STABILITY

It will be more than obvious from the preceding chapters that the processes leading to successful placements are exceedingly complex. For this reason it is not surprising that a multiplicity of theories have come and gone over the years as researchers and practitioners have wrestled with the problem of finding some consistent and stable predictors upon which to develop an approach to achieving permanence. Earlier studies focused mainly on the predictors of placement disruption: for example the characteristics of the new parents and their families, questions of family structure, the ages of the placed and birth children and the parents' motives in seeking to adopt.

As we pointed out in Chapter 1, attention has begun to move beyond the simple question of placement continuance or stability towards a concern with long-term outcomes. These include issues of social adjustment as well as questions of identity, cultural heritage and integration, especially in the case of trans-racial placements (Rushton & Minnis, 1997). As part of this new focus academics and practitioners have begun to consider such issues as the match between the children and the new parents but, so far, the results have been disappointing. Uncovering a consistent set of matching criteria has proved very hard to achieve, leading one group of experts to conclude that 'there is no substantive research about matching of children and families, and there are many different opinions about what is important' (Triseliotis *et al.*, 1997).

As the population of children thought to need a permanent alternative family comes increasingly to comprise those who are older and mal-treated, it has become clear that the problems they bring with them will not simply go away if they are given enough love and attention. In this period, when we are short of consistent research-based knowledge, it is easy to be swayed by some new approach that seems to offer an answer to previously intractable difficulties. Such 'answers' may, for example, focus on the parenting capacities and behaviours of the new parents, as if the success or failure of placements was mostly a consequence of their ability and resilience in managing problematic behaviours. Alternatively, a substantial part of the difficulties that arise in late placements may be seen as lying in a range of intractable psychosocial disorders associated with the children's early experiences, sometimes with all these being taken under the umbrella of 'disorders of attachment'.

All these factors seem likely to play a part but there are good reasons for arguing for caution as each new explanation or hypothesised major factor comes to our attention. This is an exceedingly difficult field in which to undertake systematic research studies or to choose appropriate comparison groups, let alone to plan interventions and to investigate these through controlled trials. Samples are often either small and potentially biased in various ways or large and based on data of variable consistency and quality. Studies that provide new insights can too easily be treated as 'breakthroughs', forgetting that any particular piece of research tends to 'capitalise on chance' and can produce seemingly important predictors that are not replicated in further research. For example, our pilot study found a significant association between certain early experiences and poorer outcomes, which was not repeated in the current study. This does not mean that these factors are unimportant. The lack of replication may be due to variations in practice, policy or sample characteristics across different locations and different points in time.

The factors predicting successful and stable placements have remained elusive. Moreover, even for those factors that have been more consistently shown to be related to placement instability, the *processes* linking the factor and the risk have not been the subject of much systematic research. For example, it is clear that the child's age at the time of placement is very important, with the risk of disruption increasing with age. It also seems clear that the presence of the new parents' own children, especially if they are close in age to the placed children, can be a complicating factor. Nevertheless, we know much less about *why* these factors are risks. Until we know more, placement policy, matching and post-placement support will depend on informed speculations rather than on an understanding of the processes of stability and instability.

With these caveats in mind, we want, in this chapter, to go beyond the examination of single predictors to model the processes influencing the security of these placements at the end of the first year, taking into account the most important factors identified in our earlier chapters. Bivariate analyses give a good indication of what the important factors might be but it is not possible to weigh their relative contributions if we only examine them on their own. Problems can easily arise when factors that appear to be strong predictors of outcome are highly correlated. Because of this it is necessary to consider the factors together in order to come to some conclusion about which is the most influential of them and whether the apparent effect of one is explained away by its association with the other. Multivariate analyses are an important aid in deciding which factors are most influential and what the relationships between them are. This is not simply a mechanical application of statistical procedures. It is necessary to follow the arguments through and to test alternative explanations for associations. There is an art in drawing conclusions from multivariate analyses.

CHOICE OF OUTCOME MEASURE

We decided to choose the measure of placement stability/instability, outlined in Chapter 3, as the outcome to model. There were good reasons for choosing this. First, it was clear (Chapter 8) that the changes in the children's emotional and behavioural problems were relatively slight and involved both improvement and deterioration. This complex picture made it impossible reliably to model changes in behaviour in a small sample over the year. Secondly, it seemed likely that future improvements in the children's psychosocial functioning would be quite strongly related to whether the placements became stable and secure. Thirdly, the development of a secure placement is of the greatest importance to the families, the children and the placing agencies in the short term. Finally, disentangling some of the threats to stability in the early stages of placement is likely to offer important clues on matching, on learning what parents need to know and on how to focus post-placement support.

THE ASSESSMENT OF THE STABILITY OF PLACEMENTS

The assessment of placement security was set out in Chapter 3 but it is useful briefly to review it here. Two features seemed especially pertinent to this: the parents' view of the quality of their relationship with their new child – especially whether they were becoming attached to each other – and whether the parents were satisfied with the child as part of the family. Both of these measures were interviewer judgements based on the parents' judgements. The way in which these were combined was described in Chapter 3. Of course, these judgements were not simple. In the first place there were usually two parents and often other birth or placed children. Then attachments may not have developed equally: sometimes parents may have felt connected with the child when he or she did not seem to be developing similar feelings towards them, and vice versa. We did not have the children's own views on this but it seemed reasonable to rely on the parents' accounts, since their feelings were likely to be a major determinant of whether the placement became threatened or not.

A binary summary variable, which took account of both of these elements, was computed. A clear account from the parents of either the development of a positive relationship between them and the child or their satisfaction with the placement was sufficient for the placement to be categorised as 'more stable'. Thus, placements described as 'less stable' showed little sign of a good relationship developing with either parent and low levels of parent satisfaction. Using this classification, 72% of placements were considered to be relatively secure (the 'stable' group) and 28% less secure (the 'less stable' group). The remainder of this chapter is concerned with the factors and processes that led to the children being in one or other group.

RISKS TO STABILITY

The first task was to review which characteristics of the children, the parents and the placement were related to stability at the end of the first year. These factors are shown in Table 14.1, grouped under four headings relating to the children's previous experiences, the structure of the placements, the children's psychosocial adjustment early in the placement; and the parents' characteristics and parenting approaches. The data on these variables have been presented in earlier chapters. Here we summarise the significance of the associations only. The first column shows the association of these variables as measured at one month, with placement insecurity at one year. They can thus be read as the *predictors* of security. The second column shows the association between these factors as measured at 12 months and outcome. At this point they are *correlates* of security. Of course, those factors that cannot change – such as the number of previous placements – will be related to outcome in the same way at both points in time.

The Child's Characteristics and Experiences

It is important first to note those features of the children's characteristics and previous experiences that were *not* related to stability of placement. These included: gender, ethnicity, age at current and first placement, the number of placement moves, and physical or sexual abuse. It should not

Table 14.1: One month predictors and 12 month correlates of stability at one year

Factor	1 month predictors	12 month correlates
Child's background		
Gender	NS	NS
Ethnicity	NS	NS
Age at first placement	NS	NS
Age at current placement	NS	NS
Total number of moves	NS	NS
Physical abuse	NS	NS
Sexual abuse	NS	NS
Rejection by birth parent(s)	**	**
Placement factors		
Placed on own	*	*
Placed into an established family	*	*
Age of new parents	NS	NS
Social class	NS	NS
Child's behaviour		
Total symptom score	*	***
Emotional problems	NS	***
Oppositional/conduct problems	NS	***
Overactivity/restlessness	***	***
Parenting		
Management/control problems	NS	***
Problems in responsiveness	**	***

NS: not statistically significant. $* p < 0.05$; $** p < 0.01$; $*** p < 0.001$.

be concluded from this that the markedly adverse experiences in this list did not have serious effects on the children. Rather, the lack of association reflected the fact that the *majority* of the children in our sample had very poor experiences of one kind or another, all of these finally leading to a decision to find them permanent alternative families. The findings simply mean that *within* this sample these features were not major determinants of placement stability. However, one feature of their early experiences *was* strongly predictive: the placements of children who had been rejected by their birth parents (see Chapter 4) were much less likely to be rated as stable.

Placement Factors

A number of demographic characteristics of the new parents and families did not appear to be influential. These included the age of the new parents (these fell within a usual range for adopters), ethnicity, adoptive versus foster placements and social class. There were only four lone parents, too few for statistical comparisons with two parent families, but examination of the individual cases gave no suggestion that single parenting led to more problems.

However, two features of the structure of placements *did* predict lower placement stability: the placement of children on their own and placement into established families. These two factors tended to co-occur so that it was difficult to determine which was the more influential – we especially lacked examples of the placement of sibling groups within established families – but we attempt to draw some conclusions on the relative importance of these two factors in the multivariate analyses. As far as we could tell the *relative* ages of birth and placed children were not an explanation of the increased instability in established families: these placements tended to be more problematic *regardless* of the age structure of the new family.

Initial Emotional and Behavioural Problems

Chapter 8 has highlighted the high levels of emotional and behavioural problems one month into the placement. It is important, therefore, to note the ways in which these were related to placement stability. The extent of emotional or conduct problems were *not* predictive on their own; the *overall* count of symptomatic behaviours was a *weak* predictor, but the level of overactive, restless and distractible behaviour a *very strong* one.

By the end of the year all these measures of emotional and behavioural problems were strongly related to greater placement instability. This could have arisen either because the measures better differentiated those with more persistent problems from those with more transitory adjustment difficulties by this point or because the failure of attachments and parental satisfaction to develop led to an exacerbation of the children's difficulties or because a diminution of problems went along with the development of attachments and satisfaction.

Parenting Behaviours

The final set of predictors involved the parenting approaches of the new parents. The two summary dimensions – responsivity and management or control techniques – were described in Chapter 13. Management/

control approaches at one month were not predictive of stability at one year, but the interviewers' assessments of the degree of responsiveness in parenting were. By the end of the year management/control difficulties had become strongly associated with insecurity. It should be remembered that the majority of placements (72%) were considered to be stable at one year. For those that were not the picture was apparently one of increasing parental irritation and diminished control associated with a perpetuation or increase in overt problems in the children, in the context of a failure of the development of affection and attachment between them and their new parents.

PROCESSES OF INSTABILITY

In this section we begin to weigh the relative importance of these factors and try to uncover some of the processes that led to this unhappy state of affairs. There are a number of important questions: for example, did the type of placement actually influence the level of stability or did the association arise simply because established families took on more difficult children, for whatever reason? Did rejection increase the risk of instability through its association with identifiable problems or did it appear to carry an additional risk over and above the emotional and behavioural problems we measured?

A preliminary look at the way things might have worked can be taken by examining the intercorrelations between these predictor variables at one month (Table 14.2). These correlations suggest that the relationship between instability and placement in established families may, indeed, partly be explained because rejected and overactive children – these factors were strongly correlated – were somewhat more likely to be placed with these families. However, this link did not explain the association between established families and lower responsiveness. Responsiveness was significantly, if weakly, correlated with the total count of symptoms but not significantly related to any of the other main predictors at one month (column F), including rejection and overactive/restless behaviour, which was one of the strongest predictors of instability. This means that it was improbable that the lower responsiveness observed in established families was the result of the differential placement of more problematic children.

It should be noted from the correlations that rejected children were more likely to be placed on their own – which is not surprising since they were rejected – and somewhat more likely to be placed in established

Table 14.2: Intercorrelations between the main predictors (product moment correlations)

	A	B	C	D	E	F
A. Rejected	—					
B. Symptom score	0.22 (0.08)	—				
C. Overactivity score	0.30 (0.02)	0.80 (0.00)	—			
D. Placed on own	0.46 (0.00)	0.10 (NS)	0.02 (NS)	—		
E. Established family	0.24 (0.06)	0.02 (NS)	0.14 (NS)	0.57 (0.00)	—	
F. Parental responsiveness	0.13 (NS)	0.26 (0.04)	0.22 (NS)	0.22 (NS)	0.38 (0.00)	—

Figures in brackets are significance levels. NS: not significant.

families than non-rejected children. The strong association between rejection and overactive/restless behaviour suggested that these behaviours might, indeed, have been a mediating factor between rejection and poorer outcomes. These associations might, again, have explained the relationship between singleton placements and less stable placements.

Multivariate Analyses

There are limits to the kinds of explanations that can be developed from an examination of these correlations. It is easy to propose a range of plausible models from these associations but not to decide which explanations are the more likely. In order to do this it is necessary to use multivariate analyses to try to understand the ways in which these important predictors worked. Of course, a sample of 61 – including 3 cases that had already disrupted by the one year point – provided only limited scope for this kind of analysis. Sample size was the main reason for using a simple 'yes/no', or *binary*, measure of instability.

Logistic regression was an appropriate method to use for assessing the probability that the children will fall into one or other of these outcome groups and it allowed us to consider the key predictors together in order to assess their relative importance. We used the following variables in this analysis: rejection of the child by birth parents; the overall symptom count; the level of overactive, restless behaviour; placement of the child on his/her own; placement in an established family; and parental responsiveness. That is, we were looking specifically at those one month predictors that appeared related to the security of the placement at the end of the first year. Clearly, we could not use as predictors those variables that only became associated with insecurity at the end of the year because they might themselves have been outcomes. On the other hand, the increasingly strong relationships between the children's behaviour and difficulties in parenting confirmed that our rating of placement insecurity did, indeed, reflect worsening parent–child relationships. This illustrates the advantages of a prospective design, even if it is only over a one year period.

Table 14.3 summarises the result of entering these variables into a logistic regression analysis with stability/instability of placement as the binary outcome variable. In these analyses the prediction is to *instability* and the independent variables coded so as to reflect the direction of their effect. Thus an increase in the odds ratio above one indicates that the factor increased the risk of instability when the effects of the other variables are taken into account, and an odds ratio below one indicates a

Table 14.3: Predictors of placement stability: logistic regression

Factor	Range	Beta	Significance	Odds	95% Confidence interval
Overactivity	0–10	0.357	0.005	1.43	1.10–1.94
Singleton placement	0–1	1.73	0.06	5.67	0.93–65.08
Unresponsive parenting	0–1	1.24	0.18	3.46	0.63–19.88

reduction in risk. The general approach in such analyses is to attempt to uncover the most parsimonious model, that is the one that predicts the outcome variable using as few variables as necessary. Fitting such a model in SPSS (Statistical Package for the Social Sciences) using backward selection – a process that starts with all the variables in the model and then evaluates each to see whether its removal would make the fit significantly worse – resulted in three variables being considered as unnecessary to predict instability. These were: the overall symptom count, being placed in an established family and the experience of rejection. The variables that provided the best fitting model were: overactive/restless behaviour, singleton placement and low parental responsiveness.

Because of the small sample size the parameter estimates and odds ratios were checked using the LogXact programme (Mehta & Mehta, 1993) and these are the values given in the table. It should be noted that the confidence intervals for the odds ratios for singleton placement and parental unresponsiveness were very wide. This means that we should be cautious about interpreting the *size* of these effects, even though the modelling shows that the variables are influential. That is, we can conclude that the variables were predictors of outcome but we should be less confident about saying by how much they increased the risk.

Did the results of this first analysis mean that the type of placement and the experience of rejection were unimportant? It was too early to conclude this, but the analysis did suggest that the link between these risks and placement instability arose through their association with the factors that were retained in the model, rather than through direct effects. It was not easy to know what to make of the continuing strong effects of singleton placements. This factor was strongly related to rejection and to placement in established families and may have masked the effects of both those variables. Of course, singleton placements may have been a risk factor in their own right, although this seems counterintuitive. However, in order to explore these associations further we refitted the model omitting singleton placement, to see whether rejection

Table 14.4: Predictors of placement stability: excluding singleton placement

Factor	Range	Beta	Significance	Odds	95% Confidence interval
Rejection	0–1	1.43	0.069	4.18	0.91–22.11
Overactivity	1–10	0.26	0.052	1.30	1.00–1.74
Unresponsive parenting	0–1	1.60	0.065	4.20	0.92–30.99

and placement in an established family would be evaluated differently. Omitting singleton placements did, indeed, result in the retention of rejection in the model. On the other hand, placement in an established family and the overall symptom count were still dropped. Table 14.4 provides the exact parameter estimates and odds ratios.

This analysis suggested that the association between instability and established family placements arose because of the tendency for rejected and overactive children to be placed in these families and because the parents tended to be less responsive. Of course, the converse is also true: placement in established families was not a risk when the children were not especially problematic or when responsiveness was not compromised. In addition, the retention of rejection, overactivity and responsiveness in the model meant that these factors remained as risks over and above the type of placement. We were not able in this dataset to go any further in analysis of the importance, or otherwise, of singleton placements. Different samples in which sibling and singleton placements are more equally represented in child-free and established families are needed for this.

It may be concluded from this analysis that placement in an established family was not itself a risk to stability but arose because of the confluence between it and other risks. It was not possible from a single sample to know whether this coming-together of factors was unique to this study or whether it reflected some more general pattern. For example, the association between established families and lower responsiveness might have been a happenstance of the emotional match between parents and children in our study, rather than a reflection of a predictable tendency for these parents to be less responsive, perhaps because of conflicts in their own minds between the care of their new and their established children. However, the latter might also have been so. It would not be unreasonable for social workers to presume that parents with children of their own would have a better idea of how to deal with very troubled children than those who had never parented before, whereas the opposite might be true.

LINKING THE RISKS

Although there were limits to the conclusions that could be drawn about singleton placements and placements into established families, it was possible to make more progress concerning the processes leading to instability and especially the role of rejection, overactivity and lack of parental responsiveness in this process.

As we have already pointed out, lower responsiveness at one month was *not* associated with rejection or overactive behaviour. That is, lower responsiveness was not simply a consequence of dealing with those kinds of difficulties. The inference from this was that responsiveness was likely to be important through the ways in which it interacted with the children's problems, maybe through exacerbating rather than attenuating them. Of course, this could not be the only explanation since the multivariate models showed that rejection and overactivity remained as risks even when responsiveness was taken into account. Nevertheless, the link between responsiveness and instability was an important one and we examined that next.

The first question was whether the level of responsiveness was a relatively stable feature of parental behaviour or whether it changed over the year and, if it did, what predicted the change. The answer to the first of these questions was that responsiveness was, indeed, a stable characteristic. The correlation between the measures at one month and one year was significant (rho = 0.46, $p < 0.001$).

We checked whether the level of responsiveness at one year was influenced by the other main predictors. A logistic regression analysis was performed with responsiveness at 12 months as the dependent variable and responsiveness at 1 month, rejection, overactivity and placement in an established family as predictors.

Only two of these were significant predictors of responsiveness at 12 months: rejection by birth parents and responsiveness at 1 month, which was by far the strongest predictor. These data are given in Table 14.5. We concluded from this first that responsiveness was, indeed a stable characteristic, but that there may also have been something about the behaviour and interaction style of the rejected children that led to lowered responsiveness in the long run.

Table 14.5: Predictors of responsiveness at 12 months

Factor	Range	Beta	Significance	Odds	95% Confidence interval
Responsiveness at 1 month	0–1	2.24	0.003	9.36	1.91–59.60
Rejection	0–1	1.49	0.04	4.44	1.03–23.13

The Effects of Responsiveness

The next question was whether responsiveness had a positive effect through containing or reducing problems or whether its absence led to a worsening of difficulties or whether its effect on stability operated through a different route, maybe because it reflected greater parental resilience. We looked at this first by examining whether the most predictive of the children's problems and experiences – rejection and overactive/restless behaviour – appeared to be modified by the presence of responsive parenting. For this analysis overactivity was dichotomised.

Figures 14.1a and 14.1b give the results of this analysis. These two risks were related to security of placement in similar ways depending on the presence of responsive parenting. Where rejection or overactivity was *not* present less responsive parenting made no statistically significant difference to the outcome, but it did if the children had been rejected or were overactive. When these problems were part of the picture but parenting was responsive, the placements were nearly as secure as when the children did not have these problems. However, if both less-responsive parenting *and* overactivity or rejection were present the outcome was poor. The numbers in these cells were small but the differences are nevertheless striking and statistically significant. When parenting was less responsive only 12% of the rejected children and *none* of the overactive children were rated as secure compared with 68% and 75% with responsive parenting.

The next part of this story was to ask whether more responsive parenting had this effect through leading to a diminution of problems or whether the effects on placement stability arose primarily through the greater persistence and commitment of responsive parents. By definition the more stable placements were characterised by developing attachments and by greater parental satisfaction, but were these desirable outcomes developing in the teeth of ongoing problems or as part of a

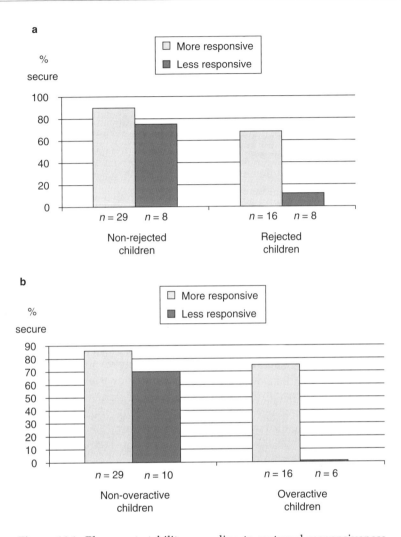

Figure 14.1: Placement stability according to maternal responsiveness.
(a) Rejected and non-rejected children. Group differences: not rejected: NS;
rejected children: $p = 0.03$, Fisher's exact test. (b) Overactive and non-overactive
children. Group differences: non-overactive: NS; overactive children: $p = 0.003$,
Fisher's exact test

pattern of diminishing ones? This is an important question for two
reasons: first, it may indicate that responsiveness promoted improvement on all fronts but, secondly, if it did not affect the level of disturbed
behaviour it is important evidence that attachments had developed in
the face of difficulties.

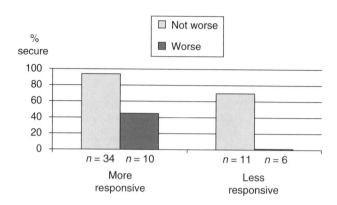

Figure 14.2: Placement stability, direction of behavioural change and maternal responsiveness. Group differences: more responsive: $p = 0.002$; less responsive: $p = 0.01$, Fisher's exact test

Figure 14.2 shows how this seemed to work. Here we used the ratings of whether behaviour got better or worse over the year, as described in Chapter 3. Lower responsiveness did appear to make some difference to whether problem behaviours got worse, although this was not statistically significant. (A similar analysis showed that responsiveness made little difference to improvement in behaviour.) On the other hand, the analysis *did* suggest that higher parental responsiveness was associated with more stable placements even when behaviour became more difficult. When the children had low or diminishing levels of difficulty, parental responsiveness was not an important factor in placement stability. On the other hand, responsiveness *did* make a difference to the stability of the placement when worsening behaviour was part of the picture. There were six placements where responsiveness was low at one month and where behaviour worsened over the year and none of these were rated as stable at a year. In contrast, of the 11 placements where responsiveness was higher, nearly half (46%) were stable despite worsening behaviour. We concluded that responsive parenting had its effect over the first year of placement by increasing parental resilience rather than by reducing children's problems.

However, there was one final critical question to be asked. This was whether the effect of responsive parenting on stability was *just* through its effect on resilience – as reflected in the parents' satisfaction with the placement – or whether the development of attachments between the parents and the children was also facilitated by more responsive parenting. This is important because, if it were so, it would show that it led to

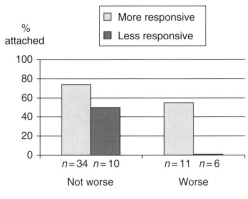

Figure 14.3: Child's attachment and behavioural change according to maternal responsiveness. Group differences: not worse: NS; behaviour worse: $p = 0.04$, Fisher's exact test

the development of attachments even when emotional and behavioural problems were present.

In order to examine this we constructed a dichotomous measure of whether the *child* was becoming attached to one or both parents. This seemed the most stringent test of whether parental responsiveness had an impact on the children's developing relationships, even if it seemed to have little effect on other aspects of behaviour.

This analysis is shown in Figure 14.3. Over half (55%) of the responsive parents whose children's behaviour got worse reported that the children were becoming attached to them, whereas *none* of the less responsive parents in this group did so. There were also fewer attachments reported by the less responsive parents than by the responsive ones even when the children's behaviour did not worsen, although this difference (50% v. 74%) was not statistically significant.

The overall conclusion on the role of responsiveness would be that it was related to the security of placement in two ways: first by its association with parental resilience but secondly through its relationship to the development of the children's attachments. The important conclusion from the last analysis was that responsiveness was able to have this effect on attachment even though it did not have a noticeable effect on the children's emotional and behavioural problems over the first year.

REVIEW OF RISKS TO STABILITY

Following through these analyses has inevitably been complex. The small sample size limited the extent to which multivariate analyses could be used and made it impossible to test for interactions between variables. Instead we had to return to bi- and trivariate analyses to explore some of the associations. It was important to do this to try to reach some conclusions about the ways in which the risks operated, rather than to rely on plausible speculation.

In this section we summarise our conclusions on the mode of operation of the various major risk indicators. As we have emphasised, there were limits to what could be concluded from this small representative sample; some comparisons were not possible because particular groups, for example sibling groups placed in established families, were not represented in sufficient numbers. In addition, a number of the factors overlapped quite strongly so it was important to try to decide which seemed to be the most important. Finally it must be emphasised that our conclusions are based on averaged or grouped effects. That is, it should not be concluded that the presence of a factor or factors necessarily means a poorer outcome. Rather, their presence increases the *risk* in a number of ways, some of which we have tried to disentangle, but the important point is to try to understand how they operated in this sample and to form some judgement on whether they reflect more general processes.

Type of Placement

The first risks concerned two features of the structure of the placements, namely the placement of children on their own and the placement of children into established families. Both of these factors were associated with lower placement stability and tended to occur together, that is the risk appeared to apply to single children placed in established families. Because these factors overlapped strongly it was not possible to decide whether singleton placements carried any especial risk or whether this was due to their association with factors in the children's backgrounds and behaviour. It was not hard to construct possible explanations of the risks associated with placement in established families: maybe parents with their own children at home experienced more conflict in their own minds because of problems in helping the new children and supporting the established ones; maybe the birth children themselves created additional stresses through their reactions to the placed children; or maybe these experienced parents were more set in their ways and expectations and were less able to adapt to the new children's needs; or maybe the children already in the home were seen by the placed children as barriers to forming close relationships with the parents.

The association between established family placement and lower responsiveness in parenting provided some indirect support for the first and third of these hypotheses, but it was necessary first to check whether the association between placement type and responsiveness and between both of these and lower placement security was simply a consequence of more experienced parents taking on more problematic children. This proved to be an important part of the explanation: parents with established families were more likely to have children placed with them who were overactive and restless and who had been rejected by their own parents. But, although this explained part of the association between this type of placement and lower security it did not explain it all. Parents of established families tended to be less responsive in their parenting and this was *not* explained by the kinds of children they took. Responsiveness had an important part to play in the story and this is summarised below. However, it is important to point out that the majority (60%) of established families were responsive in their parenting style and that lower responsiveness was a risk regardless of the family type in which it occurred. We were not able to tell from this single study whether these associations between established families, lower responsiveness and lower placement stability were specific to our study or whether they reflected more general patterns. If they are a reflection of more general patterns then they are, in part, a consequence of the placement process and, perhaps, mistaken assumptions by practitioners in the matching process.

Rejection of the Child by Birth Parents

The emergence of rejection by birth parents as a major risk to the security of placements was one of the strong and unexpected findings from this study. Once again, it was not difficult to think up plausible explanations for this association: rejected children are likely to have had particularly bad family experiences even in comparison with their maltreated peers who formed the rest of our sample. In addition, rejection would seem to be a particularly hard experience to come to terms with. The knowledge, in most cases, that there were brothers and sisters who stayed at home could feed both resentment and a sense that the rejection was in some way the child's own fault. Many maltreated children hold

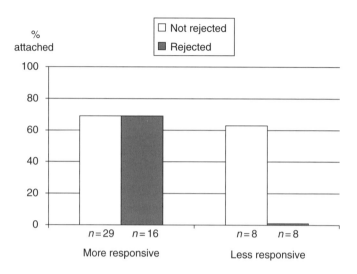

Figure 14.4: Rejection, maternal responsiveness and child's attachment.
Group differences: more responsive: NS; less responsive: $p = 0.026$,
Fisher's exact test

this belief about themselves, but for rejected children it is given the most striking and clear-cut confirmation. Chapter 9 showed how the rejected children were different from the rest of the sample on a number of psychosocial dimensions. A key question, therefore, was whether this experience had its effect through these measurable differences or whether it carried some additional risk, perhaps through a more marked effect on the child's potential for establishing attached relationships.

The first conclusion was that rejection appeared to lead to placement insecurity partly through its association with overactive and restless behaviour. The second was that rejection was not a significant predictor of whether a child would form new attachments, although there was a tendency in this direction (46% v. 68%). The next step, therefore, was to check whether rejection was a predictor of poorer attachments once symptomatic behaviour and parental responsiveness were taken into account. The answer was that it was not. Rather, rejection seemed to work, in this sample through identifiable psychosocial difficulties in conjunction with lowered parental responsiveness. On the other hand, rejection *did* appear to make the children more vulnerable to less sensitive parenting (Figure 14.4). Because rejected children tended to be differentially placed into circumstances where lowered responsiveness was more likely, their risk of poorer outcomes was increased.

Symptomatic Behaviours

The analyses relating to the children's emotional and behavioural difficulties led to a number of conclusions. First, the overall level of disturbance as assessed at one month, and especially the extent of overactive and restless behaviours, were clear predictors of placement instability. Moreover, emotional and behavioural problems were more strongly associated with instability at a year, indicating the influence of continuing or increasing adjustment problems on the stability of the placement. Secondly, these behavioural features were *not* modified by whether parenting was responsive or not. Sensitive parenting appeared to have little effect on whether problems diminished or got worse. Finally, the worsening of problems did not imply that the children were not forming attachments to their new parents. On the other hand, this latter process did appear to be influenced by the style of parenting, one of the findings summarised in the last section.

Parenting Behaviour

The final important set of predictors concerned the parenting approach of the new parents at one month. Two features were examined: the degree of sensitivity or responsiveness in handling the children's problems and in interactions with them and the extent of difficulties in control and management. Problems in the latter were not predictive of poorer outcomes, although they appeared with increasing frequency in those families where the placement was not going well. Problems in responsiveness, on the other hand, were often evident early in the placement, persisted strongly through it, and were related to lower placement stability in complex ways. As with other risk factors, the influence of lower responsiveness depended on whether it came together with other risks, rather than as a once-and-for-all effect. It was not possible to know whether responsiveness was a feature of the parents' general style or whether it arose because of particular circumstances. The different issues for established families suggested some possible routes to lower responsiveness but its early appearance and persistence in many cases suggested that it was also a reflection of personal style and circumstances rather than simply a rapid response to the children. The latter seemed unlikely because none of the other risk factors predicted responsiveness at one month.

How did lower responsiveness become a risk? The simplest answer to this is that it did *not* work by increasing the children's overt emotional and behavioural difficulties. Rather it appeared to increase the risk of instability by influencing the re-attachment process in the most troubled children. The lack of attachment and its attendant rewards for parents exacerbated the effects of other behaviours. This was particularly striking in the context of rejection (Figure 14.4). Children who were not rejected showed similar levels of attachment, regardless of whether the parenting was more or less sensitive. However, the style of parenting seemed more critical for the rejected children. Those with sensitive parenting showed levels of attachment comparable to those of the non-rejected (69%). However, *none* of the rejected children who were faced with less sensitive parenting were reported as becoming attached. Once again it was not lower responsiveness on its own that caused difficulties, it was the *combination* of lower responsiveness and particular vulner-abilities that markedly increased the risk.

It is, of course, important to reiterate the point made in Chapter 13 about the importance of context in parenting. A rating of lower responsiveness should in no way be taken as suggesting that these parents were parenting inadequately or lacked commitment to their children. The rating simply reflects the fact that some were less able than others to respond to the children in a sensitive way.

CHECK ON THE EFFECTS OF MISSING DATA

In Chapter 2 we discussed the possibility that our findings might be biased by differences between those families who agreed to take part and those who refused or were prevented from taking part in the study. The most important possible biases were those concerned with the interaction between singleton placements, rejection by birth parents and the parent-ing experience of the new families. The data were sufficient to allow a check on these. The non-participating families were somewhat less likely to have taken single children and therefore, not surprisingly, there was also a lower incidence of rejection in this group (23% of children in non-participants compared with 36% in the interviewed sample). However, when the comparison is restricted to singly placed children the rate of rejection experiences is similar (40% in non-participants and 51% in the sample). Rejected children in the non-participating families were also more likely to be placed with experienced parents and their place-ments were more likely to disrupt. Three of the five rejected children, all of whom were placed with experienced parents did so, as opposed to two of 16 placements of non-rejected children. Thus we can say with reasonable confidence that the main study findings were unlikely to be substantially different had all eligible cases taken part.

PRACTICE IMPLICATIONS

The implications of these analyses are important not only for practice but also for our models of the influences on placement security more generally. The most important analytic point is that it is essential to move away from explanations that take risk factors or indicators as representing some relatively invariant influence and to move towards models in which the risks are assessed together and in context. Of course, this is the way that practitioners and clinicians would claim to work, but it is surprising how often the risks are thought of as invariant in their effects even when we have no data on their mode of operation. For example, the relative ages of placed and birth children is often treated in this way, as is the age at placement. This is not to say that risks can simply be ignored in certain contexts but rather to argue that it should be possible to understand better the circumstances in which they are likely to be especially problematic and those in which they may be tolerated.

The second implication is that the combination of factors that may lead to difficulties can, if these findings are replicated, be identified early on in the placement and probably at a time when some help and support could be beneficial. These most notably include experiences of rejection from the birth family and high levels of overactive and restless behaviour. These seem particularly problematic when the children are cared for by parents with a pragmatic no-nonsense style of parenting. As yet we are short of good methods of assessment of key elements of parenting and of children's difficulties. Undoubtedly some children have such severe levels of disturbance following their early adversities that only specialist or highly supported environments can be expected to care for them. However, this was not the case for the great majority of those in our sample. Rather, many difficulties arose because of a mismatch between parents' style and children's needs. Our data points towards some potentially fruitful avenues for enquiry.

15

IMPLICATIONS FOR PRACTICE, POLICY, MANAGEMENT AND THE LAW

When we came to write the conclusions to our first study in this series (Rushton *et al.*, 1988) we were struck by the complexity of research into placement outcomes and recognised that we remained very far from possessing the kind of knowledge that could be used as a rule of thumb for making placement decisions and trying to secure placements. Both these observations remain true, although we should like to think that the current study has tackled some of these complexities and increased the amount of evidence about late placements in a way that has relevance and utility for practitioners and policy-makers.

We intended in this study to shift the focus away from infant placements onto children placed in middle childhood from the care system. Our findings therefore relate only to these older children, to their new parents and to the professional help provided for them. It is important, therefore, that the conclusions drawn here are not stretched and applied inappropriately to different samples.

We have divided this chapter into four sections: the first summarises the findings about pre-placement experiences for families and children; the second explores the post-placement phase for the new families including the placed children. In each of these sections we draw attention to areas that require some consideration of current policy and practice. The third section addresses management issues arising from the study findings and the final section examines implications for child care law.

PRE-PLACEMENT ISSUES FOR CHILDREN REQUIRING PLACEMENT

Pre-placement Delays

It was clear that despite 'permanency planning', there was still a considerable amount of drift for some of the sample children prior to this study. This was particularly noticeable for children who were not with their birth families for reasons of inadequate parenting or parental ill health. While these circumstances pose a dilemma for practitioners, some serious concern must be voiced when repeated attempts at rehabilitation cease to be in the child's best interests. A further problem that was noted was the frequency of delays that were due to the legal process.

The Impact of the Children's Previous Experiences on Placement Outcome

Within this sample, there were no differences in patterns of placement outcome according to the number of placements the children had experienced nor the length of time they had been 'looked after'. Neither were there any differences according to conventional definitions of neglect or physical and sexual abuse. This is not to conclude that abuse does not have serious effects, only that, as this was almost entirely a maltreated/ rejected sample, differences in outcome are less likely to be revealed.

However, marked differences in outcome did occur for children who had been singled out and rejected by their birth parent/s. This affected about a third of the sample children and a high proportion of these children were making poor progress after a year in their new family. They had not formed strong attachments, did not easily return affection and lacked genuineness in expression of feeling. This clearly caused more stress to the new parents. It may be that the experience of rejection leads to particular difficulties in later relationships and it is important to discover whether, in time, they largely disappear with accepting and stable parenting. This study was planned with the expectation of further follow-up, which is currently being conducted and may contribute to our understanding of the longer-term outcome.

This finding argues for a thorough assessment of children's early experiences and for appropriate therapeutic work to be done with the child before and during the permanent placement. Extra consideration should be given to the children's experience of rejection and how they have reacted to it. We now turn to the preparation programme for bringing together the child and the new parents.

PRE-PLACEMENT PREPARATION AND INFORMATION GIVING

The Child Social Worker's Preparation of the Child for Placement

The work conducted with children prior to placement to effect a smooth transition to the new family and to address the child's concerns and problems was found to be very variable in both quantity and quality. While we were able to give examples of knowledgeable, confident and creative practice, there were no very clear associations between the child social worker's contribution and outcome as we measured it. This should not be construed as lack of evidence for the effectiveness of the methods used, such as Life Story Work, as the quality of the social work intervention was very heterogeneous. Perhaps the broad variations in expertise, the variety of approaches taken and the limited time available constrained the possibility of a large effect on children with severe difficulties.

Moreover, the analysis showed that social worker characteristics influenced who received a high level of service more than the degree of disturbance in the placed child. These factors included the combination of training level, confidence and availability. Some children did receive a high quality preparation service but they were not necessarily receptive to the help on offer at that point in their lives. It is recognised that abused and neglected children may have difficulty in talking about internal states and may have resisted these encounters. It is clearly important to assess how amenable the child is likely to be to intensive direct work, to specify the expected benefits and to estimate how long it will take before they are apparent. These considerations need to be weighed in relation to the timescale of the placement plan.

A higher profile for direct work with children by field social workers is needed. This work proved to be highly challenging and complex in many of these cases and skilled supervision and support was often lacking. Structured assessments of the children are needed to understand their problems, to help decide how much can realistically be achieved and by what means. A considerable gap between theory, practice and research still needs to be filled. Newer methods, such as cognitive approaches, which are being adapted for use with children may be appropriate. (Reinecke *et al.*, 1996). Cognitive therapists stress a more selective approach to intervention, geared to the child's developmental level and using more standardised treatment plans.

New Parents and Preparation

The new parents were all couples, except for three lone mothers and one lone father. Two-thirds had previous parenting experience. The study revealed that some experienced parents did not feel positively about the preparation and training they received, as it did not seem to take their particular needs into account and failed to acknowledge their experience. We concluded that the adoption and fostering model was often still wedded to the preparation of childless couples.

However, we found that many children placed with experienced parents, particularly those families whose birth children were still at home, were likely to be showing more behaviour and relationship problems at the end of the year. This was not explained by more difficult children being placed with established families. This argues for a model of preparation that acknowledges parenting experience but stresses the differences involved in parenting a late placed child, especially for those who have raised children from infancy.

The preparation programme needs to be informed by research findings on the factors most likely to destabilise placements. For example, the concept of rejection and its possible consequences needs to be discussed so that new parents can anticipate the kind of difficulties the child may experience, such as problems with self-esteem, trust and relationships. There should be opportunities for anticipating possible relationship conflicts when other children are present in the home. Parents and professionals should be planning jointly for how these can be effectively addressed.

Adequate preparation should also involve the children living in the new home and address the changes that the arrival of a new sibling or siblings will bring. We found a wide variation in the extent to which the birth children of prospective new parents had been prepared or consulted. While some family social workers described extensive discussions with birth children, the task was often left for parents to complete. The difficulties in family dynamics that may develop after placement should not be under-estimated.

Information-giving About the Children Before Placement

Much has been written about the importance of new parents being given good quality information and we confirmed that where it occurred this was of great assistance in helping them to understand the history of their new child and take account of any medical, behavioural and educational problems. Possession of information enabled parents to respond appropriately to the children as questions about background arose, especially where there was no contact with the birth family. Unfortunately, information given to the parents about the placed children and their backgrounds was poor for a third of the families.

We recognise, and so do new parents, that there are times when there are genuine difficulties in determining facts about the child's history, but whatever is available should be given accurately and comprehensively and be updated as necessary. Although there is an issue of confidentiality to be addressed, prospective parents need the opportunity to discuss in detail and reflect on the experiences of children with whom they are likely to be matched. It was clear that there are occasions when new families do not 'hear' all that they are told. For this reason, we would recommend that the passing on of information should be formally recorded. Information should be available in written form, both to new parents and in due course to the children. Rapid progress in computerised storage and retrieval systems should enable bureaucratic procedures to be speeded up.

In order to achieve better quality and more accurate pre-placement information, a multidisciplinary approach to assessment is necessary, augmenting psychological and child psychiatric expertise with social work assessments. The contents of reviews of pre-placement history should pay special attention to factors that have been shown to be predictors of good and poor outcome as a means of ensuring that the most relevant information is given prominence.

Parental Stress Prior to Placement

We found that high levels of stress were experienced by the parents prior to placement, associated with initial meetings with the child and anticipation of the child's arrival. This period sharpened the focus dramatically for the intending parents and confronted them with the reality that the child was soon to become part of their daily lives. For some families the practicalities and the timing of the introductory period made for considerable difficulties. Social workers need to be more aware of the new families' existing commitments when making introduction plans. Although the stresses associated with the pre-placement period may be quickly forgotten once the child arrives, it should be acknowledged that this is a difficult period and space needs to be created to air anxieties and uncertainties without prejudice.

THE FIRST YEAR OF PLACEMENT

For most of the families and children, the placement was a long-anticipated event. However, we found little evidence of a 'honeymoon' period. Most of the children presented their new parents with at least one challenging behaviour pattern from the outset. The major concerns of new families in the course of the first year revolved around the behaviour problems of the children and how these might best be managed, the way in which relationships were developing and how the children were getting on at school. In many ways these are interlinked because behavioural problems will often influence relationships with others and, indeed, school performance.

The Children's Problem Levels and Changes Over the Year

Interviews with the new parents were conducted at one month into placement and again at the end of the first year. We were able to examine problems in the children over this period and to measure the degree of stability or change. The children started out with a multiplicity of psychosocial difficulties: extreme forms of defiant and aggressive behaviour, emotional distress, distractibility, overactivity and social and relationship difficulties. By and large, these were no greater for boys than girls. The children had very high problem scores compared with general population data but were similar to other 'in care' samples.

The problem levels of the sample as a whole hardly diminished over the year. However, this apparent lack of change masked a marked improvement for some children, maintenance of problems for some and a corresponding deterioration for others. Many of the rejected children showed an increase in behavioural difficulties over the year. We concluded that there was a group of very disturbed children in the sample who presented multiple and rising difficulties to their new parents.

In common with our previous research in the field we found that problems with overactivity and poor attention were a feature for many of the children both at the start of placement and at the end of the year.

The implications for the social work service from this section of the study are that the new parents are prepared for potential behavioural difficulties, particularly in relation to overactivity and inattention. Information concerning existing problems should be imparted to the prospective parents and, once placed, appropriate advice and targeted intervention for both parents and children should be available where necessary.

Growth of New Relationships

Barth and Berry (1988) argue that help with behaviour problems is the single most pressing need in post-placement support. This certainly needs stressing but the other important consideration is the growth of new relationships. We examined the children's relationships with new parents, new siblings and peers.

Interest in attachment theory is currently being extended to the process of re-attachment in new relationships. Difficulties in forming mutually satisfying relationships with new parents tended to be linked to an inability to express feelings openly or appropriately, with a perceived lack of trust and lack of genuine affection by the children for their new parents. Poor relationships between placed children and their new siblings presented a considerable challenge to the families involved. Whilst few placements disrupted by a year, it was clear that some were under considerable strain because of the poor development of relationships. On the other hand, the multivariate analyses showed that attachments to the new parents could develop even when behaviour problems got worse.

Knowledge is still limited on how to help the developing parent/child relationship. More needs to be known abstract how flexible the attachment system is and to what extent 'internal representations' of adult caregivers can be modified with changing experience. There has been a limited amount of work on improving attachment in birth families (Jernberg, 1989) but this has only limited relevance for much of the work in fostering and adoption. Social workers and child psychotherapists working in the permanent placement field have frequently drawn on the views of Fahlberg (1994), which stress the need for the child's emotions to be expressed rather than repressed in order to facilitate attachment. Delaney (1991), in an attempt to extend attachment theory to substitute care, advocates trying to modify the child's 'negative working model'. Delaney accepts that these representations of self and others may be difficult to modify if the child has learned to expect rejection and insensitive parenting. The child, he claims, may maintain this expectation even when new parents are accepting and nurturing.

Other attachment therapists have experimented with more intensive and less conventional 'holding' therapies (Cline, 1992). So far, these innovative programmes have not been standardised and controlled outcome evaluations have yet to be conducted. Furthermore, some authors make too easy assumptions that current difficulties are the product of insecure early attachments when they may be due to a host of other experiences, biological and temperamental factors, background factors and current relationships.

Family social workers must get to know the families well and find out exactly how they are experiencing the placement. They must judge if there appear to be misperceptions, biases or distortions or over-reactions emerging in the parenting. The children who were slow to attach frequently taxed the capacity of new parents to maintain their positive feelings. Parents need to be helped to maintain their warmth and sensitivity and not to withdraw and reject the child. If the new parents are properly listened to in the early stages of placement and the relationship concerns attended to constructively, the other problems the child is exhibiting may be more manageable. In such cases the social workers need to maintain their scrutinising and supportive role.

Relationships with new siblings

We recorded both rivalry and cooperation in the children's relationships with their new siblings, including a few examples of very extreme effects. We found that difficult sibling relationships could develop irrespective of the age gap between the placed child and the birth children. Placements of children on their own into established families were at increased risk of poor outcome, which was often associated with conflict between the incoming child and new siblings. This finding should give pause for thought to family placement workers who expect experienced families to be better used to dealing with challenging behaviour.

Peer relationships

Where the children were experiencing difficulties in forming relationships with their new parents, they often had difficulties with their new siblings or peers. Peer problems were the most common, with the placed children tending to show inappropriate social interaction with other children, for example, showing insensitivity to the feelings of others, an inability to keep to the rules of games or aggression in dealing with other children. These findings emphasise the need for more attention to be paid to children's social relationships whilst in care, since such difficulties, without adequate help, will affect their transition through adolescence and into adulthood.

Impact on the Parents

According to the parents' descriptions, the demands on them were often intense, the knowledge of the child's history and current distress were painful to witness and they had a daunting sense of responsibility. Parents were surprised by the strength of their feelings of pain, anger and frustration. The lack of someone to talk to was felt acutely. What did the families need to help them? Some wanted simply to 'off-load', to have a listening ear and to understand what they were going through. Others wanted something more specific like help to devise particular strategies to deal with problem behaviour.

We examined, in particular, the mothers' stress levels. Just under half of the mothers of children in continuing placements still felt under considerable stress by the end of the year. But, in spite of these elevated stress levels, high ratings of difficulty in the children, and some parents' unhappiness with many aspects of the placement arrangements, the majority were satisfied with the child as a family member.

Parenting Style

Over half of the new parents had difficulties with some aspect of the parenting role during the year. Most commonly, this took the form either of difficulty in responding sensitively or expressing warmth towards the new child or of problems in day-to-day management. Multivariate analyses suggested that there was a close relationship between the children's behaviour, parenting style and placement stability, with the latter being especially at risk where behaviour deteriorated in the context of less sensitive parenting. The most important feature of these analyses (presented in Chapters 13 and 14) was that in most cases these difficulties were evident in the first months of placement. This suggests that, in the course of their routine visiting in the early stages of the placement, social workers need to offer the time for parents to talk about their feelings for the child and the day-to-day progress of the placement in order that early signs of these difficulties may be detected.

LINKS WITH EDUCATION

We had reports from new parents and from teachers on behaviour at school. The new parents showed a high level of interest in the children's schooling, often giving extra help with school work at home. During the year, an improvement in reading ability and cognitive skills was observed but not in emotional or behavioural problems. Difficulties with behaviour and attention were far greater for the placed children than for control children taken from the same class at school and, if anything, worsened over the year. Past research has linked behaviour problems, such as poor attention and overactivity, to poor school achievement among children of this age.

In our direct tests of the children, we found that those who were reported to be overactive did, indeed, perform less well on tests of impulsivity and attention. However, only a small number of children were found to be inattentive in all situations. This indicates that, given sensitive support and encouragement in a classroom setting suited to their needs, many of these children have the potential to achieve more in school. Whether or not they receive such help is likely to have a major impact on their educational and social progress.

It is clear that the educational needs of children in care must be assessed and provision made for them to be met through a multidisciplinary approach. The needs of looked after children require a higher profile within schools. New parents should be informed of the new children's level of academic development before they are placed, and supported in helping these children to reach their potential. Teachers also need more training on the possible educational and behavioural problems of these children.

Information about the children's education was sometimes misleading, for within months of placement it became clear that their children's educational needs had not been adequately assessed and certainly were not being met. Some new parents were not only surprised by the level of educational difficulty but also by their response to it, speaking of the frustration they experienced in trying to help their children learn.

Education is clearly an area that needs to be more prominent on the parent preparation agenda and there is a case for closer links between social work and education in helping each to understand the interplay between home and school for children who have been in transitory placements for much of their lives. The very high levels of parental interest in education in this study indicate that such work might produce significant benefits.

CRISES AND DISRUPTIONS

Instability During the Year

One indication of the challenge of these placements is the extent of crises about the viability of the placement. Of those placements still intact at the 12 month interview, a third reported periods when they had seriously questioned whether continuing with the placement was the right course of action. The doubts of a small number of families were strong enough for them to be considering ending the placement at the time the one year interview took place.

The children's behaviour was a significant factor in all of the incidents of doubt, but was considered to be the sole cause in only two cases. Worries about the parent/child relationship were present in almost all cases and were the main factor for over half of them. Anxieties about the effect of the placement on the parents' own children were also contributing to the dilemma in all but two of the placements where birth children were resident at home.

The Disruptions

Whatever its problems as a marker of placement outcome, the disruption rate is always likely to be the most stark indicator. The disruption rate in the course of the first year in this sample was very low (5%), although if the 23 potential cases that did not enter the study sample are included the rate rises to 11%. There were also some placements within the interview sample that were decidedly unstable at the one year point. These disruption rates sit towards the low end of research-derived findings, but our one year follow-up of a restricted age sample does not encourage us to make comparisons with other studies which may be of heterogeneous placements followed for longer periods. In addition, the small proportion of disruptions does not permit statistical analysis of which factors predict it. However, the first anniversary of placement is a long way from the end of the story and it is becoming increasingly evident that outcomes cannot really be assessed until much later.

In studies such as this, disruption rates will inevitably be looked to as a guide to placement policy and will influence the recruitment of prospective adopters. It is important to consider how the risk of disruption is conveyed to practitioners and to families. Three points need to be made. Firstly, there must be a proper understanding of risk factors and disruption. Risk factors are not causal, but practitioners and families should be aware of the best evidence on predictors. Secondly, the risk level needs to be considered in comparison with outcomes recorded in alternative placement plans such as return home, impermanent foster or residential care. Thirdly, the risk rate must be understood in the context of the specific sample studied, paying attention to the nature of the sample, the length of follow-up and the level of pre- and post-placement support.

THE POST-PLACEMENT SOCIAL WORK SERVICE AND ITS IMPACT

We were able to document more precisely than previous studies of late placement the type and degree of professional support offered to the children and new parents. This was found to be a service limited largely to social work for, with some notable exceptions, there were very few other professional services involved. A considerable amount of social work time was devoted to these placements although substantial variations were revealed in the volume and quality of work.

In addition to summarising the quantitative data from the study, we have taken the opportunity, in this section, to introduce some of the thoughts that the families had about the support they had been offered. For the most part, both the child's social worker (CSW) and the family placement worker (FSW) remained involved with the new families over the year and apart from one or two cases the placing agency retained statutory supervision of the placement. However, while the parents thought the FSWs were there for them and the CSWs there to monitor the child, areas of responsibility were not always clearly delineated between the two workers. Thus, parents were sometimes unsure who to approach for advice on such concerns as child management techniques. Sometimes this lack of clarity could work in the families' favour, since they were able to choose whichever worker they expected would be more efficient, but at other times they received conflicting advice or none at all. A significant minority of families seemed to have no clear idea of what support services should be or were available.

Post-placement Work of Children's Workers

Just over half of the new parents reported that they had found the CSW supportive over the course of the year. However, there were issues raised by a number of parents that deserve to be mentioned in this context. The divided priorities evident in the preparation work of the CSWs continued into placement, and although families understood that demands of child protection work or court appearances had to take precedence, this remained a source of difficulty because of the upset caused to the children by cancelled or postponed appointments. There were frequently delays in getting the Schedule 2 reports ready to be lodged with the courts and in passing on information. Another source of discomfort was the conflicting need of integrating the child into the family on the one hand while still allowing for the continued super-vision of the placement on the other. This was of particular importance in established families, where continued concentration on the placed child could emphasise differences between them and the other children, but it was also relevant to a degree in child-free families. Although occurring rarely, there was potential for conflict where the CSW con-tinued to work directly with the birth family.

Family Social Worker Post-placement Support

The FSW support took place in a more favourable context than the CSW intervention and it appeared more uniform in quality and more con-fident and better received by the new parents. Fewer conflicts arose with new parents and the work was more rewarding. The service when categorised as high level, that is comprehensive, specifically focused and proactive, was, in general, found to be directed at the most problematic placements. However, even this concentration of effort was not related to a diminution of the child's problems or reduction on mothers' stress levels at the end of the first year of placement. It is possible that any beneficial effects may take longer to show and that even more intense and structured interventions are necessary to achieve positive effects more rapidly.

However, for the most part the new parents were provided with very little help specifically directed at enhancing parenting skills. There is a need for more specialist training in this area. We would also like to see the FSWs take a more holistic view of the family rather than be exclusively parent-focused. When there was sibling dispute and rivalry the FSWs might have seen siblings together to achieve a better understanding of the problems.

Throughout the study we were aware of the need for comprehensive assessments and appropriate formulations to ensure that practice is not determined by transient fashions or individual practitioners' idiosyncratic views. Detailed knowledge of background history is vital to developing a prospective view of the child's likely development and the services that will be needed over time, not just in the present.

Given the focus of the FSW role in the family placement we were surprised by the continuing paucity of training focusing specifically on sustaining permanent placements. There is room for a more structured approach to educating social workers about the means at their disposal for supporting placements. Greater familiarity with research evidence is needed to guide assessments and appropriate interventions.

IMPLICATIONS FOR POST-PLACEMENT SERVICES

The finding that families, and very often social workers, are unclear about their relative responsibilities in supporting placements, suggests that there is a need to debate what is meant by support, who should be providing which services and in which setting. It is important to consider in greater depth the conflict inherent in the CSW role because of the overwhelming demands of child protection responsibilities. There is also a clear need to establish with families at the time of making a placement why and how the support and supervision is to be managed.

The Social Work Service and Specialist Help

Social workers need to be open to hearing the range of needs expressed by new parents and to respond in a considered, appropriate way. They should also be aware that the family may be reluctant to tell the social worker their worst experiences and negative feelings in case this prompts the social worker to have reservations about the placement.

How are the problems the children bring to the placement to be addressed? Simply placing the child in a stable nurturing home does not have the effect of reversing past difficulties. We would argue that, as a first line of help, the social workers supporting the placement should be able to offer effective reassurance and encouragement but also be able to provide information and provide or recruit more focused help. They should be competent and confident in advising parents on sensible interventions to reduce the level of difficult behaviour. However, if the problems persist a referral for more specialist and intensive psychological help may be necessary. This is best managed by a multidisciplinary and multi-agency child mental health team who have familiarised themselves with late placement practice (Hughes, 1995). They will be able to provide a more detailed and comprehensive assessment of the roots of the problems and to offer to work jointly with the family to increase parenting skills and strategies and to modify restless and disorganised behaviour. These services should be working in partnership with parents rather than delivering prescriptive behavioural approaches.

Despite the considerable recent developments in constructing and evaluating parenting training programmes (Webster-Stratton, 1991), there are very few published examples of the specific application of these methods with substitute parents and late placed children. It may be the case that such a multidisciplinary team approach is not available locally. Kurtz, Thornes and Wolkind (1994) and the Health Advisory Service (1995) have recently criticised the lack of adequate child and adolescent mental health services for children in local authority care due to poor links, slow referral procedures, long waiting lists and insufficient access to therapeutic services. However, examples of post-adoption intervention are beginning to be published. Examples include intensive work carried out by multidisciplinary teams when placements are in difficulty (Rushton and Rushton, 1996) and a single case study of child psychotherapy with an adopted boy (Lush *et al.*, 1998). The development of Post Adoption Centres is a welcome innovation in concentrating expertise in this field (Howe, 1990) and links with other parents, hotlines, respite care and support groups should be developed. The development of appropriate, specialist and accessible resources should help to avoid reliance solely on the FSW service. We are aware that there can be considerable delays in getting referrals accepted but were pleased to hear of an authority that allows direct parent access to child psychologists for advice and counselling (Hobday & Lee, 1995).

If the assessment leads to a reliable diagnosis of attention deficit hyperactivity disorder (ADHD) some child psychiatrists may prescribe medication (psychostimulants) to reduce the child's ceaseless activity and to provide some respite for the parents. Although medication is frequently used for these children in North America there has been considerably more opposition to its use in the UK. Medication may well be prescribed in conjunction with other psychological therapies.

MANAGEMENT OF PLACEMENT SUPPORT SERVICES

In identifying shortcomings in the service, particularly with regard to the CSWs, it is not our intention to see the CSW removed from the task but for social services departments to recognise the importance and challenge of this work and to identify the skills, training and supervisory support required to sustain it. The best of the CSWs were trying to achieve this advanced level work in the context of a myriad of other competing and very different demands. The child preparation work has to be protected and the quality improved. With proper management, it may be possible to achieve this within local authority services. An accreditation process should be considered in order to operate quality control of this aspect of the social work service. In cases where preparation for placement is deficient, there may be good reason to bring in the FSW earlier to be more involved in preparing the child.

Since the legal requirement for all local authorities to set up adoption and fostering agencies there has been concern as to whether they can be adequate providers of post-placement and post-adoption support. Some doubt whether the large welfare bureaucracy, concerned increasingly with risk assessment and statutory responsibilities, can be a comfortable home for adoption services and would prefer the voluntary sector to become the main providers. Such proposals need careful consideration as to the real benefits of such a relocation of services, the unforeseen consequences of such a change and the cost of this move. Do we want specialist teams operating outside the mainstream of child welfare services? Will it achieve the goal of greater accountability? Will the voluntary agencies be any better at listening to the views of adopters and consult regularly with them and register their changing needs over the long term? Will it create more discontinuity and become an obstacle to achieving permanent placement for children who need it? Will the CSW/FSW link, despite its problems, be harder to maintain? Will the detachment of permanent placement work from social services departments result in further stripping of the statutory sector of all progressive, change-oriented work? Will, most crucially, the complex tasks of family support be more effectively accomplished? Wherever the service is provided there must be a properly founded estimation of the potential for challenge and risk in each placement and a proportionately measured support service. The work of supporting families with highly disturbed children is going to be extremely difficult whatever the setting. The crucial factor is the quality of the service. Evidence from the Oregon Social Learning Centre (Moore & Chamberlain, 1994) suggests that a comprehensive parent preparation and parenting skills programme can result in more successful outcomes in highly difficult placements.

LEGAL IMPLICATIONS

The Children Act (1989) was being introduced during the data collection period of the study. As the sample was aged between five and nine in the early 1990s, they were first admitted to care in the late 1980s prior to the introduction of the new Act. The Act has produced further clarification of when the state has the grounds for intervention (based on the concept of 'significant harm') and greater regulation of social workers in their use of emergency powers, and so it is possible that decision-making in relation to children similarly at risk may have differed after 1989. Most children are returned from care to their birth parents and only a small proportion go on to live in a permanent new family.

Although there are now fewer adoptions it has frequently been noted that they give rise to more complex placement issues and support needs. The reform of adoption legislation has been called for because the existing legislation is still too grounded in baby adoptions where post-placement support was not envisaged. The findings in the study about the uneven volume and standard of post-placement service raise the question as to whether post-placement and post-adoption service should be guaranteed to the new families by law. Any expansion of service may have cost implications, although the extent of this will not be known until cost–benefit analyses have been done. Furthermore, the introduction of contracts between families and adoption agencies may give rise to anxieties about the costs they may have to bear if they are claimed to be in breach of their service obligations. It is likely that only in response to statutory obligations will social services departments give priority to new demands. The Adoption Bill (DoH, 1996a), which was the best hope for securing progress, has to date not been enacted and without a major campaign to promote it, it will be low priority for the new Labour administration shackled to tight spending limits. The major focus has been on the Children Act and the attempt to redress the balance between child protection and family support – all of which has left adoption rather in the margins.

CONCLUSION

Much developmental psychology research has been about broken attachments and separation – this study is on the psychology of joining new families. In examining the process of transfer of a child to a new home, we have highlighted the level of challenge presented by the placed children and the need for the provision of responsive, effective services to support and secure these placements. The strongest message from our research, and one that needs to lead to fundamental change, is that the level of difficulty revealed in the children means that new parents cannot be expected to face these alone and the families and the children will need access to continuing services, often from an integrated multi-agency team representing health, social services and education. Most of the children were at high risk for mental health problems at the start of placement and the opportunities need to be taken to prevent these problems persisting into their later lives. There is a major question as to whether the current system allows for sufficiently intensive intervention. Case load size and other demands can frequently result in only low level support which may have too little impact to counteract the risks.

APPENDIX A
THE EXPRESSION OF FEELINGS QUESTIONNAIRE (EFQ)[1]

RATIONALE FOR DEVELOPING THE INSTRUMENT

A child's ability to express feelings in an open and appropriate manner is central to the development of an emotional bond between placed children and their new parents and crucial to understanding the success or otherwise of a placement. At the time of data collection for this study there was no appropriate and acceptable instrument available to us; therefore we designed the EFQ to assess parent perceptions of the child's feeling states. This appendix describes the questionnaire, the scoring system and preliminary analyses which establish areas of difference and similarity between the sample and control groups, in terms of behaviours exhibited by the child. Further statistical analysis to determine the reliability of the instrument is currently being undertaken.

The questions included in the EFQ drew on existing attachment research along with observations concerning attachment made by researchers in the family placement field. The areas addressed were the extent to which children were able to show their feelings in an open manner to their new parents and seek comfort without withdrawing into themselves or using inappropriate social behaviours. It was thought that this ability would be important in influencing the development of a mutual relationship and would reflect an older child's ability to use adults as 'a secure base'.

[1] Funding for the collection of comparison data on the EFQ was provided by the Buttle Trust.

QUESTIONNAIRE

The questionnaire is intended for completion by parents and contains 53 items, divided into four sections, designed to examine the extent to which the children are able to share feelings, indicate needs and express negative and positive emotional states to their new parents. *Section A* explores the manner and extent to which children express their feelings, *Section B* addresses the social behaviours of the children, *Section C* examines the child's ability to share feelings and accept comfort from parents and *Section D* completes the questionnaire with a series of questions designed to discover the extent to which parents feel their child trusts and cares about them and to what extent the parent feels satisfied with their relationship with the child. A copy of the questionnaire can be obtained from the research team.

Scoring the Responses

The majority of responses were scalable in terms of either frequency or intensity. Therefore, a simple scoring mechanism could be employed for each item based on the response to the question. This allowed for the summing of scores on individual sections to see group tendencies.

RESPONSE RATES FOR THE SAMPLE

Fifty-one (84%) primary carers from the study sample returned EFQs at one month, although the response rate decreased to 62% at one year. Respondents and non-respondents were compared on five outcome measures to check for bias; no significant differences were found between the two groups on any of these measures. The three placements which had disrupted by one year were excluded.

THE CONTROL GROUP

A comparison group of 54 mothers and 30 fathers were recruited from two schools in a socio-economically mixed area. There was a single father in both the sample and comparison group, whose questionnaires were included with those of mothers, allowing us to examine the responses of main caregivers in the first instance. Children within the control group who had been adopted or were being fostered were excluded from the analysis, as were step-children. There were no obvious differences between the sample and control groups. The mean age of the control group children was 7 years 6 months, with ages ranging from 5 years 5 months to 9 years 6 months. There were 25 boys and 30 girls. The mean age of the sample group was very similar at 7 years 5 months. There were 27 boys and 24 girls in the sample group, but no significant sex differences were found.

RESULTS

For the purposes of assessing the instrument's discriminatory power the control group results are compared with sample results at one month, on the assumption that this early in placement children are likely to be experiencing more difficulty in expressing emotions given the newness of their situation.

A high EFQ score denotes more or greater difficulties in the expression of feelings. This is a sum of categorical scores for each child on the basis of 0 = no problem, with the score rising in value according to the extent of the difficulty. A cut-off of 83 was determined by a comparison of the distribution of scores for the sample and control group. The majority of control group scores were under 83 and when those above 83 were excluded from both the control group and the sample group, the mean was very similar (control = 55, sample = 56).

Items that Discriminated Between Sample and Controls

Table A.1 shows significant differences between a range of items on which the sample children differed from the control children. Firstly, the sample children tended to express their emotions with less openness and appropriateness in the areas outlined above. Secondly, the sample children had more difficulty with their 'social' behaviours such as attention-seeking and over-friendly behaviours. Finally, as Figure A.1 shows, more of the sample children showed a lack of trust and caring and were less likely to have an easy relationship with their new parents.

Table A.1: EFQ items which discriminate between sample and control

	Sample children (1 month); nos vary, max 51 (%)	Control children; nos vary, max 54 (%)	Probability
High score on EFQ (> 83)	86	2	N/A[a]
Open expression anger	71	92	*
Open expression frustration	76	94	*
Open expression sadness	72	90	*
Appropriate expression affection	82	100	**
Appropriate expression sadness	86	100	*
Appropriate expression fear	79	95	*
Bottling up emotions	33	6	***
Seeks attention by:			
Misbehaving	41	15	**
Complaining of illness	27	11	*
Affection shown	86	98	*
Affection genuine	71	100	***
Attention-seeking	49	15	***
Over-friendly with strangers	49	19	**
Immature affection	13	4	*

* $p < 0.05$, ** $p < 0.01$, *** $p < 0.001$.
[a] This scoring was the means by which the cut-off was determined.

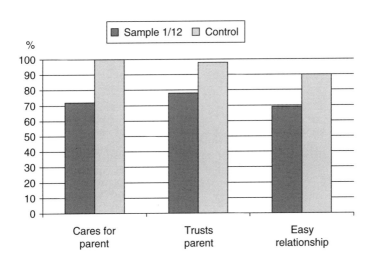

Figure A.1: Parent perceptions of the parent–child relationship. Group differences significant at $p < 0.01$ or better

APPENDIX B
PLACEMENT SEQUENCES
ACCORDING TO REASON
FOR FIRST ADMISSION

Placement chains are grouped under the main reasons for initial admission and arranged according to their length.

Abuse of placed child or sibling (17)

F	$\bar{X}$ placements 2.9 s.d. 3.7
F	$\bar{X}$ end placements 2.4 s.d. 1.3
F	$\bar{X}$ returns home 0.2 s.d. 0.4

F
F
F
R
RT
F – F
F – F
F – RT
F – F – F
F – PA – F
F – RF – F
F – F – F – F
F – F – F – F
F – H – F – F
F – F – H – F – F
F – RF – F – H – F
F – F – F – F – RT – F – F – F

Poor parenting (neglect, emotional abuse, abandonment, can't cope) (30)

F	$\bar{X}$ placements 5.3 s.d. 2.6
F	$\bar{X}$ end placements 2.6 s.d. 1.2
F – F	$\bar{X}$ returns home 1.2 s.d. 1.0

F
F
F – F
F – CH
F – F – F
F – F – F
F – F – F
F – F – F – F
R – F – F – F
F – H – F – F
PA – H – F – H – F
F – F – F – F – F

F – H – F – F – F
F – H – F – F – F
F – H – CH – F – F
F – F – R – H – F
F – H – F – PA – RT
F – CH – CH – CH – CH
F – H – F – F – RF – F
F – H – F – H – F – F
F – H – F – H – F – F
F – H – F – H – F – F
RF – H – CH – RF – H – F
F – F – F – H – F – F – F
F – PA – F – H – R – PA – F
F – H – F – H – RT – H – F – F
R – H – H – F – H – F – F – F – F
F – H – CH – F – H – CH – F – H – CH – F
RF – H – RF – H – F – F – H – F – H – F
F – H – R – H – R – H – R – F – F – F – CH – F

Physical illness (including one death) (6)

R $\bar{X}$ placements   7.8 s.d. 5.7
R – F – F $\bar{X}$ end placements   1.8 s.d. 0.9
F – H – F – H – F $\bar{X}$ returns home   2.7 s.d. 2.3
F – H – F – H – F – RT – H – F – H – F
F – H – F – H – F – H – RF – H – F – H – F – F – F
F – H – F – F – H – RT – F – F – H – F – H – F – H – F – H – F – RT

Psychiatric disorder or addiction (6)

F – PA – F – F $\bar{X}$ placements   8.0 s.d. 3.1
F – H – F – F – F $\bar{X}$ end placements   3.5 s.d. 1.4
R – H – F – H – RT – F $\bar{X}$ returns home   2.0 s.d. 1.3
F – H – F – H – F – H – R – R – F
CH – CH – H – F – CH – PA – F – F – F – F – F
F – R – F – H – F – H – F – F – H – F – H – F

Childbirth (2)

                                          $\bar{X}$ placements   13.5 s.d. 7.8
                                          $\bar{X}$ end placements   3.5 s.d. 2.8
                                          $\bar{X}$ returns home   4.5 s.d. 2.1
F – H – F – F – H – F – H – F
F – H – F – H – F – H – F – H – F – H – F – F – H – F – F – F – F – F – F

Differences in number of placements F 8.24, d.f. 4, $p < 0.0001$
Differences in number of final placements   NS
Differences in number of returns home F 9.56, d.f. 4, $p < 0.0001$

Key:
H, home with one or both parents; RF, residential family facility; F, foster care; CH, children's home; R, relatives; RT, residential therapeutic community; PA, potential adopters.

LIST OF FIGURES

LIST OF TABLES

REFERENCES

Abidin R (1992) The determinants of parenting behaviour. *Journal of Clinical Child Psychology* **21**(4): 407–412.

Aldgate J & Simmonds J (eds) (1988) *Direct Work with Children*. London: British Agencies for Adoption & Fostering.

Alessandri S (1991) Play and social behaviours in maltreated preschoolers. *Development and Psychopathology* **3**: 191–206.

Alton H (1987) Moving pictures: workbook for use with children facing a move. London: BAAF.

American Psychiatric Association (1994) *Diagnostic and Statistical Manual of Mental Disorders* 4th edition. Washington DC: American Psychiatric Association.

Andresen I (1992) Behavioural and social adjustment of 12 and 13 year old internally adopted children in Norway. *Journal of Child Psychology and Psychiatry* **33**: 427–439.

Asher SR & Coie JD (eds) (1990) *Peer Rejection in Childhood*. New York: Cambridge University Press.

BAAF Adoption Statistics Project (1997) *Focus on Adoption: a snapshot of adoption patterns in England 1995*. London: British Agencies for Adoption and Fostering.

Barth R & Berry M (1988). *Adoption and Disruption: rates, risks and responses*. New York: Aldine de Gruyter.

Batty D (ed.) (1986) *Working with Children*. London: British Agencies for Adoption and Fostering.

Baumrind D (1971) Current patterns of parental authority. *Developmental Psychology Monographs* **4** (1, Part 2): 1–103.

Beeghly M & Cicchetti D (1994) Child maltreatment, attachment and the self system: emergence of an internal state lexicon in toddlers at high social risk. *Development and Psychopathology* **6**: 5–30.

Belsky J (1984) The determinants of parenting: a process model. *Child Development* **55**: 83–96.

Berridge D & Cleaver H (1987) *Foster Home Breakdown*. Oxford: Blackwell.

Borland M, O'Hara G & Triseliotis J (1991) Placement outcomes for children with special needs. *Adoption and Fostering* **15**: 18–28.

Boyne J, Denby L, Kettenring JR & Wheeler W (1984). *The Shadow of Success: a statistical analysis of outcomes of adoptions of hard-to-place children*. Westfield New Jersey: Spaulding for Children.

Brebner C, Sharp J & Stone F (1985) *The Role of Infertility in Adoption*. Discussion Series 7. London: British Agencies for Adoption and Fostering.

Brodzinsky D (1990) A stress and coping model of adoption adjustment. In *The Psychology of Adoption*. Brodzinsky D & Schecter M (eds). Oxford: Oxford University Press.

Brodzinsky D, Singer LM & Braff AM (1984) Children's understanding of adoption. *Child Development* **55**: 869–878.

Brown G (1983) Accounts, meaning and causality. In *Accounts and Action*. Gilbert G & Abell P (eds). Aldershot: Gower.

Cairns E & Cammock T (1978) Development of a more reliable version of the Matching Familiar Figures test. *Developmental Psychology*. **14**: 555–560.

Cairns R, Cairns B, Neckerman H & Gest S (1988) Social networks and aggressive behaviour: peer support or peer rejection. *Developmental Psychology* **24**: 815–823.

Carlson V, Cichetti D, Barnett D & Braunwald K (1989) Disorganised/disoriented attachment relationships in maltreated infants. *Developmental Psychology* **25**: 525–531.

Catholic Children's Society (1983) *Finding Out About Me: games for the preparation of children for family placement*. Surrey: Catholic Children's Society.

Cicchetti D & Beeghly M (eds) (1990) *The Self in Transition: infancy to childhood*. Chicago: University of Chicago Press.

Cicchetti D and Garmezy N (1993) Special issue: milestones in the development of resilience. *Development and Psychopathology* **5**: 497–502.

Cicchetti D & Toth S (1995) A developmental psychopathology perspective on child abuse and neglect. *Journal of American Academy of Child and Adolescent Psychiatry*. **34**: 541–565.

Cline F (1992) *Hope for High Risk and Rage Filled Children*. Colorado: Evergreen Publications.

Corkum P & Seigal L (1993) Is the continuous performance task a valuable research tool for use with children with attention-deficit-hyperactivity disorder? *Journal of Child Psychology and Psychiatry* **14**: 1217–1239.

Corrigan M & Floud C (1990) A framework for direct work with children in care. *Adoption and Fostering* **14**: 28–32.

Curtis P (1983) Involving children in the placement process. *Adoption and Fostering* **7**: 45–47.

Delaney RJ (1991) *Fostering Changes: treating attachment-disordered foster children*. Fort Collins, Colorado: Walter J Corbett Publishing.

Department of Health (1989) *The Children Act for England and Wales*. London: HMSO.

Department of Health (1990) *Guidelines to directors of social services. Issues of race and culture in the family placement of children*. Department of Health Circular.

Department of Health (1992) *Review of adoption law: report to ministers of an interdepartmental working group*. London: HMSO.

Department of health (1993) *Adoption: the future*. CM228 CM228. London: HMSO.

Department of Health (1996a) *Adoption – A Service for Children*. London: HMSO.

Department of Health (1996b) *For children's sake Part I: an assessment of Local Authority adoption services*. London: DoH/SSI, HMSO.

Department of Health (1997) *For children's sake: part II: an inspection of Local Authority post-placement and post adoption services*. London: DoH/SSI, HMSO.

Department of Health/OFSTED (1995) *The education of children who are looked after by local authorities*. London: HMSO.

Department of Health, PSS and Local Authority Statistics (1993) *Children in care of local authorities*. London: HMSO.

Department of Health and Social Services Inspectorate (1991) *Adoption: in the best interests? Adoption services in three London local authorities*. London: HMSO.

Department of Health and Social Services Inspectorate (1993) *Planning for permanence? Adoption services in three northern local authorities*. London: HMSO.

DHSS (1972) *The report of the departmental committee on the adoption of children: the Houghton report*. London: HMSO.

Dodge K, Schlundt D, Schocken I & Delugagh J (1983) Social competence and children's sociometric status: the role of peer group entry strategies. *Merrill-Palmer Quarterly* **29**: 309–336.

Donley K (1984) Planning placements for special needs children. *Adoption and Fostering* **8**: 24–27.

Dubois D (1987) Preparing applicants in Wandsworth. *Adoption and Fostering* **11**: 35–37.

Dunn J & McGuire S (1991) Sibling and peer relationships in childhood. *Journal of Child Psychology and Psychiatry* **33**: 67–105.

Dunn LM, Dunn LM, Whetton C & Pintile D (1982) *British picture vocabulary scale*. Windsor: NFER-Nelson.

Eckenrode J, Laird M and Doris J (1993) School performance and disciplinary problems among abused and neglected children. *Child Abuse and Neglect* **7**: 53–62.

Egeland B, Sroufe A & Erikson M (1983) The developmental consequence of different patterns of maltreatment. *Child Abuse and Neglect* **7**: 459–469.

Erickson M, Egeland B and Pianta R (1989) The effects of maltreatment on the development of young children. In *Child Maltreatment: theory and research on the causes and consequences of child abuse and neglect*. Cicchetti D & Carlson V (eds). New York: Cambridge University Press.

Fahlberg V (1981) *Helping Children When They Must Move*. London: British Agencies for Adoption and Fostering.

Fahlberg V (1994) *A Child's Journey Through Placement*. London: British Agencies for Adoption and Fostering.

Festinger T (1986) *Necessary Risk: a study of adoptions and disrupted adoptive placements*. Washington: Child Welfare League of America.

Fonagy P, Steele H & Steele M (1991) Maternal representations of attachment during pregnancy predict the organisation of infant-mother attachment at 1 year of age. *Child Development* **62**: 891–905.

Fratter J, Rowe K, Sapsford D & Thoburn J (1991) *Permanent Family Placement: a decade of experience*. London: British Agencies for Adoption and Fostering.

George V (1970) *Foster Care: theory and practice*. London: Routledge & Kegan-Paul.

Gibbons J, Gallagher B, Bell C & Gordon D (1995) *Development after Physical Abuse in Early Childhood*. Studies in Child Protection. London: HMSO.

Harris V & McHale S (1989) Family life problems, daily caregiving activities and the psychological well-being of mothers of mentally retarded children. *Americal Journal of Mental Retardation* **99**: 231–239.

Health Advisory Service (1995) *Child and Adolescent Mental Health Services*. London: HMSO.

Heath AF, Colton MJ and Aldgate J (1994) Failure to escape: a longitudinal study of foster children's educational attainment. *British Journal of Social Work* **24**: 241–260.

Hennessy K, Rabideau G, Cicchetti D & Cummings M (1994) Responses of physically abused children to different forms of inter-adult anger. *Child Development* **65**: 815–828.

HMSO (1966) *Registrar General's Classification of Occupations*. London: HMSO.

Hobday A & Lee K (1995) Adoption: a specialist area for psychology. *The Psychologist* January: 13–15.

Hodges J & Tizard B (1989a) IQ and behavioural adjustment of ex-institutional adolescents. *Journal of Child Psychology and Psychiatry* **30**: 53–75.

Hodges J & Tizard B (1989b) Social and family relationships of ex-institutional adolescents. *Journal of Child Psychology and Psychiatry* **30**: 77–97.

Hoffman-Plotkin D & Twentyman C (1984) A multimodal assessment of behavioural and cognitive deficits in abused and neglected preschoolers. *Child Development* **55**: 794–802.

Houghton D & Houghton P (1984) *Coping with Childlessness*. London: Allen & Unwin.

Howe D (1990) The Post Adoption Centre: the first three years. *Adoption and Fostering* **14**: 27–31.

Howe D (1995) *Attachment Theory for Social Work Practice*. London: Macmillan Press.

Howe D (1996) Adopters' relationships with their adopted children from adolescence to early adulthood. *Adoption and Fostering* **20**: 35–43.

Howe D (1997) Parent reported problems in 211 adopted children: some risk and protective factors. *Journal of Child Psychology and Psychiatry* **38**: 401–411.

Hughes B (1995) *Post placement services for children and families: defining the need.* Social Services Inspectorate/Dept of Health.

Iwaniec D (1995) *The Emotionally Abused and Neglected Child*. Chichester: Wiley.

Jernberg A (1989) Training parents of failure-to-attach children. In *Handbook of parent training: parents as co-therapists for their children's behaviour problems.* Schaefer CE & Briesmeister JM (eds), pp 392–413. New York: Wiley.

Jewett Jarratt C (1978) *Adopting the Older Child*. Harvard, MA: Harvard Common Press.

Jewett Jarratt C (1982) *Helping Children Cope with Separation and Loss*. Harvard, MA: Harvard Common Press.

Kadushin A (1970) *Adopting Older Children*. New York: Colombia University Press.

Kadushin A & Seidl F (1971) Adoption failure: a social work postmortem. *Social Work* **16**: 32–38.

Kaniuk J (1992) The use of relationship in the preparation and support of adopters. *Adoption and Fostering* **16**: 47–52.

Katz L (1977) Older child adoptive placement: a time of family crisis. *Child Welfare* **56**: 165–171.

Katz L (1986) Parental stress and factors for success in older child adoption. *Child Welfare* **65**: 569–578.

Kaufman J (1991) Depressive disorders in maltreated children. *Journal of American Academy of Child and Adolescent Psychiatry* **30**: 257–265.

Kirk HD (1964) *Shared Fate: a theory of adoption and mental health*. London: Collier MacMillan.

Kurtz Z, Thornes R & Wolkind S (1994) *Services for the mental health of children and young people in England: a national review*. London: Dept of Public Health South Thames RHA.

Ladd G (1983) Effectiveness of a social learning method for enhancing children's social interaction and peer acceptance. *Child Development* **52**: 171–178.

Lush D, Boston M, Morgan J & Kolvin I (1998) Psychoanalytic psychotherapy with disturbed adopted and foster children: a single case follow-up study. *Journal of Child Psychology and Psychiatry* **3**: 51–69.

Lynch M & Cicchetti D (1991) Patterns of relatedness in maltreated and non-maltreated children: connections among representational models. *Development and Psychopathology* **3**: 207–226.

Maccoby E & Martin J (1983) Socialisation in the context of the family: parent–child interaction. In *Handbook of Child Psychology*. Hetherington M (ed.). Chichester: Wiley.

Main M (1996) Introduction to the special section on attachment and psychopathology 2. Overview of the field of attachment. *Journal of Consulting and Clinical Psychology* **64**: 237–243.

Main M & George C (1985) Response of abused and disadvantaged toddlers to distress in age-mates: a study in the day care setting. *Developmental Psychology* **21**: 407–412.

Main M & Solomon J (1990) Procedures for identifying infants as disorganized/disorientated during the Ainsworth Strange Situation. In *Attachment in the preschool years: theory, research and intervention*. Greenburg M, Cicchetti D & Cummings E (eds). Chicago: University of Chicago Press.

Maluccio A, Fein E & Olmstead K (1986) *Permanency Planning for Children*. London: Tavistock Publications.

Maughan B (1994) School influences. In *Development Through Life: a handbook for clinicians*. Rutter M & Hay DF (eds). Oxford: Blackwell Scientific Publications.

Mehta C & Mehta N (1993) LogXact Turbo. Cytel Software Corporation, Cambridge, MA.

Moore K & Chamberlain P (1994) Treatment foster care: development of community-based models for adolescents with severe emotional and behavioural disorders. *Journal of Emotional and Behavioural disorders* **2**: 22–30.

Mueller E & Silverman N (1989) Peer relations in maltreated children. In *Child Maltreatment: theory and research on the causes and consequences of child abuse and neglect*. Cicchetti D & Carlson V (eds). New York: Cambridge University Press.

Napier H (1972) Success and failure in foster care. *British Journal of Social Work* **2**: 187–204.

Nelson KA (1985) *On the frontier of adoption: a study of special needs adoptive families*. Washington: Child Welfare League of America.

Parker G, Tupling H & Brown LB (1979) A parental bonding instrument. *British Journal of Medical Psychology* **52**: 1–10.

Parker RA (1966) *Decision in Child Care: a study of prediction in fostering*. London: Allen & Unwin.

Parker R, Ward H, Jackson S & Aldgate J (eds) (1991) *Looking After Children: assessing outcomes in child care*. London: HMSO.

Part D (1993) Fostering as seen by the carers' children. *Adoption and Fostering* **17**: 26–31.

Patterson G (1982) *Coercive Family Process*. Eugene, Oregon: Castalia Publications.

Pinderhughes E (1995) Toward understanding family readjustment following older child adoptions: the interplay between theory generation and empirical research. *Children and Youth Services Review* **18**: 115–138.

Quinton D & Rutter M (1984) Parents with children in care: current circumstances and parenting skills. *Journal of Child Psychology and Psychiatry* **25**: 211–230.

Quinton D & Rutter M (1988) *Parenting Breakdown: the making and breaking of inter-generational links*. Aldershot: Avebury.

Quinton D, Rutter M and Rowlands O (1976) An evaluation of an interview assessment of marriage. *Psychological Medicine* **6**: 577–586.

Raven JC (1958) *Raven's Progressive Matrices*. Cambridge: Cambridge University Press.

Reinecke M, Dattilio F & Freeman A (eds) (1996) *Cognitive Therapy with Children and Adolescents*. London: The Guilford Press.

Richardson S, Dohrenwend B & Klein D (1965) *Interviewing: its forms and functions*. New York: Basic Books.

Rowe J & Lambert L (1973) *Children Who Wait*. London: British Agencies for Adoption and Fostering.

Rowe J, Cain H, Hundleby M & Keane A (1984) *Long Term Foster Care*. London: Batsford Academic.

Rushton A (1994) Principles and practice in the permanent placement of older children. *Children and Society* **8**: 245–256.

Rushton A & Rushton A (1996) Adoption and fostering: new perspectives, new research, new practice. In *Psychology in Practice with Young People, Families and Schools*. Sigston A, Curran P, Labram A & Wolfendale S (eds). London: David Fulton Publishers.

Rushton A & Minnis H (1997) Annotation: transracial family placements. *Journal of Child Psychology and Psychiatry* **38**: 147–159.

Rushton A, Treseder J & Quinton D (1988) *New Parents for Older Children*. London: British Agencies for Adoption and Fostering.

Rushton A, Treseder J and Quinton D (1993) New parents for older children: support services during eight years of placement. *Adoption and Fostering* **17**: 39–45.

Rushton A, Treseder J and Quinton D (1995) An eight year prospective study of older boys placed in permanent substitute families. *Journal of Child Psychology and Psychiatry* **36**: 687–695.

Rutter M & Quinton D (1981) Longitudinal studies of institutional children and children of mentally ill parents (United Kingdom). In *Prospective Longitudinal Research: an empirical basis for the primary prevention of psychosocial disorders*. Mednick S & Baert A (eds). Oxford: Oxford University Press.

Rutter M, Tizard J & Whitmore K (1970) *Education, Health and Behaviour*. London: Longmans.

Rutter M, Cox A, Tupling, C, Berger M & Yule W (1975) Attainment and adjustment in two geographical areas: the prevalence of psychiatric disorder. *British Journal of Psychiatry* **126**: 493–509.

Ryan T & Walker R (1993) *Life Story Work*. London: British Agencies for Adoption and Fostering.

Sainsbury E (eds) (1994) *Working with Children in Need*. London: Jessica Kingsley.

Salzinger S, Feldman RS, Hammer M & Rosario M (1993) The effects of physical abuse on children's social relationships. *Child Development* **64**: 169–187.

Sawbridge P & Carriline M (1978) Social work tasks in relation to placing children in new families. In *Good Enough parenting*. CCETSW (eds). London: CCETSW.

Schachar R, Rutter M & Smith A (1981) The characteristics of situationally and pervasively hyperactive children: implications for syndrome definition. *Journal of Child Psychology and Psychiatry* **22**: 375–392.

Shields AM, Ryan RM & Cicchetti D (1994) The development of emotional and behavioural self regulation and social competence among maltreated school age children. *Development and Psychopathology* **6**: 57–75.

Smith C (1984) *Adoption and Fostering: why and how*. London: Macmillan.

Sroufe LA (1990) An organisational perspective on the self. In: *The Self in*

Transition: infancy to childhood. Cicchetti D & Beeghly M (eds). Chicago: University of Chicago Press.

Taylor E, Scacher G, Thorley G & Wieselberg M (1986) Conduct disorder and hyperactivity. *British Journal of Psychiatry* **149**: 760–767.

Taylor E, Sandberg S, Thorley G & Giles S (1991) *The Epidemiology of Childhood Hyperactivity*. Maudsley Monographs Institute of Psychiatry. Oxford: Oxford University Press.

Thoburn J (1988) *Child Placement: principles and practice*. Aldershot: Community Care/Wildwood House.

Thoburn J (1992) Review of research relating to adoption. In *Review of adoption law: report to ministers of an interdepartmental working group*. Appendix C. DoH and Welsh Office. London: HMSO.

Thoburn J & Rowe J (1988) A snapshot of permanent family placement. *Adoption and Fostering* **12**: 29–34.

Tizard B (1977) *Adoption: a second chance*. London: Open Books.

Trasler G (1960) *In place of parents: a study of foster care*. London: Routledge & Kegan-Paul.

Tremitiere B (1984) *Disruption: a break in commitment*. York, PA: Tressler-Lutheran Service Associations.

Triseliotis J (1989) Foster care outcomes: a review of key research findings. *Adoption and Fostering* **13**: 5–7.

Triseliotis J & Russell J (1984) *Hard to Place: the outcome of adoption and residential care*. London: Heinemann Educational Books.

Triseliotis J, Shireman J & Hundleby M (1997) *Adoption: theory, policy and practice*. London: Cassell.

Visher E & Visher J (1996) *Therapy with Step Families*. New York: Brunner/Mazel.

Vondra J, Barnett D & Cicchetti D (1989) Perceived and actual competence among maltreated and comparison school children. *Development and Psychopathology* **1**: 237–255.

Vostanis P, Nicholls J & Harrington R (1994) Maternal expressed emotion in conduct and emotional disorders of childhood. *Journal of Child Psychology and Psychiatry* **35**: 365–376.

Webster-Stratton C (1991) Annotation: strategies for helping families with conduct disordered children. *Journal of Child Psychology and Psychiatry* **32**: 1047–1062.

Wedge P & Mantle G (1991) *Sibling Groups in Social Work: a study of children referred for permanent substitute family placement*. Aldershot: Avebury.

Wolke D (1986) *Testers' Ratings of Infant Behaviour*. University of London, Institute of Child Health. Hospital for Sick Children: Great Ormond Street, London.

Wolkind S (1979) *Medical Aspects of Adoption and Foster Care*. London: Heinemann.

Wolkind S & Rushton A (1994) Residential care and foster family care. In *Child and Adolescent Psychiatry: modern approaches*. Rutter M, Hersov B & Taylor E (eds). Oxford: Blackwell Scientific Publications.

Yule W & Raynes N (1972) Behavioural characteristics of children in residential care in relation to indices of separation. *Journal of Child Psychology and Psychiatry* **13**: 249–258.

INDEX

Index compiled by Annette Musker